FROM ZAMINDAR TO BALLOT BOX

*Community Change in a
North Indian Market Town*

FROM ZAMINDAR
TO BALLOT BOX

Community Change in a

North Indian Market Town

RICHARD G. FOX

CORNELL UNIVERSITY PRESS

ITHACA, NEW YORK

First published 1969

To JeanO, Lars, and M. S. Khan,
three friends in India

Preface

My wife and I lived in the town of "Tezibazar" from November, 1963, to October, 1964. Before leaving the United States for India, I had chosen this locality as my research area on the basis of census materials and the previous work of Professor R. L. Singh of Banaras Hindu University. After reaching India, I found no reason to change my initial choice and in a short space of time had set up my household and begun my research.

We were lucky enough (considering the scarcity of residential space in the main market area) to rent the upper story of a wholesale cloth shop almost in the exact center of the town along the main street. The social and economic life of the urban center went on transparently underneath the front porch of our house and in the backyards and public square beneath our rear veranda. The people of the town were similarly aware of our movements and equally able to watch our style of life.

"Tezibazar" is not the real name of the town, nor do any of its inhabitants appear with their real names in this book. Other geographical and administrative names have also been changed to protect the identity of the town. The problem of informant protection in a literate, unisolated complex society is difficult at best. It is immeasurably heightened when the venue of research is a small urban locale. Not even the anonymity of the city cloaks my informants in Tezibazar. Therefore I have not included any bit of political or social scandal which was not common knowledge. I have also excluded cases of moral delicts which might prove embarrassing or which were irrelevant to the purpose of this book.

My major emphasis throughout the research was on the commercial populace and business activities within the town. Clearly, many aspects of social life are underrepresented in the following account, and the qualities of businesses and businessmen have greatly influenced my work. To have sampled equally all social groups and activities, however, would have been beyond the capabilities of a single researcher, and a more focused investigation was required. Nevertheless, I believe that this presentation does deal with Tezibazar as a community, not because every activity or aspect of social life has been thoroughly sampled, but rather because those social institutions which were studied are of paramount importance in defining the town. The organization of trade and traders, the physical morphology of shop and market area, the ties of commerce and credit to rural localities all demarcate Tezibazar from surrounding population clusters. These institutions have defined and still do define the town as an urban area with a characteristic style of life and social pattern.

Throughout the text, most Hindi words are italicized or capitalized. Plurals are formed by the addition of an unitalicized English s (*mohallas*). Word spelling consistently indicates aspiration by *h* after the consonant. The letter *s* stands for dental, alveolar, and retroflex sibilants because these three phones are in free variation in the local Hindi dialect; however, the spelling *sh* has been retained for two words, "*shekh*" and "*shah*," for fear the reader would not otherwise recognize these names. Certain familiar Indian place names are given in their English forms (thus Ganges, not Ganga). A formal transliteration of the Hindi words most frequently used in the text appears in Appendix II, along with a guide to the Devanagari symbols and their English coding. Various Hindi sayings, proverbs, and caste names are also formally transliterated at various points throughout the text.

I am grateful to the Foreign Area Training Program of the

Social Science Research Council and the American Council of Learned Societies for providing the financial aid that made the research possible and for a supplementary six-month grant which allowed me to write up the field materials. The Foreign Area Training Program also kindly provided a three-month grant for the study of Hindi at the University of California, Berkeley.

I am also indebted to the Office of Education, United States Government, for subsidizing my study of Hindi and South Asia. I held a National Defense Foreign Language Fellowship in Hindi for the academic year 1961–1962 at the University of Michigan, for the summer of 1962 at the University of Pennsylvania, and for the academic year 1962–1963 at the University of California, Berkeley.

Brandeis University generously provided a grant that offset the cost of typing the manuscript and preparing the Index.

Especially to Professors Morton H. Fried and Marshall D. Sahlins, Elman R. Service and Eric R. Wolf, I owe much of my present understanding of anthropology and whatever insights into human society the following presentation contains. I am grateful also to Professors Robbins Burling and Howard Schuman for their helpful comments on the original version of this work. I am indebted to Professors William Rowe, Ralph H. Retzlaff, and O. L. Chavarria-Aguilar and to Dr. Amar Bahadur Singh for knowledge of South Asia and Hindi. In the course of many discussions with Dr. David Kaplan, I have gained greater insight into problems of preindustrial urbanism and the relationship between city and state. Finally, I wish to thank Jean Hobday for her patient criticism, most of which was very perspicacious, and some of which I heeded.

R. G. F.

Waltham, Massachusetts
May 1968

Contents

Maps

Charts

Tables

FROM ZAMINDAR
TO BALLOT BOX

*Community Change in a
North Indian Market Town*

INTRODUCTION

The Study of a Market Town

This book analyzes the changing relations of a small market town with the larger society of India. By using historical materials and studies of comparative urbanism, it attempts to portray the nature of this interaction in the past. By using data from anthropological field work, it tries to indicate recent changes and the present-day interaction between the urban community and the nation.

Anthropologists have increasingly turned their attention in recent decades to the study of "complex societies." This research has been promoted not only by the demise of the primitive world (or its radical transformation through European contact), but also by a burgeoning interest among anthropologists in economic development and modernization in nonindustrial countries. The nonindustrial complex societies of Asia, the Near East, or Latin America have been characterized in different ways and been called by different terms—"modern folk society," "great and little tradition," "part-societies," "feudal society."[1] But the problem for anthropologists dealing with such complex societies has not been definitional; it has been mechanical and conceptual. By "mechanical" is meant the difficulty in applying small-scale anthropological field technique to the study of a complex so-

[1] Elman R. Service, *Profiles in Ethnology*, p. xii; Robert Redfield, "The Social Organization of Tradition," *Far Eastern Quarterly*, XV (1955), 14; A. L. Kroeber, *Anthropology*, pp. 278–280; Gideon Sjoberg, "Folk and 'Feudal' Societies," *American Journal of Sociology*, LVIII (1952), 231–239.

ciety. By "conceptual" is meant the problem of defining the unit of analysis and research in such a society. Obviously, the latter difficulty is intimately tied to research method. The usual "solution" has been to make community studies—that is, to accept as a viable research locale a village or a city ward, and to apply the traditional intensive anthropological methodology to its study. Increasingly in recent years, however, the relevance of the community study approach to the description of a complex society has been sharply questioned.[2] Although it results in a manageable research area, the community study method only leads to a proliferation of specific, self-contained studies which even taken together do not adequately describe a complex society.

Various anthropologists have attempted to avoid the limitations of the community perspective. Thus, the social organization of a complex society has been characterized by Eric Wolf as a "web of group relations" which connects particular localities and local traditions with national-level institutions.[3] In the same vein, Bernard Cohn and McKim Marriott have described Indian civilization as comprising numerous levels of diversity whose integration is accomplished by "networks" of kinship, ritual, and trade relations which join the local community with the larger society, and by urban "centers" where economic, religious, and political specialists congregate and mediate between the local area and the next larger societal unit.[4] To study the organization of the national sphere or of the local sphere without analyzing their interrelation is to create individual community profiles, irrelevant for the characterization of the complex society as a whole. Wolf and Cohn and Marriott point to the importance of

[2] Julian Steward, *Area Research: Theory and Practice*, pp. 50–51; Adrian Mayer, "System and Network: An Approach to the Study of Political Process in Dewas," *Indian Anthropology*, ed. T. N. Madan and Gopala Sarana, pp. 266–267.

[3] "Aspects of Group Relations in a Complex Society: Mexico," *American Anthropologist*, LVIII (1956), 1065.

[4] Bernard S. Cohn and McKim Marriott, "Networks and Centers in the Integration of Indian Civilization," *Journal of Social Research*, I (1958), 1–8.

studying "hinge" groups and centers—whether religious, administrative, or commercial—as pivotal agents or loci in the integration of local traditions with national ones.[5]

My research in India attempted to go beyond the limits of the community study. I was able to study a small urban area, Tezibazar, as a market and political center. The traditional merchant castes and other social groups engaged in business within the town were viewed as hinges connecting the urban locale to regional society. The following pages present data and advance a thesis concerned with the social nature of such a market town and the commercial groups which inhabit it.

In India, interest in small urban areas as centers and their inhabitants as hinge groups has hardly begun.[6] Even though over 70 percent of all urban areas in the country have a population of 20,000 or less, and even though 23 percent of the total Indian urban population lives in them (1961 census), such localities have received little scholarly attention in proportion to their importance or magnitude. Most sociological and anthropological interest has been directed toward Indian villages; the remainder has been turned to the great urban agglomerations, the major cities of the subcontinent. In both cases, the primary orientation has been to treat these locales as more or less self-sufficient communities (except insofar as migration is considered).[7]

Recent scholarly research in small Indian urban areas has been

[5] Wolf, *op. cit.*; Cohn and Marriott, *op. cit.*, p. 5.

[6] For a general bibliography of urban studies, see William Rowe, "Caste, Kinship, and Association in Urban India," unpublished paper prepared for the 1964 symposium of the Wenner-Gren Foundation for Anthropological Research (Burg Wartenstein). For a marketing study of a small Punjabi town, see Walter Neale, Harpal Singh, and Jai Pal Singh, "Kurali Market: A Report on the Economic Geography of Marketing in Northern Punjab," *Economic Development and Cultural Change*, XIII (1965), 129–168. For a study of traditional merchants in a small Punjabi city, see Leighton Wilson Hazelhurst, "Entrepreneurship and the Merchant Castes in a Punjabi City" (unpublished Ph.D. thesis, University of California, Berkeley, 1964).

[7] See Richard Lambert, "The Impact of Urban Society upon Village Life," *India's Urban Future*, ed. Roy Turner, pp. 117–140.

the almost exclusive preserve of R. L. Singh and his fellow urban geographers at Banaras Hindu University. Their publications have broken the preliminary ground for such studies, although naturally their work and theoretical interests have been primarily geographical and therefore of limited value in discussions of social and cultural factors.[8]

Another neglected research area in India even more directly within the purview of the social sciences has been the traditional merchant castes as hinge groups in urban centers. Numerous books have appeared on the developmental economics of India, the nature of public and private enterprise, internal markets and marketing in the subcontinent, and on other equally relevant questions to the state of national or local commerce. But rarely is mention made of the economic importance or social relevance of the present-day Baniya (traditional merchant) castes—or, for that matter, much consideration given to any of the social groups involved in business. D. R. Gadgil's small publication, *Origins of the Modern Indian Business Class*, first penetrated this research area through an attempt at evaluating the present-day status and functions of traditional business groups. Even Gadgil retrenched his original investigation because "of the lack of adequate recent data," and his "interim" report was forced to bear a heavily historical emphasis.[9]

My own research attempts partially to fill the lacunae regarding the nature of Indian small urban centers as well as the activities of commercial groups. Briefly, I found that the pattern

[8] R. L. Singh and K. N. Singh, "Evolution of the Medieval Towns in the Saryu-par Plain," *National Geographical Journal of India*, IX, (1963), 1–11; R. L. Singh and S. M. Singh, "Mungra-Badshahpur: A Rurban Settlement in the Ganga-Ghaghara Doab West," *National Geographical Journal of India*, VI (1960), 200–206; K. N. Singh, "Barhaj: A Study in the Changing Pattern of a Market Town," *National Geographical Journal of India*, VII (1961), 21–36; R. L. Singh, "Ballia: A Study in Urban Settlement," *National Geographical Journal of India*, II (1956), 1–6; R. L. Singh, "Two Small Towns of Eastern U.P.: Sultanpur and Chunar," *National Geographical Journal of India*, III (1957), 1–10.

[9] D. R. Gadgil, assisted by M. V. Namjoshi, *Origins of the Modern Indian Business Class: An Interim Report*, p. iii.

of interaction between Tezibazar town and the larger society had undergone a major shift in the last half-century. In the past, the interaction of the town with the region was almost entirely mediated by local "big men"—zamindars—who created the town and its market and governed its social existence. At present, however, the zamindars are gone, and as a result, the town's political, caste, and community organization is becoming increasingly absorbed into the modern administration and cultural traditions of the Indian nation.

I wish not only to describe this changing pattern of interaction between town and nation, but also to explain it. My thesis is that the nature of the town's traditional social integration has predetermined its reaction to modern political influences. Specifically, its lack of traditional social cohesion and community has promoted the penetration of modern social ideas, the dissolution of existing custom and organization and their replacement with new formal structures, and, above all, the increasingly direct merger of the town into a regional and national society. All these changes are evident in the town's reliance on the modern political machinery of the nation-state to establish internal power and status and to arbitrate formerly intracaste and kin disputes. They are also exemplified by the alteration of the significant internal political groups on the basis of regional political organizations and national political ideologies.

Why did the town lack internal social cohesion and community? Precisely because of the traditional pattern of its integration into the larger society and as a result of the highly competitive and familial patterning of commercial enterprise. For in this market town the local overlord—invested with the powers of state authority or property ownership in British times—created the urban area, regulated its market place, and mediated between the component but socially unrelated commercial groups which were attracted to settle therein. It was these local overlords who provided internal social cohesion and political structure and through whom the town was related to the outside. Economic factors were also decisive in preventing the growth of a town community. The nature of the trading castes, the traditional organization of business ventures, and the highly competitive market of an underdeveloped economy helped fragment the social body into individually competitive family units.

Once the function of local overlord is destroyed by economic decline, so, too, is supra-town supervision and control. No conditioner of community existence emerges from the social realm or economic market of this now reduced social world. All that remains are the economically competitive, mutually "repulsed" merchant castes. The only replacement for the old local big men is the new regional and national political machinery of the state, which, although in different fashion and with different rules and results, performs the same internal leadership as did the former overlords. This reliance on the electoral process and political apparatus naturally furthers the amalgamation of the town with larger social groupings and the transformation of internal organization to fit the realities of political conflict on supra-local levels. Consequently, it also creates a growing impotency of purely local structures and groups such as castes.

The two processes of dissolution and amalgamation noted for the town also characterize the internal organization of one resident trading caste specially selected for study. Within this (Umar) caste, local usages and internal political organization have given way to a regional "caste" structure—but with greatly altered powers of social control and a widened viewpoint embracing the nation. As the local caste group's powers of social restraint have declined, many caste customs and institutions have died or changed because of individual behavior being unmuzzled from traditional sanctions.

In science, a single case is only informative, not explanatory. This book attempts to relate the present and past organization of a single market town to other urban locales in India as well as to the whole pattern of urbanism in preindustrial complex societies. Insofar as most towns in India were formed in similar manner around local overlords and with similar populations, the social characteristics of Tezibazar town may illustrate a widespread pattern. On a larger scale, insofar as the lack of traditional community can be shown to be typical of oriental urbanism, the developments in this market town are relevant to comparative studies of preindustrial urbanism around the world. Finally, the descriptive material on Tezibazar portrays an urban type neither preindustrial nor industrial, but what might be described as post-colonial: that is, the urban reflection of a society which is basically preindustrial, but which has been fundamentally altered by the presence of other, dominant (often colonial) industrial societies around it.

CHAPTER 1

Tezibazar, Town and Region

Ram-Ji called it "dog's heaven." Another man said it was his "homeland." To the city dweller it is only an insignificant way station on a rural bus line. To the villager it is the market where he buys his goods. All points of view describe the small town of Tezibazar.

THE REGION

Tezibazar lies in eastern Uttar Pradesh—one of the states of independent India formerly called the United Provinces (of Agra and Oudh) under the British. Uttar Pradesh, or U.P., is in many ways one of the most advanced regions of India, but the eastern section of this great state is sorely behind the central and, particularly, the western regions. Sophisticated townsmen note this: when they are unhappy about the persistence of a custom or at least apologetic for its presence, they say, "But in the west this is better, because they are more forward."

The area of eastern U.P. in which Tezibazar lies is fully within the plain of the Ganges River. For many miles around the town the terrain is broken only here and there by the hillocks of villages and small towns. The forty-inch rainfall isohyet passes through this part of eastern Uttar Pradesh. Most of the rain comes in the monsoon, from July to October. Eastern U.P. is one of the most fertile and intensively cultivated sections of India,[1] yet it is so densely populated that it must import food

---

[1] O. H. K. Spate, *India and Pakistan: A General and Regional Geography*, p. 501.

8

Map 1. Uttar Pradesh State, showing Tezibazar in Jaunpur district

grains. Aside from its impact on Tezibazaris as consumers, this food deficit has importance in determining business in the town. A large part of Tezibazar's trade, both wholesale and retail, lies in food grains. Some of the grain—and the term includes wheat, rice, barley, maize, and various kinds of *dal* or pulses—is imported from other states; the remainder is collected by the local merchants from nearby agriculturalists who manage to produce surpluses. The leading merchants in Tezibazar are generally dealers in food grains.

Tezibazar is a small urban locality in Jaunpur district. Merchants from the town go to Jaunpur city to pay their income and sales taxes, to see to their legal affairs, and to replenish their inventories. Halfway between Jaunpur and Tezibazar lies Baragaon, the town's *tehsil*, or subdistrict, headquarters. Here lives the *tehsildar*, the high government official most immediate to Tezibazar, and here also are various tax offices and other administrative machinery. Finally, Tezibazar is in *pargana* Sarai, an official *tehsil* subdivision which, however, has no formal administrative structure except a few low-ranking land revenue officers. Tezibazar is the functionless "capital" of Sarai *pargana*, and the town is often called "Sarai-Tezibazar."

The population density of Jaunpur district is 973 persons per square mile and that of Baragaon *tehsil*, 814. Villages are everywhere, and for long stretches the roads leading from Tezibazar to nearby cities are continuously built up with villages, small towns, and way stations for travelers. Hundreds of bicycles, oxcarts, *ikka*s, camels, trucks, and buses ply the principal routes, and the roads are always quite crowded except in the midday heat of the hot season.

Rice, both irrigated and unirrigated, is the predominant food crop in Jaunpur district, closely followed by wheat. Barley and corn rank lower. The main cash crop is sugar cane, which is often processed (against government wishes) by the local peasantry into *gur*, a crude molasses sugar. Near Tezibazar, cultivation of tobacco is a large enterprise.

Tezibazar is a small urban enclave within an overwhelmingly agricultural countryside (see Table 1). From a few miles out along the road to Jaunpur, the town appears as an irregular ridge running perpendicular to the road and lending interest to the otherwise unending flatness of the alluvial plain. The nearby country is primarily covered by rice fields, each plot demarcated by an earthen border. In the winter these or other plots are put into wheat, mustard, and peas. Vegetable cultivation predominates within a mile or two of the town, and the fields alternate between cauliflower and cabbage, carrots and eggplant, melons

and squash. The small agricultural segment of the town's population—generally Koiri, Kurmi, and Kunjra by caste—owns and
tends these fields and brings its produce into town for sale on
market days.

Table 1. Rural and urban population of Jaunpur district and Baragaon *tehsil* from
the 1961 census of India

Place	Rural		Urban		Total	
	No.	%	No.	%	No.	%
Jaunpur	1,432,982	94.10	84,191	5.90	1,517,173	100.00
Baragaon	266,446	95.20	13,540	4.80	279,986	100.00

The soil of the Tezibazar area is generally typical of the
Gangetic Plain. There are, however, also large patches of *usar*,
heavy alkaline clays that are impossible to cultivate. A local
proverb lists the *usar* as one of the four distinctive characteristics
of the *pargana:*

bacch Upadhya umar usar / ye hae*n* Sar*a*i ke dham dhusar.
(*bacch, upadhya,* Umar, *usar* / These are what make Sarai famous.)

The other three names are those of social groupings which will
play a large role in the succeeding pages: the *bacch* are the
original branch of Thakurs or, as they consider themselves,
Rajputs who settled in this area, as are the *upadhya* for the
Brahmins. The Umar are the most important Baniya or traditional merchant caste in the town.

COMMUNICATIONS AND THE TOWN

Tezibazar is a nodal point for several main roads. The metaled
road between Allahabad city and the district capital cuts the
town at its southern tip (see Map 2). This crossroads is a way
station for the constant caravans of trucks and buses which pass
through on their way to the city or the district town, both of
which are about two and a half hours away. The metaled road
from Pratabgarh city, one and a half hours distant, intersects the

Allahabad route in Tezibazar. What was formerly the main highway between Jaunpur and Pratabgarh and thence Lucknow is now an almost obliterated dirt road running through the northern midsection of the town; it was in use well over a hundred years ago when this part of Old Town was the center of the urban area. The main street of the town leads into the road north to Gopiganj, ten miles and less than an hour away. From Gopiganj this route goes to Shahganj, another important small urban center in Jaunpur district. All these routes are covered by public buses owned and operated by the Uttar Pradesh government. They offer efficient, inexpensive, and relatively quick transportation, considering the condition of the roads. About twenty-five or thirty buses pass through the town daily.

Tezibazar is also a station on the Northern Railway. Four passenger trains and numerous freights stop here each day and link the town directly with Varanasi (Banaras), four hours away, and the state capital of Lucknow, seven hours distant (this time can be reduced to five and a half hours by changing to a mail train in Pratabgarh).

The numerous surrounding villages are linked to Tezibazar by footpaths or, at a greater distance, by *ikka*s which go between villages not easily reached on foot or too distant for easy walking. Many of the goods for Tezibazar come by railway or by truck. Shipments of cloth from Kanpur, the main industrial center of U.P. and a large producer of textiles, always arrive in large bales aboard trucks, whereas raw tobacco from Gujarat or cloth from Calcutta or Bombay comes by train. The effective distance of truck transport is about two hundred miles, beyond which the railroad is usually employed. For local transportation of salt and grains, particularly to and from villages, camels are widely used; they also often travel relatively long distances (over a hundred miles). Any market day finds many of these beasts tied up in front of large grain shops or at the Gola Mandi, where food grains are sold. Bicycles are employed for small-scale local transport. A village retailer who has purchased cloth from a Tezibazar wholesaler loads the parcel on the back of his cycle.

The same is true of utensil and hardware dealers and of sugar and salt merchants. These men rarely come from villages more than fifteen miles distant, and the average is three to five. Bicycles are also used as a convenience by those villagers who can afford them when they come for retail purchases, and for many of the small village merchants, they are indispensable adjuncts of their trade. In the town private automobiles are scarce. There are only five and although they are used as business devices in some cases, it is rarely for transport of goods.[2] A merchant in Pratabgarh, however, often sends his son to collect accounts due and deliver cloth goods to his Tezibazar customers on a motorcycle.

The post office, of course, links the town to the outside world. Besides its normal mail service, the Tezibazar post office also receives and sends telegrams and has a long-distance telephone connection.

Thus the communications network of the town intimately connects it, both for purposes of trade and travel, with distant parts of India as well as with the nearby rural area. Far from being remote or removed through natural barriers or lack of transportation, the town is enmeshed in the mechanized network of truck and railway as well as the less advanced system of camel and *ikka*.[3]

THE TOWN

Tezibazar, the town and market center, is fundamentally different from Tezibazar, the official and administrative locale called the "Notified Area." The latter is an artificial and arbitrary governmental unit, originally set up under British rule and continued in independent India. It exists only in these terms, not in any intrinsic social or economic way.

Nevertheless, the Notified Area (N.A.) is important to Tezi-

---

[2] Of the five automobiles, two were hired out for use in marriage processions (*barat*), and two others were kept primarily for prestige. The fifth was used for long commercial trips.

[3] A glossary along with a formal transliteration of Hindi terms appears in Appendix II.

bazar; its political organization is for all intents the town's as well
and constitutes one of the few conditioners of a community
existence within the market center. But this official area has little
importance apart from the political reality given it by the town's
population as well as by the provincial government. Thus, the
Tezibazar N.A. consists of 775.81 acres, of which, however,
only 302.14 acres, or less than one-half, are built up—that is,
possibly constitute part of the town complex. Twenty-one and a
half acres are under water, a fraction more than twenty-five are
put into orchards, and the rest, consisting of over half the N.A.
acreage, is agricultural land.[4] Further, the Notified Area of Tezibazar includes five primarily agricultural villages—Sarai Rustum,
Palkapura, Dhaurahra, Kamalpur, and Latharia, which have
nothing in common with the town save a shared political framework—and a small commercial settlement, Gajraj Ganj, one mile
away from the town nucleus and only slightly more integrated
with the town than are the villages (see Map 2). Unfortunately,
official statistics do not distinguish the actual town or urban area
from these peripheral localities. Thus, in that it contains data on
a sizable rural land area and population, the official statistical
information given below may not always present a completely
fair picture of the town itself.

Tezibazar, the town, is essentially a long ribbon of business
development strung out along a single street for over a mile.
Along this entire length shops line both sides of the road in
seemingly endless progression. Intermittently the porches of the
shops cover the sewer drains, which also run almost the length of
the town. In slack times businessmen sit on their porches and
discuss the news of the day with their neighbors. The street is
bright and hot, and the shops seem dark and cool. The owners,

[4] For these survey figures I am indebted to Professor R. L. Singh
under whose direction in October, 1959, Tezibazar was surveyed and
mapped by a group of students from Banaras Hindu University. Professor Singh's excellent maps and survey figures aided me greatly in the
initial stages of my research, and I am grateful for his help in both a
personal and a scholarly sense.

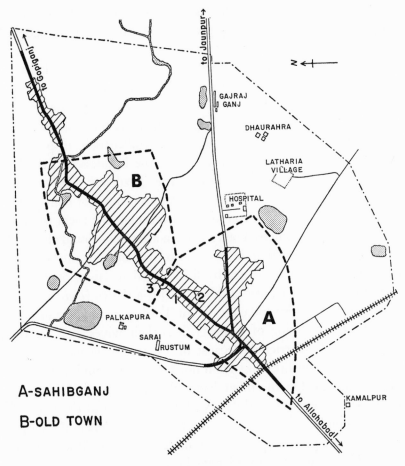

1-Vegetable market   2-Grain market   3-Leather market
═══ Main road ■■■ Extent of business survey — Secondary roads
+++ Railroad ⬤ Water ▨ Central area ·—·— Boundary of Notified area

Map 2. Tezibazar Notified Area, showing Sahibganj and Old Town;
extent of business survey (after R. L. Singh)

when they are not serving customers, lounge on the *gaddi*, or
sheeting, which partially covers the floor of each shop and which
is reserved for the money box, the owner, and more distinguished guests and customers. When buyers come, they squat on
the perimeter of the *gaddi* or, if graced by the shopkeeper with

an invitation, slip out of their shoes and sit down cross-legged upon the sheeting. For really prestigious customers or guests, the owner orders pillows and offers *pan* (betel) or cigarettes. Even the most humble shopkeeper will obtain *"laci"* (*ilaci*, cardoman) for his guests to chew as an aid to digestion.

It is not uncommon in the smaller, poorer shops for female relatives of the merchant to help conduct the business. In some commercial lines such as bangle selling, trinket trade, or parched grain sales, women commonly handle the business entirely by themselves. In general, however, the Tezibazar ideal is for women to be restricted to the back rooms or interior courtyards of the houses, and it is considered demeaning for them to have to deal with customers. Young women are rarely found alone on the streets or assisting in the shops. When they make their twice-daily trips to the nearby fields for defecation, they carefully conceal their faces and heads with a shawl (*caddar*). Although the wealthy and educated of Tezibazar espouse a distaste for *parda* (seclusion of women), it is their wives who are the most severely restricted. Because of a favorable economic position, they suffer little loss from not using the feminine labor of their families. On the other hand, the freedom of children of both sexes contrasts markedly with the situation of the women. Young children quickly learn to relieve their elders in the shops, and they are given impressive commercial responsibilities at what would be regarded as a tender age in the West.

At one point along the main street, camels unload bags of salt or grain; further on, a truck from Kanpur delivers bales of cloth or utensils; in one place an *ikkevan* solicits riders to the neighboring villages; in another, a jeweler weighs out many rupees' worth of what he is pleased to call "pure" gold ornaments. Shops are open for business even in the slowest, or "coldest," seasons; at no time do Tezibazar and its main street lose their primary commercial character. On the day of Jawaharlal Nehru's funeral in May, 1964, the municipality called a town-wide *hartal* and injunction against doing business, which was enforced by roving, almost pillaging bands of adolescents and young adults.

Even so, the local merchants collected credit returns because they chose to regard these transactions as nonbusiness. "*Lenden*," buy and sell, is the key to Tezibazar.

In construction, the main street is a curious kind of semi-*pakka* paving. Over the years various industrious N.A. committees, hampered by limited budgets, have tried to improve the deteriorating condition of the main town artery. Generally, these endeavors have taken the form of tarring and pebbling the high street—the last such effort being made just before the onset of the 1964 monsoon. Unfortunately, with the coming of the rains and the continued heat, the tar softens, the heavy bullock carts quickly rut and destroy the surface, and the road returns to its former deplorable condition. Even this limited sort of road improvement has usually been undertaken only in the section from the rail crossing to the leather market—the main commercial nexus of the town—and beyond this point the road is an uneven, deeply rutted, pot-holed thoroughfare, almost impassable in the rainy season.

Distinction in road surface marks a physical boundary in the town that has important economic and social consequences. The section of Main Street which has been partially paved lies in the new part of Tezibazar, which is less than one hundred years old. It is also the newly important market area—a circumstance which likewise is a matter of less than a century. Along this segment of Main Street are the biggest and wealthiest shops, the grain and vegetable markets, the largest houses, and most of the well-to-do residents. Here, houses and shops are highly compacted. For the most part, residence and shop are in the same building. Space is at too much of a premium to be used solely for residential purposes. If the merchant's own family does not live in the back or on the second story of the shop, he rents it out as a residence or storage area to someone else. Sahibganj, the official name of most of this part of Main Street, has the appearance of a highly commercialized and built-up market center.

On the other hand, Old Town—the name I shall use for that section of the town demarcated by the main road between the leather market and Naibazar—has a more rural aspect. Here, the line of businesses along the high road is interrupted by purely residential buildings and even empty lots. Occasional urban developments off the main street contain small pockets of houses, and, intermittently, narrow alleys run off the road and lead to the fields. In Sahibganj, Tezibazar is little more than one street in width; in Old Town, several side roads contain secondary residential and business areas. Because of the dusty, uneven road and the greater incidence of *kaccha* (mud and thatch) houses—houses in Sahibganj are *pakka* (brick and stucco)[5]—the general impression of Old Town is of a slow, sedate, but now-deteriorated market place. Indeed, businesses in Old Town are smaller and more oriented to purely local services. On the market days, when the merchants of Sahibganj are harried with commercial activity and the transaction of goods, their colleagues in Old Town are relatively unmoved.

No sharp change in house style or business activity marks the border between Sahibganj and Old Town, however. Rather, a steady south–north gradient runs along the highroad, a gradual tapering off of business and wealth. Thus, one section of Old Town, Naiganj, which is the portion of Main Street on either side of the leather market, is almost as developed commercially as is Sahibganj itself. Neither is the distinction between Old Town and Sahibganj purely geographical. Later we shall see that these

---

[5] *Kaccha* houses are small, one-story structures and usually consist of only a few rooms. The front room or rooms are used for the shop and its stock, and a back room or rooms comprise the habitation area. Often, cooking is done in a small open courtyard in the back. During the hot nights of summer, family members move their cots into this courtyard; people without such courtyards set the cots on their front porches or in the public way.

Pakka houses vary from elaborate to simple, but are larger and more expensive than *kaccha* ones. Many are grandiose, two- or even three-storied affairs, whitewashed, with many rooms, and imposing pillared front verandas. Quite commonly, they contain an interior courtyard used for cooking, around which the individual or nuclear family apartments are grouped. As in the *kaccha* houses, the front area is used for the shop.

two areas have separate histories entailing social as well as economic and business consequences and that only relatively recently has the unified entity of Tezibazar come into existence.

Offshoots of business development have recently occurred at the two peripheries of the main road. At the southern end along the Jaunpur and Pratabgarh roads, small businesses catering to travelers have grown up. To the north is Naibazar, a new market area reached from Old Town by crossing a bridge over an artificial pond. Probably less than thirty years old, it is given over primarily to the manufacture and sale of parched grain. Another road in lower Sahibganj leads to Janghai, but has little business growth along it. The same is true of the road leading to the railroad station.

The width of Main Street varies greatly and has little to do with the age of the section. In southern Sahibganj it is quite broad, but from the vegetable market it gradually narrows until it jogs to the right beyond the leather market. From here it broadens slightly but again becomes quite narrow at the turning into Gurhai ward (see Map 3). From this point the road broadens into a very wide thoroughfare and continues thus beyond the outskirts of the town. At its narrowest the road is not wide enough for two buses or trucks to pass. The side roads range in size from streets wide enough for a single motor vehicle to footpaths too small even for bullock carts.

Household wastes and garbage are emptied into the open sewage drains which line the main road (except in the Naibazar area) and parts of the Jaunpur and Pratabgarh *pakka* roads as well. These drains have been a sore point in the town for many years, for in large measure they are the source of Tezibazar's bad reputation for mosquitoes and epidemics. The side roads and Naibazar, as well as more distant sections of the Jaunpur and Pratabgarh roads, do not have these drains.

Electricity was introduced in 1952–1953 and is available all along the main road as far as Naibazar, but not to houses on the side roads or alleys. Along some of their length, however, the Jaunpur and Pratabgarh *pakka* roads are also electrified. The hospital, located some distance away along the Jaunpur road, is not yet electrified, although the still more distant Block Development Office on the Janghai road enjoys this advantage. Many of the houses and shops on the main road are not electrified by choice.

In 1963–1964 there was no municipal water supply although construction on that project was under way and completion was scheduled for mid-1965.

TERRITORIAL ORGANIZATION AND PROPERTY

Wards and *mohallas*

There are five wards in Tezibazar.[6] These are artificial units drawn up by the government for voting purposes. They do have some reality in that they are composed of one or more *mohallas* or traditional subsections of the town. Some of these *mohallas* are recognized by the Notified Area and others are not. Often *mohallas* have subdivisions, and sometimes local people use more than one name for a particular section. "Spurious" *mohallas* comprised of villages of the rural area included officially within the N.A. also exist. They are, of course, not traditional subsections of the town, but are entered as *mohallas* by the municipal committee for taxation purposes (see Table 2).

Sahibganj Ward and *mohalla*

This ward corresponds to the Sahibganj section of Main Street. Its size, both in area and population, is unusual and is perhaps attributable to its relatively recent emergence. Within Sahibganj Ward there are no *mohallas*, although there are popularly demarcated sections such as Gola Mandi, the grain market, and Sabzi Mandi, the vegetable market. This part of Tezibazar

---

[6] For the November, 1964, municipal elections there were only four wards: Sahibganj and Naiganj were merged to give greater prominence to the Muslim vote. I have retained the pre-election ward organization because it is more in accord with the *mohalla* structure of the town and sharply differentiates Sahibganj from Old Town.

contains the official buildings as well as many of its modern
facilities: the Notified Area office, post office, the Benares State
Bank, the bus station, and the Thana, or police station. Sahibganj
also contains the *rani kothi*, the former residence of one of the
founders of this ward; the largest temple in the town; a girl's
school (up to eighth grade); a *ram lila* ground; the Muslim

Table 2. Wards and *mohallas*

| Ward | Town *mohallas* | | Rural *mohallas* |
	Official	Nonofficial	
Sahibganj	(none)		(none)
Naiganj	Naiganj	Chikan	Palkapura
	Suthatti	Pasian	Sarai Rustum
	(Machargali)		Kamalpur
	Darziana		
Anjahi	Anjahi		
	Sipah		
	Kot		
	Koiran		
	Babhanaoti		
	Chamraoti		
Gurhai	Gurhai	Dafliana	
	Katra		
	Naibazar		
Pakri	Pakri	Chamraoti	Gajraj Ganj
		Gudam	(Lalu-ka-talab)
		Lalhan	Latharia
		Ahiran	Dhaurahra

graveyard near the railway crossing; and the United Club, a
social meeting place with political overtones (see Map 3).

Naiganj Ward

Naiganj ward is a political potpourri of rural sections and
town localities. The latter is that stretch of Main Street north of
Sahibganj. The town area included in Naiganj ward is second
only to Sahibganj in its business activity. Within its limits are the
leather market (Naiganj *mohalla*); the largest mosque, the Jama

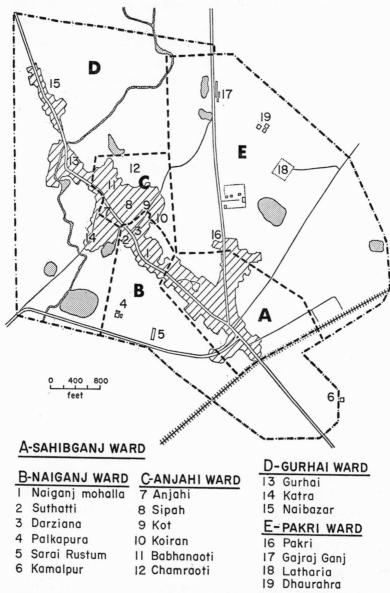

A-SAHIBGANJ WARD

B-NAIGANJ WARD
1 Naiganj mohalla
2 Suthatti
3 Darziana
4 Palkapura
5 Sarai Rustum
6 Kamalpur

C-ANJAHI WARD
7 Anjahi
8 Sipah
9 Kot
10 Koiran
11 Babhanaoti
12 Chamraoti

D-GURHAI WARD
13 Gurhai
14 Katra
15 Naibazar

E-PAKRI WARD
16 Pakri
17 Gajraj Ganj
18 Latharia
19 Dhaurahra

Map 3. Tezibazar Notified Area, showing wards and *mohallas* (after R. L. Singh)

masjid (Naiganj *mohalla*), which also contains a Muslim primary school, and the Mahajani Pathshala, or school for clerks (Suthatti *mohalla*). This ward's rural segment contains three villages as well as the area where the town's two intermediate colleges are found. In this same locality is the Sanskrit Pathshala, or traditional school for boys.

Anjahi Ward

From the middle of Naiganj north along Main Street to Anjahi we begin to enter the heart of Old Town. Within Anjahi are Kot and Sipah, the oldest *mohalla*s of Tezibazar. The latter contains the supposedly oldest monuments in the town: the remains of a fort built by the *bhar*, the alleged autochthones of this area; and the Sayad Mansur-ka-mazar, the tomb of an ancient Muslim saint and the center of a much more modern communal conflict. Sipah also contains a municipally constructed slaughterhouse and has a primary school and *ram lila* ground. These *mohalla*s, as well as Babhanaoti and Koiran, are well off the main road, unelectrified, and, for the most part, consist of *kaccha* residential buildings. Anjahi *mohalla* in this ward has some business activity, but the others have none whatsoever.

Gurhai Ward

There are nineteen electrical posts from Sahibganj to the end of Naiganj ward, only three in Anjahi, and Gurhai ward, which begins beyond the twenty-second electrical pole and around a sharp bend in the road has five. All of Gurhai ward is involved in business activities to a much larger degree than are the side-road *mohalla*s of Anjahi, but the commercial atmosphere is neither dense nor fast. Gurhai *mohalla* has a *ram lila* ground and a large temple, while Katra contains a *dharmshala* (pilgrim's rest house) and a house of prostitution. Crossing the small bridge over Lurkur Ram's tank (*talab*), one reaches Naibazar *mohalla*, almost entirely *kaccha*, thinly populated, and only recently carved out of the rural area. There is a *dharmshala* in Naibazar.

Pakri Ward

Pakri ward is primarily rural. It includes some town area along
the Jaunpur road but is for the most part composed of a small
peripheral commercial area (Gajraj Ganj) and two agricultural
villages. Within Pakri ward are the railway station and hospital
and, just before its borders, the *dak* bungalow (used by officials
on tour). Its more popular name, Lalu-ka-talab, seems to be a
tribute to a Kayasth who once lived here and built the big tank
just behind the hospital.

Property Values

There are not enough good business locations in Tezibazar to
meet the demand, and consequently those that do come on the
market command high prices. Rarely, however, are they put up
for sale at any price, and many merchants in Old Town complain that they cannot find a location in Sahibganj no matter
what they offer.

Town lands are measured in *"hath,"* each one of which equals
approximately one and a half feet. *"Hath"* is commonly translated as "hand" in English, but in fact it includes the area from
the tip of the fingers to the elbow joint. From the leather market
to the railway crossing along the main road, the average rate per
square *hath* is Rs. 500.[7] A small shop site fifteen by thirty-seven
feet in size would cost about Rs. 13,000 and a large house site
would be about Rs. 40,000. From the leather market up to Gurhai, the average rate descends sharply to Rs. 200 a square *hath*,
and from Gurhai to Naibazar it is Rs. 100. Off Main Street on
the Jaunpur and Pratabgarh roads the rate is Rs. 200 per *hath* and
further out only about Rs. 100. During my stay in Tezibazar a
large shop near the Gola Mandi was put up for sale at an asking

[7] The monetary unit in India is the rupee (Rs.) which during the
fieldwork was worth twenty-one hundredths of a U.S. cent. The fractional division of the rupee is the paesa (plural: paese), and one
hundred paese equal one rupee. Before the introduction of the decimal
system, the fractional part of a rupee was an anna; sixteen anne equaled
one rupee.

price of Rs. 28,000—a very high figure. There was a bid of Rs. 22,000, but the owner refused to sell at what he considered a discounted price.

The figures for average land values given above were obtained from one of the two *lekhpals* of Tezibazar. These men and their overseer, the *kanungo*, are government officials who keep a record of all land rights in the *mauzas*, or revenue divisions, forming the N.A. and the other areas of Sarai *pargana*.

According to the *lekhpal*, there has been little change in the ownership of plots in the main urban area between the leather market and the railway crossing. He estimated that in the last four years, 2 percent of the plots had changed hands. However, the area above the leather market in Old Town and Naibazar, has seen a 20 percent change in ownership in the last four years. Even though people have the purchase money, they cannot gain access to the main market area in Sahibganj because no one sells. Their only choice is to open up new areas along its peripheries.

CLIMATE AND THE YEARLY ROUND

The climate of the Tezibazar region is typical of the Gangetic Plain. The three main seasons are winter, which extends from November to mid-March; summer, which is from late March to late June; and the monsoon or rainy season, which lasts from July to the end of October, although the rains generally stop about the middle of September.

The mean temperature for winter is between 55° and 70° F. depending on the month. Often, however, it grows quite cold. In the winter of 1963 there were a few days when the temperature dropped slightly below freezing, causing a number of deaths from exposure and considerable damage to the wheat and pea crops. *Divali* and *dasehra*, or *ram lila*, the main festivals of this area as well as of the rest of India, occur in the early part of winter. Many *kirtan*, or group prayer and lecture meetings, are held during this season. This is also the time when Tezibazar men go out on what they call "picnics" (the English word is used)— convivial occasions in the rural area when they cook their own meals and enjoy nature. December and January are cold months: the people go to sleep early; the streets of the town are clear by ten o'clock; even the dogs are too cold to fight or howl. This season is pleasant because of the relief from the mosquitoes, although they return with increased vengeance during the transitional months of March and April. In December the championship *bubol* or nightingale fights take place in the town. These birds, which do not have the pleasant voices usually associated with this species, are matched as are cocks in other parts of the world, and the grand champion may earn several hundred rupees for its owner on this day. *Bubol* fighting, although it draws large crowds, is considered an activity of rowdies and is more or less discouraged by responsible adults. In January the famous celebration of *magh mela* takes place in Prayag, an old ritual center now part of Allahabad city. Hundreds of thousands of people take to trains, buses, carts, and foot to come to take their ritual bath at the holy *sangam*, the confluence of the Ganges, Yamuna, and mythological Sarasvati rivers. Tezibazar, being on one of the main roads to Allahabad, naturally receives many of these pilgrims, the poorer segments of whom encamp on the open field near the N.A. office. For the traditional merchant castes of Tezibazar the cold season's last months—February and March— are the time for marriages and the celebration of engagements. It is also the time when fathers begin to look for husbands for their daughters, either for marriage during the hot season or in the following year. Toward the end of February the temperature begins to climb, and by the end of March it is rarely below 90° F. at midday.

April is quite hot, but not until the end of this month or the beginning of May does the hot dry wind, the *lu*, usher in the full-scale hot season. At this time a very common activity for young boys and even some adult men is kite flying, where they try to cut each other's lines by means of a special string called *ril*. Kite flying is done in the cool of the evening in the hot season, after the *lu* has died down sufficiently. Parents tend to disapprove of it as a waste of time and money and as leading to laziness and bad habits. It is one of the few forms of outwardly aggressive behavior allowed in Tezibazar. Everything withers during May and June, and the hot wind, which blows dusty and quick through the main street of the town, prevents the people from leaving their houses between eleven and four o'clock. Now the temperature reaches 115° F. at midday, and most people sleep or relax on their cots through as much of the day as they can, while the dogs seek relief by lying in the sewer drains. In this season people rise and eat quite early; they avoid the "hot" foods such as *ghi* (clarified butter) or meat and eggs (if they eat them at all) because these make one hotter and can even derange the mind if eaten in excess. Large horseflies bred in the drains and fields invade the town at this time, and people blame them for the genesis of epidemics. Still, the market is active, for this is the marriage season (especially for villagers, after they have cut and sold the winter crop) and the best time for business. Because of the heat, activities start early or last long into the night. The merchant castes of the town also celebrate many marriages during this season, although the tendency is for these to be smaller and less prestigious than those during the cold season. The summer of 1964 was quite mild and, a number of times, was interrupted by cooling cloudbursts and heavy electrical storms.

The monsoon rains finally arrive toward the end of June, although they are not entirely predictable. In 1964, they came to Tezibazar on June 23; they were, however, intermittent and not exceedingly heavy. The monsoon rains bring relief from the heat and the *lu*, but this season can be almost as trying as the previous hot one, when it does not rain. Temperatures are not that much diminished, and the humidity is, of course, much greater. If the town seems lethargic and dull at midday in the hot season, it appears even more so during the monsoon. Business is "cold" during this season, the road through the town is often muddy, and there is little inducement to venture out on trips. No marriages take place and few all-India ritual occasions occur (except *raksa bandhan*), although during this period there are some locally important ones such as *gurva mangal* and *nag pancmi*, which is celebrated throughout the entire region. Still, this season is *basant*, spring, when greenness returns to the fields, and when, it is said, people and especially women become "sentimental." Neighboring women often come together at night to sing traditional songs (many of which the men claim not to understand) in the local dialect. The rainy season forces rats and mice out of their hiding places, particularly drains, and makes them easy prey for the feral cats who live on the rooftops and who because of them stay fairly fat throughout the year. The dogs, who dine well in the hot season on refuse from marriage feasts, now must look forward to lean days. In spite of the slight relief afforded by the fall festivals, many dogs die of starvation by the middle of the cold season.

Although Tezibazar lies on a slight rise, it still is not high enough to escape periodic flooding during the monsoon, and many places during this season are never dry. In this respect Tezibazar follows the pattern of the whole *tehsil*, which is characterized by an abundance of ponds and permanently inundated areas. The town has had a bad reputation for fevers, and in Tezibazar genealogies, entire lines suddenly end from such epidemics. Defective sewer drains add to the danger, and a local saying observes that if one can survive the Tezibazar mosquitoes, one can survive anything. These drains, which are completely stagnant (and therefore must be dredged periodically), harbor mosquito larvae as well as rats and other vermin. During the monsoon they flood onto the main street and set the town awash in filth. Under such conditions periodic outbreaks of cholera and other epidemics are unavoidable; the last came in the hot season of 1963, when nine deaths were directly attributed to this cause.

The end of the rainy season and the beginning of the cold— that is, from mid-September to November—is one of the most dangerous periods in the town. In September swarms of young mosquitoes emerge from the sewer drains and cover house walls and ceilings. At the same time, the nights begin to cool off, although the days still run hot. This is the season of fever, when many would-be informants are incommoded and unable to help.

LANGUAGE

Tezibazar lies within the nuclear Hindi-speaking area. It is on the linguistic border of several dialects, but the predominant speech is a mixture of Bhojpuri and Avadhi elements. Most men, particularly merchants, speak a regional variant of standard Hindi—with somewhat simplified grammar and pronunciation. Many can speak quite sophisticated Hindi and fill their speech with high-sounding, Sanskrit-derived words when they find a fitting occasion or listener. They also speak the local dialect, which is necessary in their transactions with the rural peasantry. This local dialect is also what is spoken by most women, who are generally illiterate. The difference between the regional variant of Hindi and the local dialect is striking. After a few months the regional speech possessed few problems for me, but I was never able to understand much of what was spoken in dialect. Similarly, many women could not understand my Hindi, and I was told that this was due not so much to lack of skill on my part as to their being unacquainted with the regional tongue. Urdu, a form of Hindi which makes greater use of Arabic and Persian words and has a more "Persianized" pronunciation, is spoken by Muslims. By a proper selection of words, Muslims can make themselves virtually unintelligible to Hindus. Many men in the town have studied some elementary English in the public schools. Only about six, however, had more than a rudimentary knowledge of the language.

CHAPTER 2

Social Bases

In 1961, the census of India enumerated Tezibazar, the Notified Area, as having 7,208 persons: 3,761 males, 3,447 females. This figure shows a rapid increase in population in the last decade. Generally the population history of the town has been relatively constant except for the impact of epidemics in the 1911–1931 period:

The population in the Notified Area and the number of houses in 1951 were surprisingly close to what they had been in 1901— and this in the face of a sizable increase in the built-up area. Only

Table 3. Population of the Notified Area, taxable houses and built-up area, 1881–1963

Year	Population	Change	Built-up area (acres)	Taxed houses
1881	6,423		218	433
1891	6,060	− 363		
1901	6,130	+ 70	249	1,135
1911	5,393	− 737		
1921	4,966	− 427		
1929	–	–	249	800
1931	5,008	+ 42		
1941	6,055	+1047		
1951	6,238	+ 183	296.1	1,163
1959	–	–	302.14	
1961	7,208	+ 970		1,697
1963	7,261 (est.)			1,677

Note: Throughout the tables, a dash indicates that data were unavailable or figures unknown.

Sources: R. L. Singh, and Jaunpur *kachehri* records.

since 1951 has the municipality shown a large increase in population and a meteoric rise in the number of taxable houses. The latter statistic may be a result of the proliferation of small properties in the rural area as an aftermath of zamindar abolition.

The Notified Area maintains records of the number of houses and population per ward. Unfortunately, separate enumeration of population for the *mohallas* does not exist, although the number of taxable houses is some indication of sub-ward population.

Table 4. Population by ward and number of taxed houses by ward and *mohalla*

Ward	Population	Mohalla	Houses 1961	Houses 1963
Sahibganj	2,014	–	459	400
Naiganj	1,226	Naiganj		100
		Darziana		55
		Suthatti		75
		Palkapura		25
		Sarai Rustum		10
		Kamalpur		15
		Total	273	280
Anjahi	1,284	Anjahi		70
		Sipah		40
		Kot		10
		Koiran		50
		Babhanaoti		95
		Chamraoti		85
		Total	323	350
Gurhai	1,429	Gurhai		130
		Naibazar		98
		Katra		136
		Total	359	364
Pakri	1,308	Pakri		149
		Gajraj Ganj		75
		Latharia		45
		Dhaurahra		14
		Total	283	283
Total	7,261		1,697	1,677

Source: Notified Area records.

Except for Sahibganj, the wards have been created so as to be more or less equal. One hundred eighty-four houses, or almost 11 percent of those taxed, are not integral parts of Tezibazar town even though included within the N.A. This figure perhaps gives some measure of the percentage of rural population included within this political unit.

In the census of 1951, 40.74 percent of the N.A. population was classified as engaged directly in, or dependent upon, commerce for their livelihood—an extremely high figure. K. N. Singh in his functional classification of urban centers in U.P. notes that Tezibazar is two standard deviations removed from the average percentage of commercial population in towns, and on this basis he rates the town as uni-functional: a market center.[1] The census further classifies the remainder of the Tezibazar N.A. population as: 16 percent engaged in, or dependent upon, nonagricultural production and manufacture; about 8 percent in transport; approximately 14 percent in miscellaneous services; 21.5 percent in agricultural production; and less than 1 percent dependent upon rental property or investment for their livelihood.

The census of India also records the number of Muslims and scheduled castes (economically underprivileged and socially ostracized groups usually equivalent to the untouchable castes). In 1951, 1,668 Muslims lived in the N.A., constituting 26.65 percent of the population; 727 individuals belonged to scheduled

[1] Kashi Nath Singh, "Functions and Functional Classification of Towns in Uttar Pradesh," *National Geographical Journal of India*, V (1959), 121–148. Although based on a different occupational breakdown and a different method of enumeration, the 1961 census indicates the overwhelming importance of commerce in Tezibazar. Of a town total of 1,953 male and 462 female workers, 735 men and 63 women (41.8 percent) were engaged in trade, whereas 337 men and 202 women (20.8 percent) were dependent upon cultivation. The 1961 percentages are also quite close to those from 1951. See Office of the Registrar General, *Census of India, 1961—Uttar Pradesh*, Part II-B, "Economic Tables," Table IVb.

castes and accounted for 11.63 percent of the population. Their distribution by ward in that year was as follows: [2]

Ward	Muslims	Sch. castes	Others	Total
Sahibganj	450	4	1,155	1,609
Naiganj	413	105	535	1,053
Anjahi	490	311	330	1,131
Gurhai	167	71	949	1,187
Pakri	148	236	741	1,125
Total	1,668	727	3,710	6,105

The Notified Area files contained a notation of the various scheduled castes and the number of families of each in 1961: Pasi —46 families; Camar—117; Musar—4; Dhorkar—1; scheduled caste total—174 families.

SOCIAL SURVEYS

An anthropologist faced with a research unit of over 7,000 individuals cannot expect to make a total census of population unless he awards undue time to this venture. On the other hand, if he samples in a situation defined by a culture and institutions with which he is not well acquainted, he is bound to leave out or miss significant aspects of the society. Just such a dilemma faced me in Tezibazar, and I resolved it by taking two surveys directly selective of businessmen. The first was a total survey—not a sample—of all the permanent businesses in the town: every shop and street-front concern; every daily shoe repairer on the public road; every owner; every servant or clerk. To my knowledge I missed some, and there was one outright refusal (some of those missed were tantamount to polite refusals). Undoubtedly, I did not obtain others which I do not know about, but I would rate these as comprising no more than 5 percent. To take only a

[2] These figures are taken from *District Population Statistics, Uttar Pradesh: No. 29 Jaunpur District*. The total population figure was later changed to 6,259, although it appears as 6,238 in the general census tables. In computing the percentages I have used the corrected total of 6,259, which must be deemed the true figure for this sample population.

limited sample would have been, I felt, to run the risk of losing valuable social material on caste and family structure, not to mention the problem of drawing a representative sample in a town as disparate socially, geographically, and economically as Tezibazar. My first survey was as thorough as possible a canvassing of all permanent businesses in the town; it did not, however, include solely market-day traders, whether town residents or not, or commercial activities (such as milk or egg sales) where there was no permanent shop or marketing base within the town precincts. My second, more intensive survey, was drawn up to provide information on various attitudes, consumption patterns, and business techniques of Tezibazar merchants. This survey was not a random sample in that I selected a 20 percent interviewing schedule from members of three specific traditional merchant, or Baniya, castes (Umar, Kalvar, and Kesarvani) which I had enumerated in my earlier survey.[3]

The total survey of businesses and businessmen can be equated with a town survey in certain ways: not in the sense of a random "slice" of Tezibazar social life, but as a considered choice or selection of the overwhelmingly important activity and grouping within the town. From its very inception Tezibazar, the town, meant Tezibazar, the market. Its political and economic base, as well as social constitution, is grounded on its market function; and the equation of town with market, and businessmen with local society, is the only legitimate valuation of its existence as an urban center. It is true that my survey and the social materials drawn from it are not a sample of the whole Notified Area[4] and that a significant minority (the noncommercial population) is ignored. It is, however, as close as possible to a complete accounting of the predominant sector of the town.

An additional factor is that the census figure of 40.74 percent for commercial population is an understatement of the town's commitment to business ventures. This figure is computed for

---

[3] See p. 285 for more information on the surveys.
[4] Map 2 indicates the territorial extent of the business survey.

the whole of the N.A., which is probably no less than 10 to 11 percent rural and noncommercial. Further, the occupational classification of the N.A. population is based on the official all-India census categories. These often do not count as business or commerce certain kinds of activities which could quite legitimately be so classified (as in fact I classified them in the survey). For the census, tobacco factories, sugar-processing plants, barbering, shoe-repairing, bangle-selling, and the making of parched grain are not commercial occupations. Further, many of the individuals classified as agriculturalists primarily grow vegetables for the town, and every market day they bring in their produce for sale. They are, to be sure, not permanent businessmen or shopkeepers, but they are just as much dependent on trade for their livelihood as are such categories of commercial population. If we were to ignore this arbitrary classification, some of the census figures of 16 percent for population in nonagricultural production, and of 21.5 percent for agricultural population would have to be added to the figure for total commercial populace. Even so, there would be no weightage for the difference between the town alone and the whole of the N.A. My own estimate would be set closer to 60 percent or above for population directly or mainly engaged in, or dependent upon, commerce.

SOCIAL ASPECTS OF WARD AND *MOHALLA*

If in the past the *mohalla* had social functions, it no longer has at the present. At *holi* time, some *mohalla*s have their own burning areas, but it is not obligatory or even customary to attend the burning in one's own *mohalla*, and anyway, this in Tezibazar is sport primarily for children and adolescents. Further, because of the vicissitudes of finding commercial space along an already crowded street front, no necessary caste or communal patterning to residential areas exists except for untouchables. Muslim and Hindu, Brahmin and Baniya castes all live intermixed or interspersed—all vying for their share of trade from the people passing along Main Street. Untouchables, mainly Camar and Pasi castes, however, are definitely distinct residentially. There are two Camar "*bastis*"—both of which are called "Chamraoti" *mohallas*—one in Pakri ward and the other in Anjahi. A Pasi settlement is located in Naiganj ward. These areas are slightly but definitely removed from their nearest "caste" neighbors and appear like small villages haphazardly tacked onto the town. They are entirely *kaccha:* the houses are small and dilapidated; and the narrow paths which lead through the *basti*s are here and there blocked by a thin goat or, rarely a half-starved calf. Many of the people look little better off than their animals.

The older, less commercialized, and therefore less space-pressured sections of Tezibazar show a degree of neighborhood caste patterning, although the social discrimination which creates the untouchable *basti*s is lacking. Darziana and Chikan *mohalla*s in Naiganj ward are named after two Muslim castes: the Darzi, or "tailor," and the Cike, or Cikuva, which means "butcher." These two *mohalla*s are not primarily inhabited by these castes, nor are these areas defined by these businesses (although it happens that the two butcher shops in the town are located in Chikan *mohalla*). Business location is defined not by traditional caste or neighborhood criteria, but by economic considerations. However, these two *mohalla*s are predominantly Muslim. Similarly, Sipah and Kot *mohalla*s within Anjahi ward are known as Muslim neighborhoods, whereas Babhanaoti, as the name suggests, is inhabited by many of the Brahmins of the town. Koiran, in this same ward, is named after the Koiri caste—vegetable gardeners by traditional occupation—and this caste does indeed congregate here. Anjahi, Gurhai, and Katra *mohalla*s are known as areas of the Umar, the predominant traditional trading caste in Tezibazar. However, the fact that the two former areas lie along the main road mediates against the dominance of any one group. Dafliana *mohalla* in Gurhai ward is named after a Muslim caste of musicians called Dafari, although few live here and the area is not even highly Muslim in population. Naibazar has no special typing except that it is primarily inhabited by Baniyas or traditional merchants as befits a commercial area. Finally, in Pakri ward, other than Chamraoti, there is a *mohalla* called Gudam which is predominantly Muslim. Lalhan in the same ward is named after the Lala, or Kayasth, caste grouping; however, the area is known as the residence of Kurmi vegetable gardeners. Ahiran *mohalla* in Pakri ward, which is more or less part of the rural area, is named after and inhabited by Ahir or traditional cowherds and milk sellers.

Thus, most of the communally or caste stereotyped neighborhoods are found in Old Town. Before the emergence of Sahibganj, this segmentation into residentially distinct caste or religious *mohallas* was much more characteristic of town morphology than at the present. No one remembers how much autonomy these *mohallas* enjoyed nor what their social or political functions might have been; but it seems reasonable that to the extent a *mohalla* was occupied by a single caste, that caste's internal organization served also as the structure of the *mohalla*.

Significantly, Naiganj *mohalla* and Sahibganj ward, which contain approximately a third of the town's houses and population, show no such caste and neighborhood patterning. These are the business areas par excellence, where economic rationality takes precedence over any desire for caste or communal association. These are also the newer areas of the town wherein the social pattern of past centuries has not been imported. To be sure, the overwhelming make-up of the population in these locales is Baniya—that is, members of the various merchant castes which inhabit the town. But this only indicates that in a market place one finds merchants, and that in India these belong to traditional merchant castes—a significant statement but irrelevant to the relationship between caste and town territory.

It should be noted again, however, that even in those relatively noncommercial and peripheral sections of the town where some caste-neighborhood congruence exists, it is a residue of the past rather than a presently significant social patterning of town society. This situation is true for all castes and communities other than untouchables.

CASTE AND COMMUNAL GROUPS

Status Groupings of Castes

Caste is a local, kinship-delimited, endogamous or hypergamous, commensally restricted, and sometimes occupationally specialized social unit which often has juridically corporate functions. A full complement of castes of this sort exists in Tezibazar. No less than forty-six castes appear in my survey of businesses in Tezibazar, and undoubtedly the figure for the entire Notified Area is higher. In a system as complex as is this one, certain mental abbreviations or short cuts are made by the population itself to portray the system for easy manipulation. Thus, a man who says his caste is "Kisan" is stating not what his endogamous group is, but what the general position of that group is in the total caste scene. This simplification is sometimes referred to as the *varna* scheme in discussions of Indian caste, although, as I shall note below, the term *"varna"* in Tezibazar refers to a specific simplification used by sophisticated and educated people who are trying to fit local usages into an all-India framework. Whatever the term used to describe them, these simplifications or categories are not groups, only mental orderings of the caste universe. Neither do they have any formal structure (but see "Muslim" below). Rules of eating, however, do tend to follow these statuses closely; if an individual can eat with one caste within a category, most often he can eat with them all. Within any one of the categories, rank may be unclear, and each caste may rate itself highest; but with few exceptions, they accept their "membership" in that status category and claim that it ranks equal to all others.

Similar systems of aggregate statuses are commonly found in Indian villages. Such mental abbreviations or typologies usually reflect the relative position of the various caste groups in the local hierarchy. As such, village status categories have a ranking and social reality apart from their merely categorizing function.[5] This sort of hierarchy is, however, absent from the Tezibazar system—absent not only in terms of popular conceptions (with some exceptions) or popular ranking criteria, but also as reflected in the rules of commensality (see Chapter 5).

Tezibazar residents speak of six main status categories: Thakur, Brahmin, Baniya, Kisan, Sudra, and Muslim.[6] The Brahmin and Thakur statuses are respectively the traditional "priestly" and "warrior" segments of the population. In Tezibazar they each have an actual uni-caste composition, so that in their cases and in this local area, a complete correspondence exists between caste and status category.[7] The Brahmins and Thakurs are supposedly of higher status than the other groups, but this position more often reflects a statement of scriptural "should-be" by the sophisticated than actual practice. These two categories are not well represented in Tezibazar, either as residents or in business (see Table 5).

The largest local status category is that of the Baniya castes' grouping and includes all castes whose traditional calling involves trade. "Vaisya" is their Sanskritic name and is used by educated people in refined conversation. "Baniya" is the most commonly used term, however, and although it sometimes carries a demeaning connotation, it is found in everyone's speech. "Baniya" has the disadvantage of sometimes referring to any

[5] Cf. Kathleen Gough, "The Social Structure of a Tanjore Village," and McKim Marriott, "Social Structure and Change in a U.P. Village," in *India's Villages*, ed. M. N. Srinivas, pp. 90, 113.

[6] Several families do not belong to any of these categories, but are generally ignored by local people because of their small population. Three such families appeared in my business survey: a family of Punjabi immigrants; and two families of Srivastava caste (the latter are classified in a locally unimportant "Kayasth" status). I have enumerated these as "Other" or "Other Hindu" in subsequent tables.

[7] This statement is true for the Brahmins represented in the business survey. There are other Brahmin castes in the area, such as Mahabrahmin, Gosain, and Bhuinhar (the latter sometimes are considered Thakurs and the two former groups are often denied as Brahmins), but none of these appeared in the survey nor are their numbers great in the town.

merchant, regardless of caste.[8] Both "Baniya" and "Vaisya" will be used here to refer specifically to a man belonging to one or another of the traditional merchant castes.

In Tezibazar the Baniya castes comprise the largest, most influential, and wealthiest segment of the resident population. They monopolize the business and politics of the urban area, and their social structures are tantamount to the social structure of the town.

Table 5. Business population by status category with the percentage of business ventures by each

Status	No. of castes	No. of families	Families (%)	Pop.	No. of businesses	Business (%)
Brahmin	1	26	4.96	197	25.84 *	4.56
Thakur	1	10	1.91	83	10.50	1.85
Baniya	13	287	54.77	1,773	327.16	57.70
Kisan	12	55	10.49	360	53.50	9.44
Sudra	3	27	5.15	171	27	4.76
Muslim	14	116	22.14	852	120	21.17
Other	2	3	.58	29	3	.52
Total	46	524	100.00	3,465	567	100.00

* Fractional numbers indicate partial ownership.

The category "Kisan"—a potpourri of many castes—is sometimes described as referring to "farmers" or cultivators, even though it contains the Hindu Nau (Nai in standard Hindi), or barber caste, and the Lohar, or blacksmith-carpenter caste, along with other castes not traditionally engaged in agriculture. This category is important in the town, not only for its control of many businesses, but also because many customers from the rural areas are of the Kisan castes. These people are traditionally lower than the Baniya, but, as we shall see, this again is more ideal

[8] The term "Baniya" is occasionally used, by extension, to mean anyone sharp with money, or someone unable to do physical labor, since Baniyas are not considered strong or physically adept. To illustrate the second usage: my Muslim cook once explained why he could not help some men moving heavy goods for me by saying, "ham banIya hae*n*"— "I'm a Baniya."

statement than practice, and even the statement is ambiguously made.

The last status among the Hindus and the one actively discriminated against in actual behavior is the "Sudra." This category in composition corresponds to "untouchables" or, as Gandhi euphemistically called them, "Harijans." Many of its component castes are classified as "scheduled castes" by the government and given special privileges. The use of the word "Sudra" affords a good example of the penetration of a Sanskritic motif into the town, and of its misuse. "Sudra" in the Vedas refers to the group below the "twice-born" castes which by birth was destined to serve the three higher groups; in no way were Sudras represented as being outside the system of caste as are those presently so named in Tezibazar. Use of this more refined and historical (perhaps venerable) name parallels the adoption of "prestige" names by individual castes. The derogatory descriptive name for the modern Sudras is *"achut."* This word has the meaning of "untouchable" or "unclean." Gandhi's euphemistic "Harijan" is heard often in the town, but exclusively denotes only one of the component castes of the status, the Camar, or leather worker. This caste is quite the largest single unit within this status category.[9]

The Muslim status category is both a little more than just a status and also a little less. What establishes the Muslim category is the unity of religion among all its component groups—unity, that is, as viewed by the Hindus, who (even the Sudras) refuse to share any form of food with them. The Muslim status is

[9] It has been customary in works on Indian caste to replace the actual caste names (Hindi or otherwise) with meaning equivalents in English: thus, Camar = leather worker, Dhobi = washerman. Undoubtedly this method has the advantage of simplicity and clarity. On the other hand, there are many castes for which no suitable translation exists. More importantly, the above method can lead to confusion of functional name with function so that a member of the leather worker caste is thought of as a leather worker. It also insinuates the idea that leather worker in Bombay is equivalent to leather worker in Kashmir. For these reasons, I choose to retain the Hindi caste names.

something less than a category because, unlike the situation in the other categories, an extremely wide rank differential which corresponds to the difference between Hindu "twice-born" and Sudra castes exists within this status. But these distinctions are significant only for Muslims, and Hindus operate as if the Muslim category were of one unitary status only, even though they are aware of the different Muslim castes and of the fact that Muslims believe there are significant rank differences between these castes.

The Muslim category is also something more than merely an aggregate status. Stimulated by the popular attitude which equates all Muslims as one and which on the part of Hindus is usually discriminatory, it has taken on the quality of a minority group: that is, a self-conscious interactive unit with leaders and an organization founded on the principle that such an entity as "Muslim" does indeed exist. This development transcends individual caste barriers for certain purposes and in certain ways. Such an organization or development in India is often called a "communal movement"; I discuss it further directly below.

In most cases, individuals using these aggregate terms are aware that they are only status levels and not real caste entities. Such, however, is often not true of many non-Vaisyas using the term "Baniya." So well has the term "Baniya" stereotyped caste distinctions that some people are unaware that they exist at all within the status. Many of my city acquaintances in India were quite surprised to find that Baniyas "had castes," and some thought that "Marvari," one of the most famous groupings of merchant castes in India, and "Baniya" were synonymous.[10]

Perhaps causes contributing to such ignorance are the total

[10] It is interesting how often this popular misconception appears in anthropological literature on India, in part as a result of the limitations of the community study approach. In many village studies, the term "Baniya" is reported as if it were the name of an actual caste characterized by trade as a traditional occupation. See Oscar Lewis, *Village Life in Northern India;* McKim Marriott, *op. cit.,* p. 90; and Pauline Mahar, "A Multiple Scaling Technique for Caste Ranking," *Man in India,* XXXIX (1959), 127–147.

identification of the Baniya with the occupation of commerce and the highly evolved stereotype, based primarily on his antisocial profit activities, which people use to characterize him. In many ways the Baniya stands apart from the rest of the society, partially by choice, partially by the distaste for him of other castes, so that his social life other than his business dealings is relatively unknown to the general populace. These remarks are most applicable to the city, where contact with the Baniyas is most functionally economic, and the villages, where the scarcity of resident Baniyas creates an anonymity for them. In the small towns daily social and political contact makes knowledge of the Baniya castes to some extent inevitable.

Informants were in general agreement about the assignment of caste groups to the categories of status, probably because such assignment carries no special social benefits. No caste is trying to move locally from one category to another, because this movement would bear no relation to rank mobility. One "Baniya" caste and several "Kisan" castes (by popular estimation) claim to belong to a "Ksatriya" status category. They have derived this term from classical Hindu tradition, but they do not employ it for social mobility into the "Thakur" category within the town. Their claims to Ksatriya status are expounded in their caste journals and in a city environment, primarily as historical rationalization rather than for contemporary mobility. Their "mobility" is geared to an all-India, classical concept, emanating from the cities and sophisticated modern caste organization, and peripheral to the local situation. Thus, these castes do not view their claims to Ksatriya status as in any way demanding changes in their commensal situation or formal social relations within Tezibazar. The reality of these categories for the Tezibazar populace lies in their summation of scriptural, historical, occupational, and behavioral characteristics thought to personify the "typical" Baniya, Brahmin, or Thakur.

The above six statuses are those commonly enunciated in Tezibazar. Another system, however, is utilized by sophisticated people in trying to make the caste network intelligible to the anthropologist. I include it here to show the awareness of all-India themes by at least the more progressive in the town population. This rating contains only four groupings: Brahmin, Ksatriya, Vaisya, and Sudra. The Muslim forms no part of this categorization; if at all, he is included under the title *mlicch* (local variant of Hindi *mlecch*), meaning "dirty or barbarian, not belonging to the caste system" (and carrying the connotation of inferiority). The Brahmin and Vaisya (Baniya) groupings as well as the Sudra correspond to those similarly named in the popular system. However, both Kisan and Thakur are merged into the Ksatriya, or king and warrior, level. The people who employ this system have learned that these four "groups," or *varna*, existed in ancient India and that from them all present-day castes have supposedly arisen by a process of outmarriage. They thus feel a necessity to find like organization now, even if to do so means the uncomfortable merging of two popularly distinct levels: Thakur and Kisan. Indeed, my informants felt uneasy about the conjunction of these two statuses, but the Kisan fit nowhere else, since Sudra was understood to be the precincts of the *achut* only. In everyday activities, they did not use this system; it is only introduced on special technical occasions to justify the present Tezibazar situation.

Terminology of Caste

The word for caste generally used in Tezibazar is *"biradari"* or *"biradar"* in dialect. This word is also usually employed to distinguish the various status levels, so that a man of merchant caste would first reply to a question about his *biradari* affiliation by saying he was a "Baniya." One would then ask him what kind of Baniya he was to determine the identity of his caste. The term *jat* or *jati*, often heard for "caste" in India, is understood but not commonly used except by relatively sophisticated people explaining matters to the anthropologist. Here again they change local nomenclature to fit their perceptions of the all-India model; thus they say the word *"jat"* refers to the category "Baniya" or "Kisan," and that the word, *"upjat"* signifies the component castes of these levels. Some people distinguish *"jati"* from *"biradari"* on the basis that the latter refers only to the local population of the caste whereas the former term includes all caste mates. Even by those who have heard of it, the term *"varna"* is never used in a local context. The double usage of the word *"biradari"* holds true among Muslims, also, where after the preliminary reply of *"musulman,"* the real caste name is given (although some Muslims then answer *"sunni,"* their religious denomination). In this book, *biradari* will always signify caste.

Another all-India influence is the employment and recognition of status level names. All Thakurs call themselves *"singh"* (lion), and many Baniyas use *"gupta"* (secret) rather than their caste name: Virendra Bahadur Singh; Badri Prasad Gupta. Brahmins employ a similar system with more variability: *pande, dube, tavari, sukla, misra* are all Brahmin names.[11] Neither the Muslims, Sudras, nor Kisan in Tezibazar use such terms, although I was told that the names *"sarma"* (formerly denoting a Brahmin) and *"varma"* were in other areas employed by Kisan. In some cases these status names replace the actual caste ones. One year's list of students in the Mahajani Pathshala (school for clerks) notes that two boys of *"gupta"* caste were enrolled.

Various titles of deferential address correspond to these status categories. A Brahmin is generally addressed as *"pandit-ji"* or *"maharaj,"* although the latter is considered somewhat villagey. In reference, a Brahmin's name is appended to the term "pandit": Pandit Mohan Lal. "Thakur" is not only the name of a status, but also a term of address and reference: Thakur Amar Bahadur. The corresponding deferential reference terms for Baniyas are Ram Nath "Sahu" or "Babu" Deota Din. *Babu* can also be used as a term of address, as *"babu-ji,"* although here its usage is much wider than the Baniya status category; almost anyone of higher status can be appealed to in this fashion. A term of address

[11] These are the names of *aspad*s or ritually important titles of *kanaujiya* Brahmins. See R. S. Khare, "The Kanya-Kubja Brahmins and Their Caste Organization," *Southwestern Journal of Anthropology*, XVI (1960), 348–367.

limited to the Baniya is *"mahajan";* however, this word is used infrequently because it implies a degree of servility for the user as between servant and master. For Sudras and Kisan there are, to my knowledge, no deferential terms of address or reference. For specific individuals who are to be solicited, the term *"sahab,"* both as reference and address can be used, or the deferential *-ji* be added to a name: Kedar Nath-ji.[12] For Muslims the terms *"sahab"* and *"miyan"* are used coupled with the name in address, as Karim-Miyan. In address without the use of the name, *"bare miyan"* is employed.

Parenthetically, it may be said that the use of titles is very exact in Tezibazar, and any sort of honor or activity carrying a title is quickly resorted to for use instead of the individual's name: Chairman-Sahab, Manager-Sahab, Inspector-Sahab, even Driver-Sahab and Conductor-Sahab (for bus employees).

Communal and Communities

"Communal" and "communities" are words which appear often in the news and activities of post-Independence India: the Congress party opposed "communalism"; "communal" riots take place; there are "communal" political parties. Often this word is used to key emotions to any deplorable situation because it has a pejorative connotation; sometimes it is used as a backhanded insult to Muslims when they cannot be mentioned as such: "members of the minority community were said to instigate the riot."

Thus the word "communal" and the idea of community are used extremely loosely in common and official parlance. Generally "communal" carries two didactic meanings: it can refer to the tendency of various distinct groups to react in the same or sufficiently equivalent manner on certain occasions or to a group actually organized and having leaders and objectives. The first usage implies no organization, no necessary leaders or corporate activities of the communal unit; it only states in effect that for

[12] In such names as "Ram-Ji" and "Lal-Ji," the last element is an integral part of the name and has no status reference.

certain activities or times, various separate groups crystallize in behavior and common action and can be treated *as if* they were a group. Thus, a Brahmin political candidate who receives the "Brahmin communal vote" is not gaining the affirmation of an organized political entity (that is, Brahmin communal vote); his candidacy has only evoked a similar response among many or most Brahmins (whose feeling of identity may be promoted by political leaders). Or, when one speaks of a Hindu–Muslim riot, these two communities are treated as if they were groups, when in fact a particular stimulus has elicited a generally similar response from various distinct groups, who thus sort themselves out as either "Hindu" or "Muslim" in reaction to a specific problem.

The second sort of "community" (and this usage is much less common than the above) is an actual, organized group co-ordinated by leaders and competing for access to political power or economic resources as a unit. Such a group is a structured entity based on the common sentiments or typical predictable reactions used to characterize the first meaning of "community." The growth of organized communities or associations from such sentiment has been a characteristic development of Indian politics in the last several decades.[13] Such communities still often depend heavily on merely common support or sentiment rather than actual organization, but the trend is there to see. In the case of the Tezibazar Muslims—to a large extent as the result of reflexive groupism due to minority pressures—the organization of the community is well developed. In the town Baniyas it is much more nascent and the Jana Sangh political party provides the

[13] See Selig Harrison, "Caste and the Andhra Communists," *American Political Science Review*, L (1956), 378–404; Lloyd I. Rudolph and Susanne Hoeber Rudolph, "The Political Role of India's Caste Associations," *Pacific Affairs*, XXXIII (1960), 5–22; Robert T. Anderson, "Preliminary Report on the Associational Redefinition of Castes in Hyderabad-Secunderabad," *Kroeber Anthropological Papers*, XXIX (1963), 25–42; Richard G. Fox, "Resiliency and Change in the Indian Caste System: The Umar of U.P.," *Journal of Asian Studies*, XXVI (1967), 575–587.

nucleus of formal organization. This significant trend—the transformation of local groups into structures mirroring political and economic alignments on the regional or national level—clearly distinguishes Tezibazar from Indian villages. On the national level, communal politics is merely the manipulation of common sentiments and reactions—and unavoidably so, given the divisive effect of size and diversity in group formation. On the local level in Tezibazar, this kind of sentiment is beginning to crystallize into politically effective associations which, like the town castes, contest in local politics.

CHAPTER 3

Economic and Political Bases

No street of goldsmiths exists in Tezibazar nor is there a cloth dealer's section or a center for hardware. Instead, shops of all styles and selling every kind of merchandise are jumbled together along the main street, and only chance, a favorable location, or the lack of a spot anywhere else dictates their position. Four locales in Tezibazar are, however, set aside for certain specific commodities. Gola Mandi in Sahibganj is the area of main concentration of wholesale and retail shops dealing in the food grains and *gur*. Further along in Sahibganj is Sabzi-Mandi, or the vegetable market—rather a misnomer since the retail fruit and vegetable sellers only occupy its periphery adjacent to Main Street. Within the *mandi* itself are wholesale and retail potato dealers, various trinket and knicknack stalls spread along the ground, and a few ovens for parching rice and other grains. In one corner several Halal-khor, members of a low Muslim caste, sell small grain winnowers made of rice straw and pig gut for home use. Near the Jama mosque in Naiganj and the southern limit of Old Town is the leather market. It is primarily an outlet for wholesale hides and such retail leather goods as shoes. The center for sale of meat and fish is also in Naiganj ward, at the intersection of Main Street and the *gali* (alley) leading to Koiran *mohalla*.

The shops in Tezibazar are open seven days a week, yet the overwhelming share of business comes in on the Thursday and Sunday market days. No one knows when or how these two days became established. They are mentioned in the Jaunpur District

Gazetteer of 1908 and undoubtedly are considerably older. In
any case, their history is of much less consequence to the Tezibazar merchant than is their economic import. The commercial
populace of the town suffers severe underemployment. During
the five non-market days of the week, the businessman can afford to take his leisure in the shops of friends, visit the city for
purchases, or sleep away his time. Generally it is a very dull and
wasteful period, during which the shop owner sits beside his
money box waiting for a stray customer to enter his shop. "We
eat for seven days, but we only work on two," as they themselves put it.

ECONOMICS AND THE MARKET

The Market

At the peak of the market, people line the streets in great
numbers, with the main congestion between the great temple in
Sahibganj and the leather market. *Ikka*s, rickshaws, bicycles,
camels, ox- or buffalo-carts, trucks, buses, and many pedestrians
contend for passage along Main Street. Rickshaws with attached
loud-speakers and sometimes with hooked-in phonographs, alter-
nately blaring *biri* (country cigarette) advertisements and Indian film songs, create a furious and deafening din as they slowly
pass up and down Main Street. The hubbub is heightened by the
loud-speakers or phonographs used by various shops to add appeal to their wares, indiscriminately adding cacophonous voices
to what already is a high roar. Sometimes the physical congestion
of the street is so great around the vegetable market that it causes
complete stoppage of all traffic except that of adventuresome
pedestrians who deftly snake through and find passage between
the axles of carts and the horns of oxen. Market-day merchants
line the road, encroaching both on the public way and on the
stoops of the permanent shops, much to the consternation of the
latter's owners. The bane of these merchants is the occasional bus
or truck which must pass through the scant roadway or the
vagrant cow or buffalo that steals a cabbage or eggplant as it is

driven by. These nonpermanent vendors come mainly from the nearby rural area or the agricultural localities contained within the Tezibazar Notified Area. They deal primarily in vegetables or other foodstuffs, and although they add to the congestion of the market, their numbers are not great in comparison with those of the permanent businessmen. From the vegetable market to the beginning of Naiganj ward, these temporary vegetable sellers pile up purple mounds of eggplant, green mounds of peas, and (the largest) deep-red mounds of chili peppers. These are the winter crops; in other seasons, squash, melons, cabbage, *parval*, *ninuva*, or mangos replace them; but the positioning of the merchants along the street remains. There is also a smaller placement of vegetable sellers near the police station. Further along in Sahibganj is to be found the Kumbhar caste of potters selling earthenware in all sizes and shapes. Toward the Sabzi Mandi are the Barai (Caurasiya) with their delicately piled rows of betel leaves, which must continuously be washed in order to remove the ever-settling dust of the fast-paced market. The Barai grow these leaves for sale to local *pan* dealers for whose business they are, of course, essential. *Pan*, or betel chewing, is extremely popular in Tezibazar, as one would expect from its proximity to Varanasi (Banaras), the famous center of *pan* in India. Slightly beyond the Sabzi Mandi sit the Muslim Curihar women, selling the brilliantly colored glass bangles which are a necessary part of every unwidowed Indian woman's dress. Bangles, trinkets, and betel leaves constitute the few commodities in which women play significant roles as traders. Further along, in Sipah *mohalla*, just before the turn to Babhanaoti, weavers and dyers from the villages bring cloth to sell. This trade proceeds on an exceedingly small basis. Here and there Camar shoe repairers and leather workers are scattered through the mass of roadside commerce, although for the most part they congregate in front of the bus station in Sahibganj and at the leather market in Naiganj. With insufficient tools these thin, prematurely aged men make minor repairs to shoes or sew patches on the leather bags used by farmers to draw irrigation water from their wells. Now and again a patent medicine or herb which aids digestion is offered for sale, sometimes from the hands of a bearded and ritually adorned saint, sometimes by a high-pressure salesman seated atop the back seat of an ancient convertible automobile.

Customers in the Tezibazar market are overwhelmingly from the nearby rural area. A large proportion are village merchants who have come to replenish their stock from larger counterparts in the town and at the same time to do their own retail shopping. Itinerant professional merchants are uncommon in Tezibazar, and almost all business is controlled by the permanent concerns in the town. Why the market days should persist under these conditions is moot, for few customers are necessarily forced to shop only at these times. In the best business periods, when retail trade increases because of the marriage season, the entire week is filled with commercial activity. In slack periods, when town merchants must depend on dealings with village shopkeepers, the differential between the market days and the remainder of the week is greatest. Perhaps the persistence of definite market days stems from convenience for village shop owners.

Under the congested circumstances, it is remarkable to what extent shoving or pushing is absent from the market place; people manage to move about without much physical contact, neatly stepping over merchandise lining the streets. However, the buses to Gopiganj which pass through the town always have great trouble and never is there more than a few feet of clearance on either side. Should a buyer be squatting in front of a hawker's display of goods, the clearance is often little more than two or three inches. Because of the noise, most such buyers are unaware of an approaching bus until hot air from the exhaust on their necks awakens them to the now-passed danger.

The most congested area is within the small *gali*, or alley, leading to Gola Mandi and the grain market. Here camels and oxcarts stand or are brought in and out, while just aside from their passage, heaps of grain are spread out on the ground. To pass through this alley, persons are forced to scramble over bags of grain, around or even underneath camels, and, of course, over the displayed merchandise. However, the amount of steady traffic here is not as large as on Main Street.

Beyond the Sabzi Mandi and particularly past the leather market, the great volume of traffic lessens but in no sense to the level of the rest of the week. Nevertheless, most stores in Old Town are primarily for the use and needs of the local populace and draw less of the market-day business (see Table 6). There is

Table 6. Estimates by merchants of the percentage of customers from rural area and from town

Area *	No. of merchants	Rural customers (%)	Town customers (%)
Sahibganj	20	85.4	14.6
Gola Mandi	3	87.0	13.0
Naiganj	3	96.7	3.3
Old Town †	5	47.9	52.1
Naibazar	1	100.0	0.0
Total	32	81.2	18.8

* This material was drawn from a 20 percent sampling of merchants belonging to Umar, Kesarvani, and Kalvar castes. The areal distribution is therefore random and tends to reflect business location in the town.

† Includes Anjahi, Gurhai, Katra.

a small resurgence of the market in Naibazar, however, where, by allowing a measure of barter sales, various town traders siphon off some of the customers headed for the main market.

Thus position and physical location are central to Tezibazar business. Merchants say that people prefer to shop in Sahibganj because they can find both a variety of shops and many of the same sort of shop in one place. This proliferation gives greater room for higglehaggle and comparison shopping by the customer, as well as an easier satisfaction of his various requirements. Therefore, in Tezibazar the first requirement for successful business is a location near the center of the market. The discussion of land prices above will also have helped to clarify this point.

SPATIAL AND SOCIAL ASPECTS OF A SHOP

In every shop, whatever the caste of its owner, regardless of whether it is wholesale or retail, *pakka* or *kaccha*, two important areas orient the store spatially and socially: the money box, which is equivalent to the owner's seat, and the *gaddi*, or matting which covers the floor.

The *gaddi* is any covering put over the bare floor, upon which the merchant places his strong box and on which he and his prestigious guests or customers sit. Usually the *gaddi* consists of a coarse matting covered over by a special white sheeting. But this is not essential, for the *gaddi* is a ritually and socially delimited area of the shop whose existence is not conditioned by the material expression of its presence.

The *gaddi* is *pavitra*, or pure, and so can be defiled. Muslim and untouchable customers were formerly not asked to sit on it for fear they might pollute it. Even now, many either do not step upon the *gaddi* or sit very close to the edge. The characteristic pile of shoes in front of every shop on market day is also an expression of the purity of the *gaddi*. Shoes are made of cow-hide, and the cow is sacred to Hindus. To wear shoes onto the *gaddi* would therefore be to pollute it. Egg or meat sellers engaged in hawking their wares cannot step over the threshold of the shop or onto the *gaddi*. I was told that in the cities, Marvari merchants did not even permit smoking on their *gaddi* and often had a separate sheeting for Camars and Muslims to sit on, while they and the money box rested on another.

To disobey any of these restrictions is supposedly to bring the businessman bad luck. Upon the *gaddi* is placed the strong box in which the merchant keeps his cash and accounts. The money comes from the goddess of wealth, Laksmi, and the money itself —that is, the actual coinage—symbolizes or is an idol of this goddess, whom all Hindu businessmen worship. By extension, the fact that the money box is placed on the *gaddi* sanctifies it, so that anything against the values of Hinduism, such as the wearing of leather shoes or the selling of meat, is a direct insult to

Laksmi and thus brings down bad luck upon the merchant. Note that the money box itself is not *pavitra,* but only its contents. These remarks apply to Hindu businessmen only, because Muslims obviously do not operate within the same belief or value system. But even in Muslim shops, some area is demarcated as the center of the shop by the placement of a mat or sheeting. It is also customary, although not mandatory, to take off one's shoes when entering a Muslim shop.

The *gaddi* and money box in combination also serve to establish status: merely to sit on the *gaddi* indicates some prestige, although informants say there is now little discrimination in this matter. But the closer to the money box and owner's position a customer or guest is invited to sit, the more prestige he has. The right side indicates higher rank than the left, and for those of highest status or deserving of greatest deference, pillows are brought for use as backrests. There is an expression, "gaddi-par bae*thna*" (to sit on the *gaddi*), used to indicate that someone holds an individual in high repute.

The *gaddi* and strong box condition the presence of the store, but there are other ritual embellishments and ordinary decorations. Because all business is done in a squatting or sitting position on the floor, most shops do not have chairs or tables. An interesting exception are the drug shops, or "medical halls," as they are called in Tezibazar. These stores always have a bench and table to simulate a Western, or *angrezi* (English), atmosphere, complementary to the western-style medicines purveyed. In Hindu shops, a typical wall motif is

लाभ ऴ शुभ

which freely translated means "Profit–Welfare–Auspiciousness." Usually there is an image—sometimes gilded—of Mahalaksmi and of the elephant-headed god, Ganes, caretaker of auspicious beginnings. Muslim businessmen hang quotations from the Koran on their walls. All these items have definite and important ritual connections with the business and businessman. A popular, purely decorative device is the use of calendars, which are distributed by most of the wholesale houses and "factories" in Tezibazar. These portray in exotic colors various high gods, national political figures, and buxom movie stars. A few business-men have photographs of the particular ancestor who founded the family business.

TEZIBAZAR: A BANIYA MARKET

The business survey strikingly demonstrated the extent to which the traditional commercial castes control the main avenues of business activity in the town.[1] Almost 55 percent of the total number of families are Baniya by caste: over 63 percent, if only Tezibazar residents are considered (about 13 percent of the families engaged in town business are nonresidents). The largest single grouping after Baniya is the Muslim, which accounts for slightly over 22 percent (see Table 5). The same holds true for the respective percentages of businesses owned: almost 58 per-cent for Baniya; only 21 percent for the next largest category, Muslim. The Baniyas, then, are represented in trade almost three times more than is the next largest group. Even this figure is deceptively small in one sense: the computations above include not only trading concerns (cloth shops, groceries, and so forth) but also services such as barbering, tailoring, and utensil repair-ing. If only trading concerns and not services are counted, Ba-

---

[1] See Table 8 for a list of Baniya castes. It should be noted that some castes termed "Baniya" in Tezibazar are sometimes reported as artisan in villages: Teli (oil presser); Kalvar (distiller); Bhuj (grain parcher); and others. However, these groups also sell their products and com-monly operate shops. Majumdar refers to Kalvars in a U.P. village as "bania" (D. N. Majumdar, *Caste and Communication in an Indian Village*, p. 32). The ethnographic surveys of Crooke and Sherring often list these castes as small traders or even Vaisyas and remark about the difficulties of separating the "higher" artisans from the Vaisyas or business men (W. Crooke, *The Tribes and Castes of the North-Western Provinces and Oudh;* Rev. M. A. Sherring, *Hindu Tribes and Castes as Represented in Benaras,* pp. 292–302). Perhaps the difficulty stems from the use of "Baniya" as a caste name in many community studies (see Chap. 2, n. 10). This means that such castes as Teli, Kalvar, and Bhuj are not "Baniya" by definition, and the category is thus artificially re-stricted to such general merchant castes as Agarval, Umar, or Kesarvani.

niya castes carry on 71.41 percent of all such ventures in the town. They are owners of over three quarters of all wholesale businesses in Tezibazar. The Baniyas as a whole account for 72.39 percent of all families engaged in multiple businesses (see Table 14); and the only three castes that carry on over 25 percent of the total *types* of businesses are Baniya (cf. Appendix I, Table 23).

The Baniyas are not an entity or real group, and it is incorrect to deal with them as if they were anything more than a demarcated status category. Nevertheless, these figures show that commerce in Tezibazar—and by extension, wealth and political power—are the preserve of the Baniya castes. It also indicates that the organization of the town's economy is along traditional social lines: that is, the persistence of the Baniya as the primary merchant. Insofar as this is the case, when, in the following pages, I note various customs or attitudes of Baniya castes, I note in fact those of the business class; conversely, when I describe popular beliefs or notions about the business class, I am, at the same time, describing those holding for Baniya castes. This identity is accepted completely in India—obviously more so than fact would warrant; nevertheless, at least for Tezibazar town, it holds true in good measure.

Why Baniya castes should remain monopolists of business activity is a matter compounded of the tradition of centuries and, perhaps in good measure, of economic factors growing out of the particular Baniya social stance. A main factor is the present-day attitude of non-Vaisya castes toward business. It is considered demeaning and servile, antisocial and leechlike. A Brahmin who was one of the biggest wholesale merchants in the town never allowed his sons to enter the shop for fear that they would take an interest in the business. As the Baniyas say: Other castes do business because they have to, but Baniyas do business because they like it. They feel that they are better merchants than any other caste category—a sentiment shared by non-Baniyas as well. Exactly why this should be true is a much more difficult question to answer. Some say it derives from their having lived in a business environment all their lives—but then they cannot explain why they regard a member of another caste, raised in similar circumstances, their commercial inferior. Sometimes they attribute it to something innate, a gift from god which allows Baniyas to do business in a superior fashion, but what especial trait or quality is god-given they do not say or know. At best they refer to their greater "interest" in business, a quality which no other caste has. This explanation, of course, reverts to the original suggestion that distaste for business on the part of other castes is a major factor in discouraging their entrance into the business world.

Throughout much of the world, social, religious, or ethnic distinctions often separate the merchant community from the surrounding society.[2] In predominantly premarket economies the taking of profit is considered socially illegal. Profit signifies the introduction of economic rationality into a system which is based on the rationale of kinship and family. Whatever group undertakes business and the making of profit accepts to some extent social ostracism and develops over time social traits which allow it to withstand the slings and arrows of its noncommercial neighbors (and victims) as well as traits which maximize that production of profit which is socially so disreputable.

So, too, with the Baniya of Tezibazar. Most people agreed that their commercial superiority was manifested in a complex of traits invariably associated with Baniyas, usually as an exaggerated stereotype. These traits include: (1) extreme miserliness; (2) extreme passivity and avoidance of aggressive personal relations; (3) cultivation of an anonymous personal, family, and caste image and a relative disinterest in caste and family history; and (4) the containment of much of life within the compartment of the joint family and the avoidance of larger social or

---

[2] See Weber's concept of a "guest" or "parish" people as applied to merchant communities and the comparison of the Jews as a "guest" people to the "Vanias" of India (Max Weber, *From Max Weber: Essays in Sociology*, ed. H. H. Gerth and C. Wright Mills, p. 66, and *The Religion of India*, p. 112).

ritual entanglements.[3] Even the well-known devoutness of the Baniya takes a passive form: the endowment of temples or religious shrines, rather than the financing of religious feasts and group rituals.

These social traits comprise the traditional stereotype of the Baniyas elsewhere in India—and mean more than just that they are all misers, or "*kanjus.*" These are traits complementary to a profession where every personal entanglement with others, such as friendship or feasting, places a possible limitation on the ability to exploit this person at a later time. Obligation—either as a result of accepting someone's hospitality or having asked for or received a favor—is strongly felt in Tezibazar and perhaps all through India. In a system where one's allegiance is tied primarily to the family, a favor or a consideration from someone not part of that immediate group entitles the giver to expect something equal to it in return. The receiver of the favor is put into a position of definite inferiority until he reciprocates. So hospitality not only leads to social involvement beyond the joint family —which in itself is dangerous because such entanglement may prove a limitation in business or personal aggrandizement—but it also puts one under an obligation to a host. That is why social interaction with food is almost entirely limited to the normal round of ceremonial occasions such as marriage, birth, and death.

Every show of anger or violence may catapult a merchant into a difficult and dangerous position. His profit taking, whether legal or illegal, is deemed antisocial. It can evoke resentment from the part of the population which he, the merchant, often sees as an illiterate, tasteless, but potentially dangerous horde (the peasants, or *dihati log*) or as half-dacoit (the Thakurs and Brahmins). My Baniya informants said that one of the most important if not the most important aspect of good salesmanship is always to speak "sweetly and softly" to the customer, never to try to bully him, always to attempt to cajole him, and in general to make one's own feelings and personality as unobtrusive as

[3] Cf. Crooke, *op. cit.*, I, 174.

possible. Within the town itself conflict is also sharply avoided, although not from fear of physical reprisal for shady business dealings. Enmities are long remembered and political reprisals are common and meaningful. The Baniya feels that above all it is better to be peaceful, but he interprets this to mean a kind of behavior (or lack of it) that other groups call cowardly. On a number of occasions I have seen various Vaisya sit more or less passively while members of other castes berated the miserliness and corruption of the "Baniyas." Many Baniyas are somewhat ashamed of the general appraisal of their courage, and they counter such claims with the idea that some "castes" are meant for fighting and others, including the Baniya, are not.[4] They paint the Thakurs as blood-and-thunder men without much brain, and much of the delight of the Thakur in being a commander of men is paralleled by the Baniya's pleasure in the command of wealth, most of it being gotten from such "martial" groups as the Thakurs.

The anonymity of the Baniya means a number of things. The less overt the personality, the less there is to like or dislike. He is only a small man with a money box dispensing items, not someone of flesh and blood, taking what to many rural people in India still appears an illegal thing, a profit on his investment. This effacement or lack of overt expression of the self tends to discourage friendship as well as enmity, both equally destructive for the merchant: "banIya mItr na vesIya sati" (As a prostitute cannot be a "virgin," so a Baniya cannot be a friend). By extension, Baniyas are quite unknowledgeable about their family and caste history and also unconcerned about them. To be proud of past or caste is to assert one's self. Naturally, exceptions and variations in these traits exist. One town Baniya lineage, because of its long history of landownership and town leadership, contained some men who were very interested in their caste and family history. But even in this group only one old man really knew much about his caste and family. Typical of the younger

[4] One young Baniya claimed that wrestling and other athletics were dangerous because they made the bones brittle in old age.

generation in this lineage—divorced from landownership and more completely identified with the social role of a well-to-do Baniya—was Ram Keso, a cloth merchant who knew neither his clan name or what the Hindi term referred to nor the name of his grandfather. These were "old things" which he was willing to admit might be valuable and interesting to know, but he for one did not have the time to pursue the matter.

To illustrate further this matter of family pride, the only man who lied to me about family income and expenditure by excessively *raising* the figure was a Brahmin merchant who wished to make his family in this way more prestigious. And the only people to lie to me about their landholdings by *increasing* them were a Thakur and a Brahmin who wanted to impress me with the greatness of their families. Whatever pride Baniyas felt in these matters was easily surmounted by their business acumen.

The traditional merchant castes are suspicious of those who are interested in their past. One informant told me many of the most damaging stories about political opponents, but refused to give me his own genealogy. He could conceive of my interest in the former, but what could be my concern with the latter?

The most distinctive trait of the Baniyas in the opinion of other castes and even of themselves is their miserliness. *Kanjus* is the usual Hindi term for miser, but to describe their distance from the normal in this matter, some Baniyas in jest would refer to themselves as *makhijus*—someone who would look at a fly in his soup as an additional gift of god. The term is probably an example of folk etymology, since *makhi* means fly. I also heard this word used by non-Baniya individuals in reference to traditional merchants—but not in jest. The Baniyas indicate their attitude toward wealth and its acquisition when they say: "pae-sa-hi Izzat hae," (Prestige is only money). The Baniya is preoccupied with the quest for profit, and there is no lack of "profit motive" here, expressed in a high rate of savings and an amazing creativity in strategies of chicanery and adulteration. The Baniya sums up his propensity for saving and his desire for money in these words:

camri cali jay / damri na jay.

(Let your body waste away / but not your money.)

These social traits are congruent with the type of commerce the Baniya castes pursue and the kind of society in which they live and trade. I do not speak of a simple causality here, for undoubtedly there is much mutual reinforcement of the economic with the social traits of the group. It is only a recognition that, over generations, these particular groupings have developed traits which adapt them better to their specific position or niche and that, insofar as this statement is true, it explains the continued presence of the traditional merchant in an economy that has to some extent outgrown the economic and social situations which gave him birth.[5]

POLITICAL AND CIVIC ORGANIZATION:
THE NOTIFIED AREA

The formal structure of politics in Tezibazar is based on the ideal of a democratically elected, secular, local governing body. Since 1907, Tezibazar has been a Notified Area, a status which entitles the town to elect a governing committee. The latter supervises sanitation, lighting, roads, and the town's general condition and is empowered to levy taxes on property and income as well as other cesses according to rates decided upon by the state government. The composition of the committee and the method of its election have undergone numerous and substantial changes over the years, particularly since Independence. At present it consists of ten directly elected members and one chairman, who is chosen by the committee itself and need not be an elected member. Two members are chosen from each of the wards except the now-combined Sahibganj-Naiganj, which sends four. The present Chairman is also from Sahibganj. However, a candidate need not stand in a ward in which he is resident. Members

---

[5] Some of the materials on Baniyas in this chapter have been more fully explored in Richard G. Fox, "Family, Caste, and Commerce in a North Indian Market Town," *Economic Development and Cultural Change*, XV (1967), 297–314.

of the Notified Area committee receive no official salary. The last election before 1964 was held in late 1957, when eleven Congress party men were returned to the committee. Between 1958–1964 new elections on an all-state level had been postponed twice for various emergency reasons. But in November, 1964, the N.A. elections were finally held, and again a full slate of Congress party candidates were returned, and the incumbent Chairman re-elected.

Finances and Expenditures of the Notified Area

The greater part of the N.A.'s income comes from its property and income tax. The rates as fixed by the Uttar Pradesh government are:

	Yearly income	Tax rate
Rs.	0– 500	tax exempt
	501–1,000	1.55%
	1,001–2,000	2.50%
	2,001–3,000	3.00%
	3,001–5,000	4.00%

No tax can be levied on any income above Rs. 5,000 yearly. The municipal tax is in addition to the sales tax collected from all merchants by the state government and the income tax charged by the national government.

Other sources of funds are: (1) *tehbazari*—an impost is put on all temporary hawkers occupying the market square, 12 paese for each; (2) pounds—any cattle lost or let loose in the town are kept in this open area near the N.A. office, and the owners must pay to retrieve them; (3) manure—the compost periodically dredged from the sewer drains is sold as fertilizer; (4) contributions—these are amounts paid as dearness allowance (d.a.) by the central government to help offset the salaries of the local committee's staff; (5) road grants—these large amounts (Rs. 5,000 to 10,000 annually) are given to the municipality by the provincial transport service for keeping up the roads; (6) licenses—this tax is for the licensing of carts, rickshaws, and *ikkas*.

An inspection of the N.A. finances over the years quickly indicates the stability of the amount received from town property and income tax, considering postwar inflation and the rapid rise in population since 1951 (see Table 7). In fact it is more a political football than a tax. Proper reward for a political follower is to charge him little; proper punishment for an opponent is to tax him severely. As we shall see, the municipal impost is

Table 7. Income and expenditure of the Notified Area, 1944–1962

Year	Property tax	Total income	Expenses
1944	3,783	4,830	5,020
1946	4,226	7,087 *	7,316
1948	7,077	11,468	12,558
1950	5,833	10,654	10,863
1952	10,014	13,677	12,790
1954	9,359	11,638	15,132
1956	7,402	20,536 †	9,359
1958	11,173	25,468 †	–
1960	8,958	27,160 ‡	15,043
1962	10,589	24,507 §	22,882

* In this year, d.a. allowance added by government.
† Includes Rs. 10,000 road grant.
‡ Includes Rs. 13,005 road grant.
§ Includes Rs. 5,000 road grant.
Source: Notified Area records.

and has been a seething question in the town, more an adjunct of power politics than a money-raising technique.

The expenses incurred by the Notified Area are not extensive. The N.A. employs one *jamadar*, or sanitation foreman, two cartmen, or garbage collectors, four drain sweepers, eight road sweepers, and two replacements for the above, or "rest-givers" as they are officially designated. Each morning this staff moves up the main street, sweeping and clearing the rubbish and dumping it into buffalo-drawn carts. All these individuals, some of whom are women, belong to the lowly Muslim castes of "Shah" and "Halal-Khor" (traditional names: Fakir and Bhangi). The office staff of the N.A. consists of a secretary-bookkeeper, a clerk who assists him, and a tax collector. Besides its employees' salaries, the N.A.'s other major expense is for the electricity used by the streetlights of the town.

In 1963–1964 the municipality undertook a number of construction projects. It began to build sewer drains on the Jaunpur-Allahabad road and metaled, in a halfway fashion, the main street between the leather market and the police station. Its major project, however, is the construction of a town water supply, an undertaking which has meant borrowing a large sum of money from the Uttar Pradesh government. Before my departure, ditches had been dug for water pipes as far up as Naiganj *mohalla*. I have been informed that as of November, 1965, the town's water-supply system was completed and operating efficiently.

ZAMINDARI ABOLITION AND TOWN PROPERTY

In 1951 the U.P. legislature passed a zamindari abolition bill, which made it illegal to have landholdings above a certain size.[6] This law, however, did not cover lands within the Notified Area. Only in 1956 was legislation put into effect which restricted property holdings within the town.[7] Not until July, 1963, was the law applied to Tezibazar. Up to this date, much of the town's land was held by various zamindars or given out by these landlords to occupancy (or permanent) tenants in a tenure locally known as *rahandari* (in Hindi, life-long). This 1956 law, like the zamindari abolition bill of 1952, invests occupancy tenants with the ownership of their rented lands. But if the land in zamindari is actually *sir* of the landowner—that is, within his own holdings and not given out to tenants—he may retain it, as long as the amount does not exceed the limit set by the bill. If

[6] Cf. Neale, *op. cit.*, pp. 211–260.

[7] This act is entitled the U.P. Urban Areas Zamindari Abolition and Land Reforms Act, 1956, or U.P. Act No. IX, 1957. See Baljit Singh and Shridhar Misra, *A Study of Land Reforms in Uttar Pradesh*, p. 72.

any property is found neither to be *sir* of a zamindar or owned by any other individual, it passes to the municipal corporation, just as under the 1952 law such lands came under the control of the village statutory *pancayats*.

The effect of the 1956 zamindari abolition has been to unleash many legal suits and controversies regarding landownership within the town. Raging disputes about a section of the Sabzi Mandi, several plots in Katra, and other town areas go on; disputing claimants carry their property conflict into the political arena; and it is said that present municipal authorities use their official positions to better their legal situation vis à vis these lands. That property which is still owned as *sir* by zamindars is usually given out to businessmen for use as shops. Rent is charged on the occupation of buildings, however, and not on the land.

At this point it should be noted that the official organization of land in Tezibazar is separate from that both of the town and of the Notified Area. The lands of the N.A. fall into six *mauzas*, or revenue "villages," artificial entities drawn up by the land revenue department during the British Raj and left more or less unchanged by the Indian government. Tezibazar, the town itself, is parceled among five *mauzas*, which also contain a great deal of land neither in the town nor in the N.A. (see Map 4).

In addition to the 1963 act, the original zamindari abolition bill has had fundamental effects upon the town. Many Baniya residents owned considerable zamindaris in the neighboring rural area; these were for the most part abolished by the zamindari act. These individuals, who were previously able to live off rental incomes, have been forced to take up business again, and their prestige and political role in the town, although still great in some cases, must now rest on their business success and wealth from commerce. Since the Second World War, rich merchants, many times of recent origin and without landholdings, have moved into power positions in the town contra the old established zamindar families of Baniya or other castes. The zamindars' incomes were relatively inflexible, and they did not profit

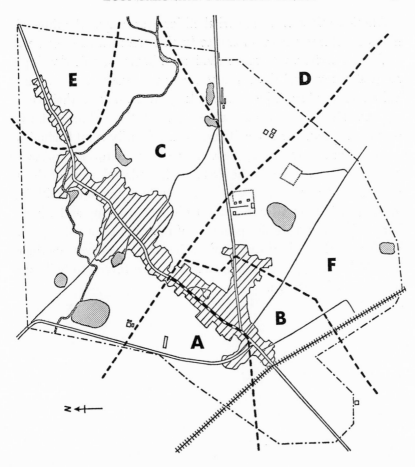

A-MAUZA SARAI RUSTUM   D-MAUZA DHAURAHRA

B-MAUZA KAMALPUR   E-MAUZA MUNGARDIH

C-MAUZA TEZIBAZAR   F-MAUZA PAKRI

Map 4. Tezibazar Notified Area, showing approximate boundaries of *mauza*s, or revenue divisions (after R. L. Singh)

so extensively in the black market and rationing days of the last World War. The zamindari abolition act of 1952 merely hastened and made final what was a natural evolution. Independence in 1947 also tended to demolish this system by introducing adult suffrage.

Another effect of zamindari abolition was to spur the flow of new capital into the town and to further the formation of new businesses and new business sections. Naturally, this development also increased the scarcity of good business locations and bid up their values. The ex-zamindars, divorced from their land incomes, looked for new investment possibilities and found business in the town attractive. These men, primarily rural Brahmins and Thakurs, have been the source of funds for the present construction boom along the Pratabgarh road, and many of them have opened small businesses in the southern section of Sahibganj. New businesses such as short-distance trucking and a lumber yard–saw mill are also products of this recent flow of capital. Because of the lack of openings in the established areas or their prohibitive cost, the ex-zamindars have been forced to build up new areas of the town.

CHAPTER 4

History of Tezibazar

Tezibazar can be considered an urban locale because of the primarily nonagricultural and commercial nature of the population, the presence of sophisticated political and educational machinery, and the existence of service institutions such as bank, post office, and rail and bus stations usually associated with an urban area. In fact, the town as an identifiable entity or community is defined by its political, administrative, and service institutions rather than by any traditional social cohesion. The interrelations of the traditional merchant castes and the other castes engaged in commerce are not mediated by any customary ceremonial or economic system such as the *jajmani* which links castes within a village, and there is no feeling that the town exists as a social unit made up of coexisting merchant castes. Nor is there a hierarchy of caste rank or commensality to designate superior or inferior groups. The Tezibazar castes only work within the same political-administrative unit and the same bazar from which they derive their livelihood—but not within the same traditional social status or ritual system on a town-wide basis.

This picture of the town resembles the recent description of Indian villages shattered by the advance of the modern world and its economy and political structure, although the rural area is not in so advanced a stage as is Tezibazar.[1] Yet there is every reason to believe that the present community organization of the

[1] See F. G. Bailey, *Caste and the Economic Frontier* (1957); T. Scarlett Epstein, *Economic Development and Social Change in South India*, section on the "dry" village, Dalena.

town (or the lack of it) is no recent development, but has existed at least since the turn of the century and perhaps from the very inception of the urban locale.

In India, much of the history of town formation has to do with a local *raja, navab,* or big zamindar who established a town or created a market. This sort of petty nobility or local strong men endowed towns and began market places and, traditionally, provided supra-caste integration to them. Tezibazar is an excellent case of this type of urban formation. In all probability the lack of community in the town is an old situation, and up to very recent times the substitute for it was the control of the market and the town by the local zamindar, who imposed a sense and structure of community upon what was an amorphous collection of primarily merchant castes, attracted by economic opportunity. After the demise or departure of the original founder or zamindar, his place was taken by smaller landowners, who inherited his position of authority in an informal manner based on the respect and homage of the population for their prestige and wealth. Finally, once even these small overlords are removed by impoverishment or zamindari abolition, the urban locale becomes merely an unstructured collection of caste groups bounded now only by political and social institutions emanating from the modern state.

The history of the present town of Tezibazar is in reality the chronicle of two separate areas, Sahibganj and Old Town, which until relatively recently were distinct. Most residents of Tezibazar do not know this fact, and much of the confusion and contradiction in the popular recitals of town history stem from a failure to distinguish the separate development of these two areas. Distinct as they are historically, Sahibganj and Old Town are similar functionally: they both developed into commercial areas, and their process and organization of growth, under the aegis and control of a local overlord or zamindar, is remarkably similar. No official recitals of the town's origin and development exist: all the following information, then, is based on oral tradition. Undoubtedly, dates and specific events before the Mutiny

(1857–1859) are totally untrustworthy, but there is every reason to believe that the pattern of development is more or less faithfully recorded, as it matches the origins of so many similar towns.

THE FORMATION OF OLD TOWN

Old Town—the area above the leather market excluding Naibazar—is a very ancient place. According to popular estimates, about one thousand (*sic*) to four hundred years ago, in the time of the Moghuls, all the area now called Tezibazar was jungle. Here lived a Sudra caste called *bhar*, warlike and pugnacious dacoits, who raided caravans for a livelihood. These people drank whiskey and were unclean. A caste of the same name and habits is said still to inhabit parts of eastern Uttar Pradesh. The *bhar* lived in what is presently Sipah *mohalla*, and the remains of their fort and *dih*, or shrine, still stand. The earliest name for the Tezibazar area was "Lorak Dih," and there are nearby villages which still retain such allegedly *bhar* titles, as, for example, Mungardih, just beyond Naibazar. The *bhar* people had become such nuisances to trade that the Moghul emperor Akbar (1556–1605) dispatched an army under Divan Vazid Khan to pacify them (a reference to the capture of Jaunpur in 1559?). The subsequent destruction of the *bhar* is variously described as the result of a siege or of a treacherous feast given by the Muslims at which the *bhar* became intoxicated and were then slaughtered.[2] After the victory, however achieved, Divan Vazid Khan and his army marched onward to Jaunpur and, afterward, to Delhi, where the Divan suddenly died. His body was returned to Jaunpur and buried there, and in his honor a *mohalla* in this city—Vazidpur—is named after him. This same Divan suppos-

---

[2] Another version has it that the Thakur clan of *bacch* dispatched the *bhar* in this fashion and were later, in turn, displaced by the Muslims. Undoubtedly, the first Muslims in this area were the Afghan rulers of Delhi and Jaunpur, long before the Moghuls. The Jaunpur District Gazetteer suggests that one of these rulers established the town, but there is no evidence for this in the oral traditions of Tezibazar and, as far as I know, no written substantiation.

edly began the formation of a commercial center in what is now Old Town. However, it was not until the first *miyan*, or governor, was appointed by the Moghul court that a real town development began. The first governor, Havi Viyar Khan, whose descendants still live in Tezibazar and held land in the Notified Area until July, 1963, was given a zamindari of approximately one thousand acres. In Moghul times, this Khan family gave no money to the government for their landholdings since they had various administrative posts and the zamindari (or more correctly, *jagir* [3]) was in lieu of a salary. But when the British came, they fixed a revenue settlement upon them. This family has a written genealogy which shows a fifteen-generation span between the first governor and his present-day descendants. They had remained a power in the town until the 1920's. The Khans claimed to have had copper plates from the Moghul emperor investing them with the deed to the Tezibazar area which, unfortunately, were now lost. The existence of these plates was attested to by other people as well.

Havi Viyar built a large complex of residential buildings in Sipah *mohalla* near the former *bhar* fort. "Sipah" supposedly comes from the Persian word "sipahi" (soldier) and refers to the governor's troops permanently stationed there. He also built the Jama mosque and near it a market place, now long since disappeared (or perhaps the location of the modern leather market). The old grain market of the town was in present-day Anjahi *mohalla* just in front of Sipah, and this construction also owed its existence to the Muslim governor. "All the property of Tezibazar was in the hands of these Khans, who gave the land to till and to occupy to whomever they wished," is the way one informant expressed this family's role in the creation of the locality. Note, too, that the functional center of the town consisted of religious and administrative edifices, around which the markets were built as a secondary phenomenon.

The construction of the town and market places by Havi

[3] See Irfan Habib, *The Agrarian System of Moghul India*, pp. 257–258.

Viyar Khan soon attracted merchants, whose arrival is dated to Akbar's reign. At that time Brahmins, Koiris, Telis, Bhuj, and Kunjra settled here, most of whom became tenants to the Khans, and some of whom engaged in trade. The caste *mohallas* of Old Town—Babhanaoti, Koiran, and probably Chamraoti—date their origins to this period. The Umar arrived during the rule of Aurangzeb (1658–1707). These merchants settled in Katra, An-jahi, and Gurhai and transformed the town into a prosperous community. The Khan family as overlords controlled both the market and the nascent town as well as the agriculturalists in the surrounding rural area. They were the arbiters of disputes and the purveyors of the laws. Only through these landholders was the town linked to the state administration.

When the British took control in the late eighteenth century, the Khan family sided with them and were left in possession of their proprietary holdings. From the Mutiny onward, the family fortunes deteriorated, and in the last part of the nineteenth century, the Khans were forced to sell almost half their holdings to various town Baniyas, mainly of Umar caste. The latter thus became the first local Baniyas to be zamindars in their own right, although they held the land in a form of tenure wherein they were still obliged to pay the Khan family an annual quitrent. In the early years of this century, the family fortunes were irrevo-cably destroyed by the extravagance and lavish policies of Ahmad Ullah Khan—a leading figure of the town at that time. Also at this time the political and commercial center of Teziba-zar began to move to Sahibganj. Today the descendants of this once-powerful family, completely stripped of whatever they had left by the zamindari abolitions of 1952 and 1963, somehow exist in the ancient, tumbled-down *kaccha* houses of Sipah, which in the time of the first *miyan* had been so fine.

THE FORMATION OF SAHIBGANJ

During the entire period of Old Town's development, the area now called Sahibganj was totally rural and agricultural. The surrounding country was held by a Thakur clan called *bacch* or *bacchgoti.* These people now claim to have been in the lineage of the famous Rajput ruler in medieval Rajasthan, Pritvi Raj. This great king was a Rajput of *cauhan* branch and of *gotra* (exogamous clan) *vats.* The corrupted pronunciation of *vats* is *vacch,* whence the present name *bacch.* Their story goes that when Pritvi Raj was defeated by the Moghuls, his clan scattered and had to hide their real identity because the Muslims had sworn to leave no trace of them on the earth. Since they did not want to hide their identity completely, they only gave up their branch name of *cauhan* and began using instead the clan appellation. *Vats gotra* came to be known as *bacch* or *bacchgoti* in some areas and *bachalgoti* in others. The present-day *bacch* of Tezibazar claim to have come to eastern U.P. and defeated the *bhar* and then turned to agriculture. They also claim to have begun the construction and occupation of the southern sections of the town. It is true that the *bacch* Thakurs owned the land around Sahibganj before the formation of the town therein, but their further suppositions are an oversimplified version of the actual complex ordering of events leading to the inception of Sahibganj.

Before the Mutiny—how long before is unknown—while the Khan family controlled the rural and urban area to the north, various *bacch* Thakur landowners occupied the territory to the south. One such, Kalandar Singh, was zamindar of Navadanri, a small village one mile from present-day Tezibazar. This man opposed the British during the Mutiny and, after the pacification of the countryside, was captured and duly executed. His skull supposedly once rested in an old tree in front of Hindu Intermediate School, across from a large field called "the camping ground" where the British army bivouacked and tried traitors. The lands of Kalandar Singh were confiscated and then auctioned off by the British, and the part of them which now comprises *mauzas* Kamalpur and Sarai Rustum (which together form Sahibganj) was purchased by the Shah (Muslim) family. This family once rivaled the Khan family in prestige and control of the nearby country, and its members still live in Tezibazar.

The Shahs may also have bought some lands from Kalandar Singh before the Mutiny. At the time that Mohammad Akbar Shah bought *mauza*s Sarai Rustum and Kamalpur (see Map 4) only a small settlement was located there, and revenue came only from the rents of the agricultural tenants. The latter were mainly Thakur, Camar, Ahir, Kurmi, and Pasi castes.

A few years after their original purchase—that is, about a century ago—the Shahs gave some part of their holdings in Sarai Rustum and Kamalpur on lease to an Englishman. This man utilized the area for indigo cultivation and also constructed a small processing mill on it. To him the honor of having named Sahibganj belongs, for he was generally referred to as "*sahab*," and his indigo plantation occupied the very area of the present-day town ward. The Sahab, however, limited his interests to indigo cultivation; he played no part in the formation of the urban area.

The indigo market soon declined, and the Englishman departed or died; in any case his enterprise and occupation of the land ended. About ninety to ninety-five years ago, Rai Udai Baks Singh, the Raja of Bilampur (ten miles distant), purchased the same property, which ran from the present-day police station to the leather market. Udai Baks was a Thakur of *bacch* clan, a fact which affords the only substantiation of a *bacch* role in the formation of the market area—not, however, in that of original landowners as local Thakurs suggest. Udai Baks soon began to transform the primarily rural area into an urban complex. He built the large temple in Sahibganj and, behind it, the *rani kothi*, an imposing *pakka* building where his daughter, the Rani Sahiba, lived until her death in 1916. (Udai Baks had one son who died heirless, as did also his only daughter.) [4] From 1916 to 1936, the

---

[4] No exact date can be fixed for the construction of Udaiganj market, but it must have occurred sometime between 1866, when Udai Baks inherited some land in Jaunpur district, and 1899, the year of his death. A revenue map, dated 1878, in the Jaunpur district offices, shows a section of Sahibganj called "Udaiganj" (H. R. Neville, *Pratabgarh: A Gazetteer; Pratabgarh District Notes And Statistics, 1931-2;* H. R. Neville, *Jaunpur: A Gazetteer*).

building was used as a hostel for the Hindu Intermediate College; now it is totally abandoned.

Sometime after the Mutiny, at about this time, the commercial possibilities of Sahibganj were immeasurably improved by the metaling of the Allahabad road running through the southern nexus of the area. Later, in 1898, trade in this area was further enhanced by the construction of the railway line. The Raja of Bilampur decided to build up the locale into a commercial center and profit from the increased tax receipts. Udai Baks constructed Udaiganj, the present-day Gola Mandi (there is no local explanation why the name has been changed). He also located the *gur* market along the main road just north of the present police station. At the turn of the century, *gur* was one of the most important products of the town. The Raja offered land *muft* (free) to all merchants who would settle there and carry on their businesses. Despite British law, the rural area at that time was dangerous for merchants. They were often beaten by debtors; they had little protection for their lives or possessions. So they quickly took advantage of the opportunities in Udaiganj. Raghu Das narrated the story of his grandfather's coming to the town:

Ninety years ago my paternal grandfather (*baba*) lived outside the town and did business in *gur* and sugar for eight months a year. He used bullocks to carry commodities to Allahabad, Rae Bareilly, and other places. Then he moved to Sahibganj to take advantage of the Raja's offer. The market in Sahibganj was very good. My grandfather set up as a general merchant of *gur*, sugar, rice, and oilseeds. The Raja protected all the merchants living in Sahibganj at that time.

Under the control and stimulation of Rai Udai Baks, the market and Sahibganj prospered. Many of the Baniya castes now inhabiting the town date their arrival to this period. Thus, the Kesarvani moved to Sahibganj after the deterioration of the market in Phulpur, a small town ten miles away. A well in Sahibganj dated 1889 is said to bear the name of the first Kesarvani immigrant. Similarly, the Kalvar or Jaisval caste was attracted, as were many Hindu Halvais, Agarval, Bhuj, and other Vaisyas. Some Umar and other Baniyas resident in Old Town moved into Sahibganj—much to their own profit, as is indicated by the relative poverty today of those family branches which remained behind. At this time an important social and demographic factor in the town came into existence: Sahibganj became the primary residential area for Kesarvani and Kalvar and a host of other, smaller, Baniya castes and Old Town remained the preserve of the Umar.

After the death of Udai Baks his land passed into the hands of the Rajas of Bhagvanganj and Tulgaon. Since zamindari abolition in the Notified Area, former tenants now own their once-rented lands, but nonresident Rajas still collect rental from buildings on that land.

In 1907, when Old Town and Sahibganj were put under a single political and administrative unit, the official bonds which now unite these formerly distinct sections came into existence, and Tezibazar (as the market center) became a reality. Yet, there are definite social and economic remnants of its divergent origin, as, for instance, the differential in economic organization of Sahibganj and Old Town and the demographic ordering of the various Baniya castes.

The element of striking similarity in the origins of Old Town and Sahibganj is, of course, the role in each case of a local landowner and strong man as founder and protector of the town and market and arbiter of its social organization. The zamindar attracted merchants to his market place by guaranteeing them protection—by overseeing the "peace of the market." He provided social control and organization for his artificially created urban locale. The landowner was a ritual leader of a sort as well: the main *ram lila* ground in Tezibazar was situated until 1920 in front of the *rani kothi*. This community festival was supervised and in large measure financed by Udai Baks or his daughter. After the latter's death, the festival site was changed to the open space in front of the house of the then largest Hindu zamindar.

Traditionally, Indian rulers, both large and small, regulated the ranking and much of the interaction between the castes within their purview. Concerning Poona city, Gadgil writes:

The State or secular authority intervened in inter-caste or inter-communal disputes and superimposed or rather interpreted the pattern which contained the autonomous community groups, and helped to delineate the details wherever it became necessary to do this for particular groups. Though it was true that non-Hindu communities could not be fitted into the Hindu hierarchical gradation they also functioned to a large extent, as autonomous groups in social matters. . . . Their relations vis à vis each other or vis à vis elements in Hindu society were also under regulation of the State. . . . The Muslim and Maratha rulers of Maharashtra might have exercised this power in different ways and with differing results but the significant point in this context is that they both held it and exercised it.[5]

How true this situation was for the zamindar-overlords of Old Town and Sahibganj, it is difficult to say at this remove. To judge from the social responsibilities of the smaller zamindars at a later date, their duties must have been extensive in these matters.

In the early decades of the twentieth century, as the town became more prosperous and local merchants grew rich from trade and invested in land, control by the old zamindars waned. Udai Baks was dead, and the Shah family, as well as the Khans, had fallen on evil times and were forced to sell some of their property holdings to town Baniyas. Even then, however, the zamindars, whether old or new, retained many of their former powers of social control and political influence, and their town prestige remained the same. Thus, in the early years of the Notified Area committee, the zamindars occupied all the positions. At this time the committee was not elected; the District Magistrate as representative of the British colonial government appointed the outstanding men of the town to the seats. In choosing the zamindars, the British Raj merely made the official politi-

[5] D. R. Gadgil, *Poona: A Socio-Economic Study, Part II. Social*, p. 173.

cal structure the mirror of the informal one. Moving the place of the *ram lila* ground also symbolized a continuing interest by the now smaller zamindar in the community's ritual. Babu Tribeni Lal, whose family (Baniya-Umar caste) inherited on a diminished scale the social position of Udai Baks, notes the social and political duties and powers of his ancestors:

When Gaya Din [his paternal grandfather], Chaurasi Din, and the other brothers were joint, they used to do *sadarvrat*, which means they used to distribute clothing and food among the poor people every day. At *magh mela* time every year, they gave food and provided lodging for the pilgrims. The Umar caste temple and the *talab* behind the Jama mosque were built by them. At that time they were zamindars of twenty-nine villages, and in about fifteen they constructed wells for irrigation and also three wells in Tezibazar. This kind of activity in those days was the symbol of the wealthy. . . .

My ancestors were also bankers and owned sugar factories. As a boy I was told that one time Gaya Din heard from his servants that more sugar was in the shop than should be. Gaya Din thought that his son who was in charge of the shop must be cheating on the weight. He thought this would cause Laksmi [wealth] to desert him. He had all the extra sugar and some food mixed and he distributed this among the poor. Even persons who were not so poor were given some.

From Gaya Din's time up to Narain Das [his classificatory *caca* or grandfather's brother's son], any dispute in this town was referred to them and no man challenged their decisions. They always tried to avoid conflict, and most times they found a compromise. After the death of Narain Das [October 7, 1940], there was no person able enough to do this. After the breakup of the joint family under Gaya Din, Narain Das was the only man who was big enough to uphold the traditions, prestige, and status of the family. He was a religious and honest man. He did *sadarvrat* and was also a leader of his caste.

But even in the last years of Narain Das' life, the power and influence of the zamindars were being still further eclipsed. The Second World War hastened this process considerably by providing many opportunities for the small Baniya shopkeeper to

black-market and to engage in other illegal or semilegal activities
that were highly profitable. One ex-zamindar explained that
since these people were not wealthy before, they had no prestige
to retain and therefore could entertain every vile and antisocial
trick to increase their gain. However, families such as his which
were old and respected were severely limited by their fear of
lowering themselves. Less pasionately and perhaps more importantly, the inflation which the war brought was detrimental to
the zamindars, whose rental income was fixed both by tradition
and by the revenue laws of the British government. The zamindars were those, of course, whom the British both expected to
give and coerced into giving large sums to meet the war cost. By
the end of the war, on the one hand, a highly moneyed Baniya
class without the social antecedents of *noblesse oblige* and all the
social disqualifications of *nouveaux riches* had developed,
whereas, on the other, the position and status of the old zamindars had sharply deteriorated. Independence, the advent of adult
suffrage in 1947, and zamindari abolition in 1952 completed the
destruction of the former ruling elite. Gone from the town were
the old zamindar-overlords who had guaranteed the market;
gone were their successors, the big Baniya merchant-zamindars
who, if they did not direct and control to the same extent, still
had important town political functions. From the 1930's, Tezibazar was reduced to component castes which, artificially drawn
together and controlled by the overlords, had never developed
any political or social ordering of existence except the continued
maintenance of their individual caste identities. They had come
together in the town fortuitously because it was a good place for
business. This economic activity, due to its market orientation,
did nothing to condition a community existence separate from
that offered by the zamindars. On the contrary, the traditional
organization of business ventures and of the Baniya castes promoted separatism and competition, as I shall note below. A
necessity to replace the old rule of affluence by the zamindars is
the reason why acceptance of modern political machinery has
been so easy in Tezibazar. By the time the political structure of

independent India came to the town, no traditional order remained to resist it; people had no fears that it would augment or lead to social disharmony as has been the case in villages, because there was no indigenous community or cohesion to disrupt.

Many people are not entirely happy, however, with this new style social control, which is decided at the polls and mediated by regional and state political figures and parties. What has replaced the structured paternalism of the zamindar is a system of politics and town social control where there are no touchstones beyond the personal ambitions of small men who align and unalign themselves and their followers according to wherever and whenever the wind of aggrandizement blows. Social control and ethical direction in the town as it emerges from this system implies, at its worst, the oppression of the losing politician by the winner. At best, it is the outcome of many random manipulations by various men all directed toward the same political goals: local government office. This situation constitutes, however, no argument for the zamindari system, which has many black marks against it in the memories of my informants. The point is that the end of the zamindar's control has led to total adoption of modern regional political apparatus, with which, however, many people have become dissatisfied because they see it as resting upon undisciplined and uncontrolled competition. Yet, because they had no traditional system of social order aside from zamindari (which is now dead for all time), they see no alternative for the present political process save in the rise of some vaguely defined "new morality."

CHAPTER 5

Caste Ranking and Commensality:
The Absence of Hierarchy

No one knows the exact number of castes or *biradari*s in Tezibazar; certainly the figure is around fifty. Table 8 gives a total listing of all the castes which appeared in my business survey (Part A) as well as a few others which did not (Part B).[1] It also notes the total number of families, the traditional occupation (if any) of the various castes, and those which have recently adopted "prestige" names. Table 21 gives the complete list of castes appearing in the business survey, the total number of families (both resident and nonresident), and the population in each group.

Prestige Names

The newly acquired "prestige" names of various castes are symbols of a desire for legitimate status in the caste system or for a name without the pejorative connotations of the traditional one. Thus the Camar call themselves by Gandhi's name, "Harijan"—"the children of God"; the Bhangi Muslim calls himself "Halal-khor"—that is, "one who eats lawfully or correctly"—to emphasize that his sustenance is honestly gained even though his station is low. Generally, people continue to use the traditional name except in the presence of an actual caste member who

[1] This list makes no pretense of being complete and contains only the names of castes which came to my attention in the business survey or those whose members I met in the course of other interviewing.

Table 8A. Tezibazar castes included in business survey

Status category and traditional caste name	Traditional occupation	Prestige name (if any)	No. of families
Brahmin			
1. Brahmaṇ (kanaujiya) *	Priest		26
Thakur			
1. *ThakUr*	Warrior		10
Baniya			
1. Umar	General merchant		98
2. Kesarvani	General merchant		39
3. Hindu halvai (kanaujiya) *	Candy maker and merchant		35
4. Bhuj (kanaujiya) *	Grain parcher		34
5. Kalvar †	Distiller and wine merchant	Jaisval, haehae ksatriya	31
6. Teli (biyahUt) *	Oil presser		22
7. Kasodhan	Utensil merchant	AyodhIya	8
8. Sonar	Ornament maker		7
9. Agarval (marvari)	General merchant		6
10. Agrahari	Grocer		3
11. *Thather*	Utensil maker and merchant		2
12. Kasera	Utensil maker and merchant		1
13. Madhesiya ‡	General merchant		1
(Baniya total)			(287)
Kisan			
1. Ahir (gUal) §	Cowherd, dairyman	Yadav	10
2. Barai	Betel grower and pan seller	Caurasiya	10
3. Koiri	Vegetable gardener	Mauriya	8
4. Hindu nau	Barber		5
5. KUrmi	Vegetable gardener		5
6. Bari	Leaf plate maker		5
7. Lohar	Blacksmith-carpenter	Visvakarma	5
8. Kevat ‖	Cultivator		3
9. Mali	Flower gardener and seller		2
10. Kahar	Porter, watercarrier		1
11. Pal	Cultivator		1
(Kisan total)			(55)
Sudra			
1. Camar	Leather worker	Harijan, jaisvar	19
2. Pattahar	Pig herder		4
3. Dhobi	Washerman		4
(Sudra total)			(27)

Table 8A (cont.)

Status category and traditional caste name	Traditional occupation	Prestige name (if any)	No. of families
Other Hindu			
1. Hindu kayasth (srivastava)	Clerk		2
2. Arora (Punjabi)	Merchant and cultivator		1
(Other Hindu total)			(3)
Muslim			
1. Shekh	(None)		25
2. KUnjra	Vegetable seller	Sabzi-faros	24
3. Julaha	Weaver	Ansari, shekh	18
4. Muslim halvai	Tobacco and sweetmeats		10
5. Fakir or darbes	Burial and scavenging	Shah	6
6. Fakir	Scavenging	Shah kalandar	3
7. Curihar	Bangle seller		7
8. Muslim nau	Barber		6
9. Darzi	Tailor		6
10. Khan (pathan)	(None)		2
11. CIkUva	Goat butcher		2
12. Chipi	Dyer		1
13. Muslim kayasth	Clerk		1
14. Bhangi	Scavenging and sweeping	Halal-khor	1
15. Uncertain identity			4
(Muslim total)			(116)
Grand total, 46 castes			524

* Names indicating local endogamous groups or *bans*.

† Kalvars claim they are Ksatriyas and not Baniyas.

‡ This is probably a *bans* name rather than a caste, but the respondent claimed it was his *biradari* name.

§ Three respondents claimed they were Gual Yadavs, which they said was the same caste as Ahir. Usually, in the literature, Gual is reported as a separate caste.

‖ Informants disagreed about the placement of "Kevat," and some claimed they belonged to the "Sudra" rather than the "Kisan" category.

might find it offensive. However, some names such as Harijan, Ansari, and Jaisval have become accepted and are used about equally with the traditional names.

One Baniya group had changed its name and, in fact, claimed not to be Vaisya at all. The Kalvar, who were traditionally *sarab* or "wine" sellers and still engage in the business (there is an expression, "Even milk in the hands of a Kalvar seems like whiskey"), decided at a caste council some thirty years ago to adopt the name of a single branch, "Jaisval," as the name for the whole caste. Subsequently they began to propagate the story that they were not Baniyas at all, that, in fact, they were Ksatriyas of the *haehae* branch who at the time of the Muslim invasion were defeated and scattered and later forced by economic necessity to take on the degrading business of the wine trade. The

Table 8B. Tezibazar castes not included in business survey

Status category and traditional caste name	Traditional occupation
Kisan	
1. KUmbhar	Potter
2. Nuniya	Salt maker and house construction
3. Gadariya	Herdsman
Sudra	
1. Pasi	Pig herder and watchman
2. Musar	Leaf-dish maker
3. Dhokar	Basket maker
Muslim	
1. Behna or dhUniya	Cotton carder
2. Dafari	Musician

Kalvar have launched a vigorous attempt to remove the stigma (of sentiment) attached to their former primary occupation and at least in Tezibazar, where they are wealthy, are on equal footing with other Baniya castes. Only the Kalvar take their claim to Ksatriya origin very seriously; and many young Kalvars do not even know or care about their new "Jaisval" status.

A short explanation is also necessary regarding some Muslim caste names. The Julaha caste decided to rid itself of the lowly associations of its traditional name by adopting the cognomen "Ansari." They have tried to establish historically that they were really "Shekh" and that "Ansari" was merely an ancient family surname such as Shekh "Mansuri" or Shekh "Sidiki." Many

Julaha now answer a question regarding their caste with the name "Shekh"—only upon further questioning do they admit to "Ansari." Some Muslims refuse even to give their caste names at first, because they say there is no caste in Islam. These individuals are not necessarily members of the lowest castes and ashamed of their origins; often, in fact, they are among the better-educated groups. Their disavowal of a quite apparent reality is part of the Muslim communal image, reinforced by the need for minority unity in the face of Hindu hostility.

The *Bans*

A far more important point emerges from the study of caste names. One Baniya group, the Kasodhan, are seemingly known by another name, "Ayodhya," as well. Some individuals who use the latter title claim, however, that they are an endogamous group separate from the Kasodhan. I could never find conclusive proof for either position, although it is common for a caste name to refer really to several endogamous divisions spatially distinct and with nonoverlapping distributions. For example, "Hindu Halvai" is given as the *biradari* name, but in fact the de jure endogamous group is the *kanaujiya* branch of this Halvai unit. The same situation applies to Kalvar, Teli, Bhuj, and many other castes. I shall discuss in detail this further complication to caste structure later on in the section dealing with the Umar, who are an excellent example of such multi-endogamous group organization. Generally, only one such branch is resident in a particular locale, so that the use of the name "Hindu Halvai" for the local endogamous group is in no way misleading as long as it is remembered that in other areas a caste named "Hindu Halvai" may, in fact, not marry with the Tezibazar branch. The Kasodhan represent the only case of such a dual existence in the town, and they are immigrants of the last twenty years. Then, too, if Kasodhan and Ayodhya are absolutely separate entities rather than different branch names, no problem arises in their classification. I have, however, assumed that they refer to two locally endogamous branches of the same caste category which happened both to migrate to the same town.[2]

The Hindi word usually employed to denote locally endogamous branches within a caste category is "*bans*" or "*gotra*." In the literature the latter word is generally taken to mean "exogamous clan," but at least in Tezibazar, and particularly among Baniyas, it indicates an endogamous, localized entity. In contradiction to this usage, however, local Brahmins use the term "*gotra*" to mean exogamous clan, and "*bans*" as employed by the Thakur means the same. In the involved caste system of the town, terminology becomes an extremely complex matter.

A most vexing but illuminating point in trying to establish to what "*bans*" or section a particular local caste belongs is the comparative ignorance of its members about it. The Baniyas are particularly—though not exclusively—in this position, and in the cases of the less populous business castes, I never did determine what their *bans* were. This situation illustrates the lack of interest and knowledge about caste which I specified earlier as a prime characteristic of the Baniya castes. A further difficulty with the Kalvar arose from the fact that those men who knew

[2] For a more detailed discussion of the differences between *biradari*, or "caste," and *bans*, or "subcaste," see Adrian C. Mayer, *Caste and Kinship in Central India*, pp. 151–161, especially pp. 160–161. Mayer maintains that caste as a group and as a role-definer is primarily significant within the village or local context, whereas the subcaste (*bans*) is important from a regional viewpoint. Thus, he avoids the question regarding which is the real "caste," *biradari* or *bans*. Mayer's data differ from the Tezibazar situation in the smaller territorial expanse of the subcastes and the greater number of subcastes which are coresident. Further, his formulation does not explain how to handle the *biradari* on a regional rather than intra-village level. Since the *biradari* on a regional level is never an endogamous, commensal group, Bailey's concept of "caste category" (see Chap. 13, n. 1) would seem more suitable. From this viewpoint, the localized, endogamous *bans* become the true castes. This is the position I have adopted in respect to the Umar in Chapter 13. See also Richard G. Fox, "Resiliency and Change in the Indian Caste System: The Umar of U.P.," *Journal of Asian Studies*, XXVI (1967), 580–581.

the *bans* name refused to tell it because the caste council had decreed that the name "Jaisval" be used exclusively.

CASTE RANKING

In Indian villages, the various castes are bound together, as well as distinguished and graded for status, by a hierarchy of rank.[3] Much dispute may exist over relative positions in the system—which, indeed, has been transformed into an even more fluid state by the economic, social, and political innovations of the last century. Nevertheless, the *ideal* of such a formal structure remains, and individuals accept the fact that there is one rank location for a particular caste; the dispute only concerns which specific one.

Such a situation of hierarchy does not seem to exist in Tezibazar, either as a commonly accepted *ideal* or as a basis of behavior. The castes of the town, other than Sudra and Muslim, are interrelated in a system structured on "mutual repulsion" (to use C. Bouglé's term) and caste distinctiveness. This system merely continues to buttress caste separatism and endogamy in a situation where most of the hierarchical aspects of caste never held or no longer hold. There are individuals who still rank castes—it is human to judge one's neighbors, and perception in terms of caste is almost mechanical in India—but the behavioral concomitant of the ranking system is absent, as are consistent or popularly accepted criteria for it.[4] The one point of agreement is that Muslims and Sudras are inferior status levels; but note that this does not carry assignment of a lower or lowest rank to these groupings *within* an all-embracing system of caste status hierarchy. The Muslim and Sudra are considered lowly and as altogether different entities: *mlicch* (standard Hindi, *mlecch*), or "dirty person," for Muslims; *achut*, or "polluted," for Sudras. They are

[3] Mayer, *op. cit.* (1960), pp. 33–60.
[4] For a similar ranking situation among Indian immigrants in East Africa, see David F. Pocock, " 'Difference' in East Africa: A Study of Caste and Religion in Modern Indian Society," *Southwestern Journal of Anthropology*, XIII (1957), 296.

not lower in rank within a hierarchy; they are only more separate, more repulsed than other groupings.

In Tezibazar when a man is asked to rank the town castes, he
generally replies in one of two ways. Either he says that all castes
are equal now, or he states that according to Hindu scriptures
the Brahmin rank highest, then Ksatriya or Thakur, next Vaisya,
and, finally, although not belonging with the three preceding
twice-born groupings, the Sudra. The latter statement indicates
that the individual is acquainted with the all-India tradition and
says little for his beliefs vis à vis town castes. Usually, if he is
further asked what is the highest-ranking caste in the town, he
will reply with the name of his own, be it Thakur, Brahmin,
Baniya, or Kisan. "Every caste thinks itself the highest," he will
say, in explanation and justification for the various differing
opinions regarding the town *biradaris*. The individual accepts as
equable the fact that all castes should feel themselves equal. As
for the contradiction with the traditional system—that was for
the old days; now a "new wind" is blowing, and everything is
changed. Sometimes a man will maintain that he must rank
Brahmins higher in their role of priests, and some Baniyas rated
Brahmins and Thakurs superior because they felt that to deny
this would be to deny their religion. These minor manifestations
of an ideal sentiment are not, however, followed up in the
behavioral sphere.

That generally, in the Tezibazar caste rank system, each caste
(except the Muslim and Sudra) thinks itself superior is just a
more involved method of noting that all castes are different and
distinct. This point is further elucidated by the criteria used to
buttress the position of one's own caste as the highest. Normally
I asked informants to tell me the order of castes below their own
and why they were so placed. Such discussions placed great
strain upon the patience of my informants; they often found it
extremely difficult to explain why they had selected their various
assignments of rank. Sometimes they ranked on the basis of
wealth, sometimes by political prestige. Often they would combine the above criteria with traditional Indian occupational cate-

gories and food habits (use of meat and alcohol). Usually such procedure would quickly lead to an intricate tangle of contradictions which they themselves acknowledged as they gave up in disgust and told me to see one of the old men of their lineage or family—they themselves knew no better. Many did not even get this far; in fact, they had no reason for most of their rank designations, and a few were willing to leave it to the anthropologist's opinion in the matter. Samples of opinions follow:

Ram Nath Kalvar (Jaisval), age *c*. 65:

Brahmins are the only caste higher than the Vaisya, as they are priests and it is according to scripture. All Baniya castes are of the same status although naturally each one thinks itself higher than any other. Morally, castes which do not eat meat or drink are considered higher—[that is] the individuals of any caste who do not so do. No entire caste is considered of superior status to us [that is, Kalvar, who eat meat and drink] because it is vegetarian and nondrinking.

Ram Murti Umar, age *c*. 55:

The various groups rank: (1) Brahmin, (2) Ksattri, (3) Vaisya, and (4) Sudra, because this is according to scriptures. But at the present time if any person of lower caste has money, he will consider himself the equal of a higher caste. Now wealth outranks caste. Within the Vaisya, the Umar rank first because they do not use dirty things such as liquor or meat. [But he would not rank beyond this because the individual rather than the group mattered].

Ram Prasad Umar, age *c*. 50:

The Vaisya rank above the Kisan because the Kisan eat meat. [But he had no answer to my questioning why the Kisan were lower than either Kalvar or Hindu Halvai when both these Vaisya castes were known to eat meat.]

Sita Ram Agrahari, age *c*. 48:

The "castes" are ranked as: (1) Brahmin, (2) Ksatriya, (3) Vaisya, and (4) Sudra, because in the Hindu scriptures the Brahmin is the mouth, the Ksatriya is the shoulder, the Vaisya, the belly, and the Sudra, the feet. This is the traditional order, but nowadays the three twice-born "castes" are all equal in status and only the Sudras are inferior.

Few people really cared to consider their caste ranking system. My assistant, an educated although somewhat orthodox village Brahmin, remarked: "These people are foolish. They do not take these matters seriously." [5] In fact, the reason they did not was because I was asking them to think about the town caste structure in a way which was unusual and irrelevant. To the extent that they complied with my request, this was an indication that they knew a caste ordering of this sort might exist and were attempting to formalize Tezibazar's amorphous organization into all-India terms, such as they had done before with caste terminology and the *varna* system. I was more successful in getting patterned rankings of castes within a status category, although here, too, the absence of any standardized criteria with which to buttress ratings based primarily therefore on personal whim is clear:

Malukh Das Kesarvani (M.A., Allahabad University), age 32:

Within the Vaisya, the castes are ranked: (1) Kesarvani, (2) Umar, (3) Kalvar, (4) Marvari, (5) Halvai, (6) Kasodhan and Teli, (7) Bhuj, and (8) Agrahari. The Umar rank below the Kesarvani because the dowry system still exists in that caste whereas there is no question of dowry in the Kesarvani and anyone can marry with anyone else [*sic*]. The Kalvar rank lower than Umar because the dowry system is even stronger in this caste. They also eat meat. The Marvari [Agarval] rank below because I am vague about their customs and they also have the reputation of being cheats. Actually the Halvai rank higher than the Marvari since they are not cheats and their customs are better known to me. I really think of this business of caste ranking as a matter of individual opinion, and probably

[5] The fact that my first assistant was a Brahmin obviously affected the statements of informants about caste and caste ranking. Out of deference to him, they would accent the formal or, as they called it, "scriptural" aspects rather than some of their own ideas. Therefore even these weak statements of the traditional order are perhaps overemphases drawn out by the presence of a Brahmin.

every person would disagree about which castes are highest and which lowest. But to go on: the Teli ranks so low because they have preserved harsh treatment for caste defaulters which is unfitted to this modern age. The Kasodhan is equally low because they take bride-price, not dowry. The Bhuj rank below them because their economic condition and standard of living is much inferior to that of the Telis. The Agraharis rank lowest because they cheat in business and rob people. [Interview taken in English.]

Candrasekhar Kalvar, age 19:

The Vaisya castes are rated in this order: (1) Jaisval (Kalvar), (2) Kesarvani, (3) Umar and Sonar, (4) Teli and Bhuj, (5) Thather. Jaisvals do not take meat and do not do evil deeds, and this is why I rate them first. Formerly people of my caste ate meat, and some still do, but I think they should not. Of course persons belonging to a vegetarian caste are higher than a nonvegetarian caste. [When the obvious contradiction in this statement was shown to him, Candrasekhar became confused and could not give reasons for the ranking of the other Vaisya castes. He showed more and more puzzlement about what the ranking should be and finally suggested I see his grandfather.]

These and other responses seem to show that the caste ranking system is unstructured, a matter of personal opinion, of personally chosen criteria, replete with contradictions because it is not an integral part of the organization of town castes. The Tezibazar castes and their ranking system appear to reinforce only one aspect: the separation of the individual caste bodies and their distance from each other. Hierarchy as an ordered and regulated ideal exists neither in a partial reality of behavior nor in the individual's societal perceptions.

CASTE RANKING AND COMMENSALITY

The rules of interdining and commensal restrictions are usually considered in India an important technique by which the various rank positions in a local caste hierarchy can be discerned. A caste which takes food from another is either its equal or inferior; conversely, to refuse food from a caste is to claim an equivalent or superior status to it.

The rank designations of commensal rules are further determined by various socially defined types of food, some of which are more widely acceptable than others. In Tezibazar two types of food are distinguished: *kaccha*, consisting of rice and *chappatis* (unleavened wheat cakes) and anything boiled in water or baked; and *pakka*, meaning food fried in *ghi* (clarified butter) or *dalda* (vegetable shortening) such as the generally served *puri* (*chappatis* cooked in oil) or *kachori* (a *puri* filled with pulse). *Kaccha* food has a much more limited transferability among castes than *pakka*, which is why the latter kind of food is usually served at marriage feasts and other festivities. When *kaccha* is also served on these occasions, its purposeful choice indicates the commensal equality and unity of a specific group, generally a caste faction or caste.

In Tezibazar, the ideal statement of commensal restrictions and what they are in actual practice is fairly identical. There is little disagreement and contradiction or verbal jockeying for better position. Undoubtedly it is because the system of commensality, like that of caste ranking, is not based on a hierarchical ordering of caste. Aside from Muslim and Sudra, the town's commensal regimen seems only to distinguish, differentiate, and alienate castes; it does not rank them.

There are two other significant aspects of commensality in the town. One is the importance of personal or individual commensal predilections. A common statement in Tezibazar is, "I eat all foods with any caste Hindu even though my caste does not permit it." Often such egalitarian sentiments are never put to the test, but sometimes such a philosophy is put into practice, particularly by young men. Thus the individual as well as the caste is an operative or determinative unit in discussing commensal rules observed in the town.

An extension of the above point is represented in the commensal customs that characterize political occasions and politicians.

In situations where it is politically important to show a free commensal spirit with otherwise avoided groupings (Muslim and Sudra), a special kind of feasting procedure has developed which, although it mostly evades the problem of interdining with despised status levels, nevertheless is of sufficient departure from the normal to deserve attention, and I shall discuss it below.

On some occasions and in some places, normal commensal restrictions are relaxed. Generally this relaxation occurs on visits to neighboring towns and cities, where in the numerous tea shops and hotels no control over the caste of server or owner is possible, and little selection in this matter exists for the most part. An institutionalized occasion for the relaxation of commensal rules in the town is the men's "picnic" during the cold weather season.

The Commensal Norm

The commonly accepted rules as well as practice of commensality are simple in Tezibazar. Brahmin, Thakur, Baniya, and Kisan status categories can all take *pakka* food from each other freely, but none will take *kaccha* food from any other. Sometimes Baniya castes say they will take *kaccha* food from their family priest or *purohit* (of Brahmin caste). A few old men said they would take *kaccha* food from all Brahmins, but other people denied this, and I never witnessed such a case myself. All castes who eat *pakka* food together do so in the same line: there is no spatial separation to indicate superiority-inferiority. However, even if these castes were to sit in separate lines they would not share *kaccha* food. All these castes will accept water from each other but will not smoke from the same *hukka* (water pipe). Thus, the picture is of a system which places its entire stress on distinctiveness rather than hierarchy.

Neither Brahmin, Thakur, Baniya, nor Kisan will take any sort of food from Muslims and Sudras, nor will they take water from their hands. When members of these two status levels attend *pakka* feasts given by caste Hindus, they must sit in a clearly demarcated and separate feeding line. The distinction in food lines is always a lucid enunciation of the caste and commensal inferiority of Muslims and Sudras, but the status of the individual often forces this severe denotation to be ameliorated. Although a prestigious Muslim must sit in a separate line just as do his lower-status brethren, he usually is personally attended to in all his wants by an older, ranking member of the host family or lineage. Although the public stigma of his Muslim status cannot be removed commensally, it can be relieved in a private fashion by an unusual solicitude for that individual's desires or wishes at a feast. It is said that Muslims and Sudras will accept *kaccha* from all status levels, although such is explicitly denied by some Muslims and Sudras. Perhaps this statement is more an ideal to round out the caste system than a reality. In any case few opportunities for such commensal exchanges occur.[6]

The social distinction between *pakka* and *kaccha* is both strong and meaningful to town people. At a well-to-do marriage, the first feast, usually given on the first night, is *pakka;* all the guests of whatever caste can partake, and many of them leave afterward. But the next day, after the actual nuptials, a *kaccha* feast is given and indicates the unity of the particular caste whose marriage it is. All guests of other castes eat separate meals, generally *pakka.* In one marriage group (*barat*), I by mischance did not eat with the other non-*biradari* people, so I was invited to sit in the *kaccha* feast by some men in the groom's party. This created such a furor in the bride's family and so much denunciation of "people who undermined the caste rules" that had not the main party already eaten and had we represented anything but a few stragglers, and (most important) had it not been a question of a foreign guest, I would not have been permitted to take my meal there at all.

[6] The town commensal system is quite distinct from the practices of neighboring villages. At a *pakka* marriage feast given in a village one mile from Tezibazar, the Brahmin guests (the parties to the marriage were Brahmin) were fed before and thus separately from the other castes. The latter were fed as a group with no distinctions made save for Muslim and Sudra. Characteristically, a Brahmin from the town refused to eat with his rural caste mates. Instead, he took his food in the same line as the other castes at the second serving.

Thus the rules of commensality define two spheres of food sharing: one in which almost all castes can participate; another in which none but one's own may take part. Here again, as in caste ranking, the system is based on equivalence but distinctiveness. All caste groups, save Muslims and Sudras, are reinforced in their specific identities by the *kaccha* regimen, whereas they are unified in the *pakka*. In neither food system are they arranged hierarchically or graded as inferior and superior. Most of my informants claimed this situation to be recent—a result of the propaganda of Gandhi and the Arya Samaj. They declared that thirty years previously their caste had not taken food from this or that caste, which in these modern days of caste degeneration they now accept as commensal equals. Statements such as these are common in Tezibazar. They indicate a willingness to perceive great social change, which in itself is a significant social statement. But as real history these statements are nearly worthless, for they are based on a perception of what the past should be rather than on information or remembrance of how it really was. In the absence of written records no way is available to substantiate truly commensal change or stability in the town. However, one elderly man in Tezibazar was unusually dedicated to the preservation of historical data on his caste and was famous for this in his community throughout Uttar Pradesh. Tribeni Lal had also kept an annual diary from 1914, the year of his father's death. His opinion was that differential commensality had not been used to indicate the hierarchy of caste status for from three to four hundred years (*sic*). He remembered, however, that the present rules for interdining in Tezibazar were those which applied in his youth, and that the only substantial change was a tendency for young men to eat defiling foods such as meat and to ignore the commensal restrictions on *kaccha* food. Probably commensal change as noted by others is based on this latter sort rather than any fundamental metamorphosis in the formal structure. It is quite likely that the existent system of interdining, lacking in hierarchy but maintaining caste distinctiveness, is not of recent development, but instead an old usage in the town.[7]

Politics and Commensality

Because the vote of a Muslim or Sudra equals the vote of any other caste, politicians, particularly since Independence, have had to orient their commensal behavior so as to solicit or at least appease these groupings without endangering their own (political) status in either the caste Hindu community or their own caste. Various techniques of circumvential commensality have originated for the politically ambitious caste Hindu of Tezibazar.

On January 29, 1963, the untouchables celebrated the birthdate of an untouchable saint, Ravi Das, or Rai Das, who lived during the reign of the Moghul emperor Akbar. In attendance at the festivities were an untouchable Member of the Legislative Assembly (M.L.A.) of Uttar Pradesh, and an untouchable Member of Parliament (M.P.). Their presence, quite apart from the lengthy oratory lauding a new era of equality for the "Harijan," made at least a token food sharing necessary for the local Congress party leaders who were at the ceremony. After the public meeting, the high-ranking official guests were invited into the N.A. office to take tea and *namkin* (a salty snack food made from fried pulse and wheat noodles). This food, although technically *pakka*, merely accompanies tea and is hardly thought of as food at all. The *namkin* was served in disposable earthern dishes. Neither the food nor dishes were from an untouchable's house. One Harijan, a young B.A. student at Allahabad University, did serve food, but only to the other "Harijans." The N.A.

[7] Crooke, writing in 1896, reports that Barai and Bhuj castes would accept *pakka* from Brahmins, Ksatriyas, and Vaisyas, but would only take *kaccha* from their own caste mates. Unfortunately, he does not provide commensal information for most other castes (W. Crooke, *The Tribes and Castes of the North-Western Provinces and Oudh*, I, 181; II, 15).

baksi (a Brahmin) served the others and poured tea for every-one. The only untouchables served were the M.L.A. and the M.P.; and the only caste Hindus in attendance were the leaders of the local Congress party. As the N.A. Chairman said after-ward, "Usually even my colleagues on the committee run away from this function."

The same sort of token commensality has been developed to help caste Hindus weather those Muslim feasts which they are politically or socially bound to attend. Ali Raza, a distinguished and respected Muslim of Tezibazar, gave a feast in the town to celebrate his son's recovery from injuries received in an automo-bile accident. At this feast, all the Hindus ate before the Muslims. The food they consumed was served on leaves prepared by a Sudra caste, not on dishes from the host's kitchen. The food itself was *pakka* and had been made by, and purchased from, a Hindu Halvai. However, there was one departure from custom: the Muslim men of the household served the food. As soon as they had eaten, the Hindus departed, and then the Muslims sat down together to a meat feast. Many more men are willing to attend such a feast than would have come to the Harijan tea, mainly because at a feast they eat in a completely separate line— temporally if not spatially—from their impure hosts. Even this limited commensality was confined to the leading men of the town, who were constrained to attend out of respect for Ali Raza and political obligation to a leader of the Muslim commu-nity.

These devious techniques indicate that politics and political considerations can at least partially bridge the commensal gap. They also show the breakdown of the traditional forms in the face of political necessity. The influence of modern political machinery in the town is powerful enough partially to suppress old habits and to force the origination of new ways to hide the distinctions of the past. It is, however, not sufficiently strong to change completely such traditional habits, and the transforma-tion which has occurred is mostly a method of avoiding that greater change, the total suspension of commensal restrictions.

The Personal Element in Commensality

To my knowledge only one family in the town completely ignored all interdining restrictions. The brothers Jamna Prasad and Ganga Prasad are Hindu Halvais and therefore should accept neither *pakka* nor *kaccha* food from Muslims. In fact, they eat both sorts of meals with their many Muslim neighbors and with any other caste. At the feast of Ali Raza described above, the "brothers Prasad" were the only Hindus to stay behind and eat together with their Muslim hosts. Jamna Prasad and Ganga Prasad are also unusual for their deep friendships with certain Muslims, such as the injured son of Ali Raza. These two brothers are extreme examples of a not insignificant personal element in the application of interdining rules. Another case is that of a high status Umar who sat in the Muslim line near a friend at a marriage feast. Generally people are not so "forward" as to question these matters openly at a feast; in more private circumstances, the opinion of the individual comes to the fore. Thus, many of my caste Hindu visitors did not refuse tea made by my Muslim servant and some even ate dinners cooked by him. At a private feast given by the N.A. Chairman, various Muslims and Hindus ate *kaccha* food together, although in separate lines. In their own homes, people may share foods with other castes with whom they will not partake in public. However, the restraints on public commensality do not come from fear of caste outcasting or other positive action from the caste body. Rather, it is only a matter of individual susceptibility to the generalized disapproval of his fellows. One of the reasons that Ganga and Jamna Prasad can be so commensally free with Muslims or that the Umar Prem Nath can sit with a Muslim friend in a marriage feast is that their castes take no sanctions against them. Such people often humorously remark that if their caste *caudhari* (ritual leader) were to see this, he would outcaste them on the spot. Of course, they do not entertain this as even a remote possibility, but it makes a good joke which adds spice to the meal. The lack of caste-structured disapproval such as outcasting for breaking commensal regulations is just one aspect of a general deterioration of intra-caste social control. I shall show this deterioration even more clearly later on in discussing the Umar.

Another case of personal modification of commensal rules concerns business partners of different castes. Although such commercial ventures number only a handful, I was told that such partners would be completely free in their interdining, no matter of what caste they were. I knew of instances of Brahmin-Umar and Umar-Kalvar partnerships, where such suspension of commensal interdictions was the rule.

The Picnic

There are occasions when commensal rules are followed less strictly than in the formal observances of the marriage and other such feasts. The infrequent men's "picnics" held in the cold season are examples of such times. The picnic is an informal feast consisting of "*dihati*" (peasant-type) food cooked by the men themselves. These are small-scale festive occasions which (generally young) men look upon as affording a chance to meet away from their wives and to prepare their own food. The picnic also allows them to eat foods and with people the women might not permit in their homes. At the picnics I attended, *kaccha* food was served regardless of who was there. At one, men prepared meat, which was not eaten in their homes because the women were strict vegetarians. In another, Muslims and Hindus ate together. Usually, two castes which normally accept *pakka* from each other go on picnic and eat *kaccha* food together. These excursions into the country are definitely regarded as informal and pleasant times where conviviality takes precedence over strict adherence to caste interdining restrictions.

THE TEZIBAZAR *JAJMANI* SYSTEM

The *jajmani* system represents the reciprocal service relationship between the castes of a village. Ideally each caste has a hereditary occupation or occupations. Some are agriculturalists or blacksmiths; others are barbers or washermen. The several castes in a village reciprocate their specialized labor products. Various families of washermen are associated with various families of agriculturalists in a hereditary alliance not only covering economic reciprocity but also ritual and ceremonial obligations. The *jajmani* system, then, symbolizes the organization of cooperation within a village.[8]

A form of caste labor exchange called *jajmani* exists in Tezibazar, but its organization is fundamentally different from that found in the village. The difference lies not in the services and ritual offices exchanged nor even in the fact that in many cases the hereditary aspect of the relationship is neither observed nor binding. This sort of deterioration is also largely present in Indian villages. What is distinctive is that the Tezibazar *jajmani* system is organized not on the basis of family alliances but on the attachment of a particular service caste family to a specific geographical area of the town. Sometimes the same sort of emotional attachments and loyalties which characterize village *jajmani* relations exist in the town. But the organization and deployment of service castes depend on totally different principles. The *jajmani* relationship in Tezibazar is no closer to the village system than is the provision of neighborhood services by ethnically distinct groups in the United States (Chinese laundryman, Italian barber, Irish cop) except in terms of duration due to the relative immobility of the population. Further, the town *jajmani* network is highly contractual. No yearly grain or money payment is binding as is the case in the village, and payment is made only upon use. Thus, even in a part of the town's social structure which resembles a traditional system of familial social cohesion elsewhere, the organization is merely that of long-standing, pat-

[8] Rudra Datt Singh and Morris Opler, "The Division of Labor in an Indian Village," *A Reader in General Anthropology, passim;* Thomas O. Beidelman, *A Comparative Analysis of the "jajmani" System;* Oscar Lewis and Victor Barnouw, "Caste and the Jajmani System in a North Indian Village," *Scientific Monthly,* LXXXIII (1955), *passim;* Harold A. Gould, "A Jajmani System of North India: Its Structure, Magnitude, and Meaning," *Ethnology,* LII (1964), 12–41.

terned commercial and residential identification based on the needs of an urban Hindu population for various services.

The *Purohit*

The most consistently followed *jajmani* relationship in the town is that between *purohit*, or family priest, and *jajman*, the recipient of the services. Invariably, the priest is of Brahmin caste.

According to my informants, six generations or a century and a half ago the *purohit*s of Tezibazar signed a pact which stated what priest had jurisdiction over which families and area for performing ceremonies and sacrifices. This allotment was done mainly on the basis of geographical area and the number of houses within it. No priest was assigned any contiguous houses or any single area. The Brahmins described the method used as an attempt to equalize the number of rich and poor families or houses for each priest. Further, each house might not be as successful or gain as much prestige, and some areas of the town might prosper more than others.

This method of distribution has led to strange results in the present. My landlord, Makhundi Lal, had one *purohit*, Rudra Narain, for his store, and for his house directly behind the shop he had another traditional priest, Beni Ram. When a ceremony takes place in his house, Makhundi Lal uses Beni Ram, but when it must take place in his shop, Rudra Narain presides. He uses his house *purohit* as the main priest for marriages. Makhundi Lal and his three nearby neighbors do not have a common priest among them. I was told that such distribution on the basis of area rather than of families as in villages was the common method of allocation in towns.[9]

In the allotment of six generations ago, Sahibganj was also given out, even though only a small settlement existed there at the time. In fact, all houses, even presently unoccupied ones, and all land, even if it is not built up, are distributed to particular

[9] Harold A. Gould (*op. cit.*, p. 23) also notes the importance of location in structuring *jajmani* ties.

priests. According to informants the pact of one hundred fifty years ago had been preceded by many before and is indeed only the latest in a long chain. Allotment on the basis of areas was also said to be an old institution.

If a family vacates a house, it cannot keep the same priest, even if it relocates in another section of Tezibazar. The priest is attached to the house within his jurisdiction and serves the newly resident people when they come. The latter also must use the priest traditionally attached to the house; otherwise no one will perform the functions for them. Caste makes no difference so long as the new owners are Hindus other than Sudras (who are not served by Brahmins). Even if a migrant were from a nearby village where he had a traditional priest, he would have to use the Tezibazar *purohit*. If the village priest tried to infringe upon the rights of those in the town, he would be stopped by force. However, my informants said, mutual restraint and the rules of both town and village Brahmins made such an occurrence unlikely.

I was told that copies of the one-hundred-fifty-year-old pact were in the hands of several priests, but that they did not like to show them because they had taken over areas not theirs originally and did not want anyone to discover their poaching. Their newly acquired "prebends" came from Brahmins who no longer act as *purohit*s or whose families had died out. I was told that at the present individuals no longer feel the same concern over retaining an area as they did thirty years ago, when the *purohit*s squabbled incessantly about their respective jurisdictions. Now many Brahmins prefer to train for government service or business and have little interest in priestly duties. Brahmins who still perform the role of *purohit* are considered somewhat inferior by virtue of being dependent on the charity of others for their livelihood.

Some ceremonies can be performed by any Brahmin; others, particularly the life-crises rituals, can only be done by the hereditary *purohit*. These latter include the birth, funeral, sacred thread, and marriage ceremonies; also many *puja*s, or solicitations of specific gods, the determination of auspicious days, the preparation of a horoscope, the figuring of the exact time of birth and its auspiciousness, and the family *pujas* at the main festivals such as *dasehra, divali,* or *raksa bandhan.* If the hereditary priest is incapacitated or unwilling to work, he can allot another *purohit* to perform these ceremonies either without payment or on a share basis, but in any case the option is with the priest and not with the *jajman.*

Of all *jajmani* servitors, the traditional priest is the one most retained unchanged by Tezibazar Baniyas (see Table 9). He is

Table 9. Employment of traditional service castes by Tezibazar Baniya merchants

Traditional castes	Employed		Not employed	
	No. merchants	% merchants	No. merchants	% merchants
Brahmin	29	87.88	4	12.12
Nau (barber)				
For ritual and shaving	4	12.12	3	9.09
For ritual only	26	78.79		
Dhobi (washerman)	17	51.52	16	48.48
Mali (gardener)	28	84.85	5	15.15
Lohar (carpenter)	12	36.36	21	63.64

generally paid by the job, although some landowning merchants, particularly the ex-zamindar Baniyas, said they gave an annual grain share. Most people do not establish such a structured relationship with their traditional service castes. Their prescriptive right is to be employed when and if an appropriate occasion for their services arises, but they do not enjoy any customary right to earn a specified cash amount or grain payment. What is true of the Brahmin *purohit* is true of the other service castes also.

The Barber

The Hindu Nau (standard Hindi, Nai), or barber, is expected to visit his *jajman* at every ritual and ceremonial occasion and to perform certain duties. He must welcome the guests of his *jaj-*

man, for example, and carry messages and invitations for him. The Nau and his wife (Naun) have especially important duties during a marriage and at its preliminary functions such as the *tilak*. At the latter ceremony, which is performed at the groom's house, the date of the marriage ceremony is announced and part of the dowry received. The barber comes with the girl's representatives to the *tilak* and carries a large brass dish, or *thali*, filled with rice, wheat, cocoanut, betel, and money. The barber's pay for such work is called *bidai* and amounts to about three to five rupees. The Nau is only paid when his services are used. When the Naun takes part, she receives a new *sari*. The barber aids the family priest at many ceremonies, and the Naun has charge of a bride's deportment during the marriage ceremony.

Previously certain areas and houses were allotted to particular families of Nau. But at present this rule is not often observed, and *jajmans* may change barbers both for shaving and for performing ritual duties. In fact, my survey indicates that retention of the traditional Nau for haircutting and shaving is quite unusual. This change supposedly began about thirty years ago, because some barber families died out and others were not competent to perform the ceremonies. The Naus do not, like the Brahmins, delegate their duties to others, and so some totally new barber must be called into the employ of the *jajman*. Moreover, unlike the Brahmin case, the *jajman* has the choice of which new Nau to hire. Still, as Table 9 indicates, there is a strong tendency, at least among the Baniyas, to retain the traditional Nau, if only for ritual performances.

The Mali

The duty of the Mali, or gardener, is to provide flowers daily to families who do *puja* or worship as often as this and otherwise to prepare floral decorations at festive or ceremonial occasions. He should also be present at the weddings in his *jajman*'s family. The Malis are also given allotted areas of the town, and since they are few in number, their sphere of control is extensive. If the Mali provides flowers daily, he receives a fixed yearly remuneration in grain or cash and at festivals is given gifts of money and food. If he is employed only occasionally, like the barber the Mali will be given a cash amount per job.

The Washerman

An area is also allotted to the Dhobi, or washerman, but this distribution is now not observed for normal washing of clothes, and *jajman*s are free to change their Dhobis. The washermen themselves try to regulate this competition, but they can in no way coerce the *jajman* to accept a washerman he does not wish. Often, however, violent squabbles break out among Dhobi families over infringements of territory.

The allotted traditional Dhobi is, however, often called when a birth takes place in his *jajman*'s family. He must wash the clothing worn by the woman during delivery and also that used on the sixth and twelfth day after the birth. The traditional Dhobi is sometimes invited to his *jajman*'s weddings because in so doing the Hindu shows respect for the *ghat*, or bathing place. On these occasions, the Dhobi is given some money and clothing. For performing ritual washing, the Dhobi receives a fixed sum in grain or cash; for every day, non-*jajmani* washing, however, he may be paid a flat monthly fee or a per piece rate. Many *jajman*s have dispensed completely with the services of their traditional washermen, and this patterned service relationship is not well preserved in Tezibazar.

The Carpenter

The Lohar, or carpenter-blacksmith (neither the term nor the caste *barhai*—carpenter—seemingly exist in this area; Lohars perform both functions) makes agricultural implements for the agriculturalists resident in Tezibazar. For others he supplies various wooden implements or decorations at the time of marriage or other ceremonies: for example, the raised wooden plank on which bride and groom sit. He is paid in cash by the job, and the traditional nature of his ties to particular *jajman*s or areas is now more or less defunct.

The basis of the *jajmani* reciprocities remaining in Tezibazar is not the interrelation of families of *jajmans* with particular service castes but rather merely a mechanical distribution of the latter by town area or house—an attachment constant not to a group of people but rather to a house or house plot. In villages, the *jajmani* system serves to interrelate castes and their specific labor or craft products. The *jajmani* system in Tezibazar also performs this function to a limited extent. The organization of the town system, unlike that of the village, is consistent with and does nothing to contravene the lack of community in Tezibazar. For *jajmani* relations in the town are not structured on the basis of social mutualities between families of *jajmans* and families of service castes. What is called the *jajmani* relationship in the urban locale is merely a traditional allotment of employment possibilities among the service castes by a predetermined spatial distribution. It tends to be a commercialized (to the extent it becomes contractual) and depersonalized sorting of various services required by most Hindus. When an individual arrives in Tezibazar and finds Brahmin, Dhobi, Mali, and Nau assigned to his house site, there is no question of any social tie other than the acceptance of a service distribution favorable to the well-being of the various service castes and the impersonal satisfaction of the individual's ritual and practical requirements.

CHAPTER 6

Conflict and Social Control

In addition to caste ranking and commensality, other negative factors impede the growth of civic organization in Tezibazar. Several such divisive forces which more concretely curtail a community structure in the town will be described in this chapter. One of these forces is caste conflict and competition: that is, the opposition of town castes on a more or less group basis.

KESARVANI AND UMAR CASTE CONFLICT

In Tezibazar, caste conflict involves two Baniya castes: the Umar and the Kesarvani. The Kesarvanis can claim as allies many of the smaller Baniya castes in the town (and including some maverick Umars), whereas the Umar have been able to rally the Muslims to their side in larger political dealings. The Kesarvani, in fact, are at the forefront of a multi-caste (generally Baniya) grouping based on feelings of economic and political persecution by the wealthy and numerically dominant Umar. For various demographic and historical reasons, the conflict has crystallized about the Kesarvanis.

Ever since the Kesarvanis came to Tezibazar from Phulpur, a small town nearby, they and the Umar have been in conflict. The Kesarvanis were attracted by Udai Baks's market and arrived about the turn of the present century. A great deal of business competition and sharp dealing went on between these two groups, and it seems clear that the entrenched Umar tried to force them out of the market. However, because they settled in Sahibganj, the soon-to-be market center, the Kesarvani pros-

pered, while many of the Umar businesses decayed as Old Town
lost its economic pre-eminence. This background explains an
important ethnic and business distinction between Old Town
and Sahibganj. Of all Kesarvanis engaged in business, 68.18 percent are located in Sahibganj, whereas only 41.56 percent of all
Umar are situated there; the Kalvar caste is represented by 50.70
percent; and in total over half the merchants of thirty-six castes
are located in this main market center. Thus Sahibganj shows a
very large number of castes and an unusual concentration of one
caste, Kesarvani, as well. Naiganj, the next largest ward, has
only twenty-five castes. The Umar are not so heavily concentrated in any one section but are fairly evenly distributed over all
areas, regardless of their business activity or market importance.
In the latter sense, the Umar are highly concentrated in Anjahi-
Katra, where they carry on 37.78 percent of all businesses; in
Gurhai, where they own 57.70 percent of all concerns; and Gola
Mandi, where 47.92 percent of all shops are in their hands.
Clearly, then, the Umar-Kesarvani and allied Baniya castes' conflict has geographical connotations—the Baniyas of Old Town
versus those of Sahibganj, the former rulers of the market versus
the newcomers who have now gained economic primacy.

In 1964 a rallying point for the Kesarvani was afforded by a
legal suit between the Kesarvani Hari Har Prasad and the Umar
Chairman of the N.A., Moti Lal, regarding ownership of some
property in Katra. The intricate details of the dispute are not
necessary; even a brief survey will highlight the depth of antagonistic feelings engendered on a caste basis by this purely personal
conflict.

Hari Har Prasad had a garden and house in Katra which had
been "pawned" to him about eight years previously. The man
who had mortgaged this property subsequently died without
issue. The N.A. Chairman was zamindar of this area (in *mauza*
Sarai Rustum), and the dead man had held the property in a
permanent subsidiary tenure (*rahandari*). Chairman Moti Lal
asked Hari Har Prasad to agree to a quitrent or some other
settlement by which Moti Lal would agree to give up all his

claims to the property in favor of Hari Har Prasad. But Hari Har Prasad thought he was entitled to the property outright and refused to compromise. Then Moti Lal transferred the property to his own name (some say with the help of his position and contacts as Chairman). Hari Har Prasad instituted legal proceedings, and Moti Lal won the case. The Chairman started to occupy the house, whereupon several clashes occurred between the two contestants. The house was then boarded up by the police, and during my stay in the town a new suit was in progress. The legal confrontation began about one and a half years ago and was touched off by the impending zamindari abolition in urban areas. Hari Har Prasad claimed that various civil servants favored the Chairman's case, and he is said to have had a recent subdivisional officer transferred for showing undue preference.

No litigation of this sort goes on on a single plane. In June, 1963, Ram Deo, servant to Moti Lal, filed suit against Hari Har Prasad for allegedly refusing to return eight *tolas* of gold he had pawned for Rs. 400. Hari Har stated that when Ram Deo came to collect the gold, he did not have the key to the safe and that the servant for this reason beat him. Hari Har Prasad thus had filed a countersuit against Ram Deo.

The details of the dispute are not so interesting as are the emotions it aroused, particularly among the Kesarvanis, who, being in the minority, have a much more organized and mobilized local caste body than do the Umar. The latter are more disparate, much less an actively unified caste body in town politics. As one Kesarvani, Baij Nath, narrated:

The Umar are sly and deceitful. Even in their own caste they often cheat and do not help one another. The only reason is that it is part of their natures. Not only as individuals but on a group basis they are bad. . . . As an example of their deceitfulness, if you buy something from an Umar shopkeeper and you leave it with him, if the price goes up before you return [with full payment] to claim it, he won't sell it or give it to you, but if the price goes lower, he will push the item on you [at the pre-agreed higher price]. . . .

This [the Hari Har Prasad dispute] is a question simply of caste. All the Kesarvanis are behind Hari Har Prasad, and all the Umar are with Moti Lal, except for a very few of them.

Baij Nath's concluding remark is a gross simplification of the actual situation, wherein caste conflict is just another aspect of political alignment in the town. His statement does indicate the perception of an argument between two individuals as really pertaining to two castes.

Because the Umar *biradari* is much less a unity than the Kesarvani, individuals of this caste did not phrase the dispute as largely a confrontation between two castes. Rather they looked upon it as a feud between Kesarvani and Umar wherein, however, because of internal enmity, various Umar of the Chairman's patrilineage (*khandan*) opposed him and sided with Hari Har Prasad. Thus the structural level at which the individual commentator fixes his attention in this dispute is in part a result of the organization of his own reference group. I shall note this even more distinctly in analyzing politics in Tezibazar.

The Kesarvani are joined in their distaste for the Umar by most of the other small Baniya groups, particularly those resident and doing business in Sahibganj. Ram Svarup Agrahari had just won a long court case against his *cacera bhai* (father's brother's son) over the ownership of a shop in Naiganj. In this dispute he was backed by the Kesarvani, whereas his *cacera bhai* had the support of the Umar. In the following comments Ram Svarup identifies these two castes with rival national political parties—an important point which becomes more apparent in Chapter 11:

The most important castes in this town are the Kesarvani and Umar. Both have rich and poor within them, and each wants to get supremacy over the other and the town. The Umars are deceivers and jealous. They want to suppress all the other communities in the town. There are really only two parties in Tezibazar: the Kesarvani, who are Praja Socialist [P.S.P.], and the Umar, who are Congress.

The cases of Hari Har Prasad and Ram Svarup do not reflect the competition of the opponent castes on a group basis but rather as they crystallize around an already existent personal conflict. In the contest of the N.A. elections, however, the Umar and Kesarvani emerge as definite contestants, recognizable entities within the larger coalition of factions, castes, and communities which compose a political party in Tezibazar.

HINDU-MUSLIM CONFLICT

Hindu-Muslim conflict and hatred is comparable to caste antagonisms in its divisive effects on the town, although not in the organization of the groups involved. In Tezibazar such feelings run very high, and shortly after *id ul fitr* (a Muslim festival celebrating the end of *ramzan*) in 1964 (February 13), fears of communal violence grew to the point where some Muslims began to send their wives away. The history of Muslim-Hindu ill feeling as well as the organization and behavioral manifestation of it fit better under the rubric of town politics, and it is in that section that I discuss it fully. Here I wish to note the quality and intensity of the mutual hatred, which so effectively divides Tezibazar town.

In the deeply felt distaste which characterizes Muslim-Hindu feelings, it is invariably the Hindus who pose the problem aggressively. They argue that the Muslim can never be a real citizen of India because he is loyal first to his religion and only secondarily to his country. The Muslim, they feel, is always capable and ready to perform traitorous acts if they will benefit Pakistan. As proof, various flamboyant stories about supposed Muslim betrayal of India to China in the Himalayas are brought forth. There is also a social distaste for the *musulman* which is evidenced in the statement that they are (physically) dirty. More sophisticated people in the town claim that their commensal avoidance of Muslims is based not on a wish to maintain caste rules but upon their displeasure in eating with someone dirty.

Tezibazar people openly describe the Jana Sangh national political party as a Hindu communal group with announced anti-Muslim policies, even though the formal party leaders would deny this in public. Most of the leading Jana Sanghis in the town are severely anti-Muslim, although this feeling is not limited to them alone. The most anti-Muslim of status categories are the Baniyas and the Brahmins. In fact, most of the Jana Sangh following in Tezibazar and, for that matter, the whole district derives from these two groupings.

Local people say that Baniyas and Brahmins are especially anti-Muslim because these castes most retain the spirit of Hinduism in social habits and ideals and are therefore most inimical to Islam. Both Muslims and Hindus rejected outright the supposition that since Muslims are the second largest trading community in the town, therefore the ultimate cause of communal conflict might be business competition. Indeed, although a good deal of overlap exists in the nature of their commercial ventures, Muslims and Hindus do tend to specialization and mutual exclusion. The Hindu Baniyas undertake trading businesses, whereas Muslims mostly perform services.

Unlike the Hindus, the Muslims do not openly betray their resentment of the Hindus. They uphold the idea of a secular state where there should be no communal feelings. Most often when faced with an extreme anti-Muslim statement, they will say, "If Jawaharlal Nehru thinks us all right, why don't these people [Jana Sanghis]." Although no Muslim admitted an allegiance to Pakistan, many were sympathetic and felt that their situation would be much improved there. "What is the point of being a citizen in a country where you are despised, and where another community gets all the jobs," remarked one of my informants. Only one Muslim, however, voiced what was undoubtedly the covert hatred of the others. This man, Mohammad Akbar, was extremely wealthy, a Muslim leader as well as Sectional (Mandal) Congress party head. He also had many friends in district administration and politics. As an expression of his distaste for Hindus, he would at feasts turn to me and say, "They [the Hindus] are *bakri* [goat], we are *sher* [lion]; they eat grass, we eat meat." Even openly (although in supposedly humorous fashion) Akbar would tell Hindus that they were goats and he was a lion, and that *sher* by their nature ate *bakri*. In my presence he was the only Muslim to phrase his enmity to the Hindus positively and aggressively either openly or secretly. Fear of the overwhelming Hindu majority constrains the Muslims to silence. Their only solace is that they comprise a large enough segment of the town population (approximately 25 percent) to give them a powerful voice in local politics. In this respect and others, the Muslims have an organizational advantage over the Hindus, who only operate in unity against Muslims on sporadic, usually volatile, and sometimes violent occasions. Nevertheless, the mutual hatred of Muslim and Hindu is another important source of disharmony in the social life of the town.

THE PERCEPTION OF EVIL: SOCIAL CONTROL IN THE TOWN

Prevalent themes in most discussions in Tezibazar are assertion of the impossibility of trusting anyone and avowal of the principle that "might makes right." [1] Indeed, by virtue of almost incessant repetition they constitute a kind of description of town social interaction which in turn points to another aspect of the lack of community: the absence of any traditional organization of social control within the town. "JIski lathi, Uski bhaens" ("Who wields the stave, owns the buffalo") and "dhan-se dosti" ("Rich men have many friends") are local sayings which delineate two facets of the matter. Some people see the absence of traditional social control within the town as essentially negative: an unwillingness on the part of most people to defend the moral ideals and ethics of the society—"Now money is everything. Who will listen to anyone's troubles; everybody is interested solely in their own gain." Others look upon present conditions as a result of a positive unconcern for any other human and a desire (based upon motives of envy and greed) to suppress any other individual's advancement: "Nowadays if a man thinks his next-door neighbor is earning more than he is, he will try to cut him down, whether or not they are in the same business." Such lack

[1] G. M. Carstairs reports a similar situation for a small town in Rajasthan; The Twice-Born, pp. 41–43.

of an internal discipline is also manifest in business ethics, where there is no town supervision either by caste bodies or any other traditional organization of trade and commercial techniques. Generally, people do not complain so much at the absence of traditional social control; they accept it matter-of-factly if with distaste. What they do dwell on is the absolute corruptibility and lack of ethics of local police and government officials. However true their evaluation may be, what is interesting is that Tezibazaris look to these external organs of government to provide some element of morality or at least control within the town. They do not expect it to emerge from the town population either in behavior or ideal. Thus, what was formerly the precinct of the zamindar has now become the inheritance of a modern state, which, however, is organized neither upon the same principles of paternalism nor to the same degree of local efficiency.

In 1964 one case of moral inaction by the town population dominated all others and was cited to me many times as an example of the degraded ethical condition of Tezibazar and its populace. Mohammad Ali, Akbar, and Barku were three brothers of Muslim Halvai caste who jointly owned a prosperous tobacco business. Their father, now dead, was a native Tezibazari of impoverished antecedents who emigrated to Burma but later returned to his natal home. In Tezibazar in the early 1940's (during which period the father had deserted the family) Ali (the middle brother) and the mother began a tobacco business on a very small scale. Barku, the eldest brother, had run off to Burma, but soon returned and put the business on a sound and profitable footing. Akbar, the youngest brother, was still too small to take much part in the family concern.

During and especially after the war, the business prospered, and by the early 1950's the three brothers were all respected and wealthy men of the town. Seven years ago, however, Akbar, with the compliance of Barku, had begun to turn against his brother Ali. He won Ali's wife to his side (some people said he had seduced her) and then persuaded Ali to divorce her. According to Muslim law, no divorced husband and wife should occupy the same house; but instead of sending the woman home to her father, as was the usual custom, Akbar retained Ali's wife in the joint household and asked Ali to take up residence in one of their shops.

Akbar had the responsibility and power of overseeing the joint family and of determining what would be best for it. He enjoyed this privilege because he had been given the authority of *malik*, or "treasurer-supervisor," of the joint household in earlier days when Ali and Barku had continually been at odds and Akbar had acted as mediator. Without question he had the right —in fact the obligation—to ask his brother to live in their shop if he felt his presence at home would be detrimental to the family's well-being. Ali maintained that Akbar was plotting against him all this time, and many people joined in his opinion. In any case, what Akbar subsequently did to his brother set people astir and made them vigorously condemn him.

Although he did not live at home, Ali was still a member of the joint household, and Akbar in his role of family *malik* provided him with food and clothing. Ali declared that at this time he expected his brothers to find him a new wife. In fact, they wanted him to remarry his former wife and three years previously (1960) had approached him with such a proposal. At first Ali agreed but then refused when he found that everything was conditional upon his promising to make his wife his sole heir. Whereupon Akbar threw him out of the joint family.

For three years Ali had lived like a pauper, at times sleeping on the streets, mostly penniless, and often hungry. All this time Akbar refused to partition the family holdings and give his brother a share. People vilified Akbar in private for what was seen as inhuman treatment of a brother—elder at that. Yet Akbar was rich, and so he sat on the *gaddi*, while his brother barely subsisted on secret handouts. Many individuals criticized the town and themselves for what they considered was shabby treatment of a generally pitied man, but the only one to help destitute Ali was Yogendra Nath, the local leader of the Jana Sangh party, who used him as a political weapon against Akbar and the Muslim community.

Ali illustrated the moral situation in this fashion:

Yogendra Nath is the only man who has really been my friend and helped me. This is for two reasons: first, because he is an honest man, and second, and more importantly, because he is an outsider and has no interests in the town. All the other people in Tezibazar only befriend me to blackmail Akbar—by scaring him into thinking that they may take my side, and then Akbar will bribe them with money or by favors into remaining loyal to him. Surely there are other honest men in Tezibazar who would not do this. But those who are honest are afraid of Akbar and do not come out on my side. Generally, whoever is your enemy is my enemy if we are friends, but everyone switches allegiance to suit his own interests alone.

In 1964, because of Yogendra Nath's help and Akbar's alienating some of his important allies, many townsmen began to take Ali's side openly. But Ali had no illusions about this development:

A few years ago even the Chairman [who had recently become a strong advocate of Ali's case] and Akbar were excellent friends because Akbar had lent the Chairman a large sum of money. Then Akbar sat on the *gaddi* in the Chairman's shop, and I was considered a very disreputable type. But now that the Chairman and Akbar have split [over the repayment of the loan], and because of Akbar's other disgusting acts, he is in disfavor throughout the town. And now I am not considered so bad anymore.

It is true that at first I did call a *pancayat* of my caste, but Akbar so insulted them that they left without deciding anything and also did not ever want to meet again. How could Akbar get away with insulting them? A rich man can do anything because now money is everything.

This frank statement was not made in private; it was given at a public tea shop in Tezibazar and was heard by two or three other people, some of whom were Hindu. Far from disagreeing with Ali, they only shook their heads in assent, and one man said, "Now everything is deceitful and corrupted [kharab]."

RITUALS AND VOLUNTARY ASSOCIATIONS

Rituals

The cohesion of a community is often dramatized in public rituals which bring together and align the disparate segments of the population and at the same time emphasize the distinctive social roles of the various groups.[2] Very few such occasions exist in Tezibazar, because most ritual occasions are performed within the joint family household rather than as communal undertakings and because of the divisive effects of caste and communal antagonisms, which are rarely bridged successfully.

In the past, several calendrical festivals dramatized the unity of the community. Significantly, these festivals were celebrated under the aegis of the zamindars, who supervised their performance, assigned social roles, and financed them. The great Hindu festival of northern India, the *ram lila*, was always formerly celebrated in Tezibazar with dramatic readings from the Ramayana by professional players. It was performed in front of the *rani kothi* and was underwritten and supervised for the most part by the Rani Sahiba, the daughter of Udai Baks. Every year a committee was chosen from among eminent townsmen to organize the presentation, and it was considered a distinct honor to be selected. After the death of the Rani Sahiba, the *ram lila* ground was moved to the open space in front of a wealthy Umar zamindar's house. Soon, however, caste rivalries and the absence of supervision by a powerful overlord undermined the unity behind this ritual. Shortly after 1922, another Umar family fell out with the sponsoring Umar zamindar. As a mark of scorn and independence, they set up their own *ram lila* ground and imported their own professional company. At present, this *ram lila*

[2] For an example, see Epstein, *Economic Development and Social Change in South India*, pp. 183–184.

is still held separately. There is now also a third performance area in the town, used by caste groups antagonistic to the Umar. All my informants reported a steady deterioration over the years in the *ram lila* of Tezibazar and advised going to Allahabad to see a "really good" one. The cohesion which the *ram lila* performances now symbolize is a cohesion of caste or subcaste groups, not of Tezibazar town as a whole.

Politics has also begun to influence public rituals. The boisterous, exuberant holiday of *holi* is the festival which above all others breaks down the barriers of caste and community, of wealth and poverty, of high prestige and lowly status. The reduction of all people to an equal level is symbolized in the theoretically indiscriminate throwing of colored water or mud and offal and in freedom to say anything to anyone. Expectedly, *holi* is the most genuinely communal festival in Tezibazar. The town *holi* is rather quiet, however, except for the areas around the bus station or where packs of children gather. Many people stay at home, and much of the dousing with water occurs among relatives within the household. On the outside, Tezibazar people say *holi* often degenerates into mere mudslinging, and any feeling of mutual attachment is replaced by impersonal aggression or practical joking.

In 1964 politics supervened in the *holi* celebration. There was some disagreement about the correct day for the celebration. As it was explained to me, the festival dates are fixed according to the phase of the moon (since both the Hindu and Muslim ritual calendar is based on a lunar year). If the night sky is overcast, it cannot be determined with certainty (that is, within one day) whether the moon has reached its fullest or its greatest wane. In 1964 the Chairman of the Notified Area and his political allies celebrated *holi* on one day. His political opponents and their followers celebrated it a day later. The Chairman's group took out a procession through the town on their day; the opponents took out their own on the following day. Since, as will be made clear later on, political opposition within Tezibazar primarily derives from caste and communal antipathies, the two *holi* performances indicate another division of community ritual by the town's internal social fragmentation.

Other important town celebrations are *divali*, "festival of lights" in worship of Laksmi, goddess of wealth, a traditionally important holiday for merchants; *gurva mangal* and *nag pancmi*, during which Shiva is worshiped in the form of the *lingam* and homage is also paid to snakes; *khichari*, a winter festival when brothers send their married sisters special foods; *raksa bandhan*, a monsoon festival where brothers and sisters exchange gifts; and the birthdate of the god Krishna. On these occasions most of the religious performances and ritual dining take place within the individual households and are not held communally. On some of these occasions processions are taken out, but they consist of a few dedicated adults and a majority of children who troop through the town carrying banners and singing appropriate songs. Often, even such seemingly innocuous activity has been a battleground for town social conflicts. Many times, the two intermediate colleges in Tezibazar organize independent processions as an extension of the wider town political conflict in which they are engaged.

Wrestling matches are a traditional part of the *nag pancmi* celebration. They are underwritten by the wealthier merchants of the town. Large crowds gather for this entertainment, and here the fissiparous nature of caste, community, and neighborhood alignments is significantly overcome.

The foregoing festivals are Hindu celebrations from which Muslims are for the most part excluded. Another great division in Tezibazar's ritual life comes from this communal distinction. Forty or fifty years ago, Muslims and Hindus seemed to take much greater part in each other's rituals, perhaps as a result of their mutual regulation by the town zamindars. But just as the last several decades have seen a widening political enmity between Muslim and Hindu, so too has cooperation in ritual observances turned to overt hostility.

The Muslim festivals reflect a much greater degree of communal cohesion than do those of the Hindus. Because of their minority status, the Muslims have been forced to identify as a unit even more than their common religion might mandate. The celebrations of *id ul fitr* and *muharram* especially bring out all Muslims in a common ritual front against the Hindus.

At *id ul fitr*, the celebration ending the month of fast (*ramzan*), Muslims throw open their doors and feed Muslims and any other castes which will eat with them. This, too, is one of the times when alms are given the poor as a religious duty.

Although *muharram* is a festival for Shi'ite Muslims (to honor the martyred sons of Ali, whom the Shi'ites recognize as *imam* and Caliph in descent from Muhammad), the entirely Sunni Muslims of Tezibazar celebrate it with great show. They march en masse along Main Street, carrying gaudily adorned floats representing the tombs of Hasan and Husain, Imambaras, horses, and other religiously significant items. Periodically, the procession stops, and small groups of men give exhibitions of drumming and stylized portrayals of martial skill. A typical motif in the latter display is the unarmed man who dispatches four swordsmen. In 1964 the protagonist in most of these "duels" was a small, short boy crippled in one leg. The message was clear: one Muslim is worth four Hindus. Thus, *muharram* directly portrayed the minority status of the Muslim and yet his invulnerability. This festival as well as *id* strengthen the bonds of Muslim community to an extent which no Hindu celebration nor any town celebration does for the urban community as a whole.

Voluntary Associations

Richard K. Beardsley has shown that the analysis of voluntary associations is important for describing community organization in Japanese and Spanish villages.[3] In Tezibazar it might be expected that the absence of commensal and caste rank hierarchies

[3] "Ecological and Social Parallels Between Rice-Growing Communities of Japan and Spain," *Symposium on Community Studies in Anthropology* (Proceedings, 1963, American Ethnological Society), pp. 55–56, 61.

and a *jajmani* system of family mutualities would be counterbalanced by a profusion of voluntary associations. On the contrary, there are few formal voluntary associations in the town. By "formal" I mean those which have a continuing membership and policy or activity and whose organization is on more than an ad hoc basis. Many informal ties exist: neighbors exchange food or chores; men go on picnics or to the city cinemas together; women neighbors have folk-song sessions; *kirtan* or devotional meetings are held; people go to the same temples for *puja;* men meet in tea shops. No doubt these activities interrelate townspeople, but they only integrate small groups at a time, and most of these activities are structured on the basis of caste, community, or neighborhood as well.

Most of the voluntary associations which do exist are also defined by caste and communal conflicts. For example, I have already mentioned the political conflict behind the hostility between the two intermediate colleges. Chapter 12 shows this hostility to be in large part caste and communally based. It has riven the voluntary educational institutions and their managing committees. Again, many of the town temples also have managing committees, but since individual castes own the temples, the basis of membership in these committees is caste-ascriptive.

An organization called the "United Club" exists in Tezibazar and describes itself as a "recreational meeting place" open to all residents of the town and nearby villages. It rents a small hall at the southern end of Main Street where its members gather and chat or play some of the table games which the club owns. Its membership is not limited to a single caste or community. During the Christmas school vacation of 1963 it financed several nights of *kavali* (a Persian poetic form sung to the accompaniment of music) which attracted great masses of people. The club also sponsored a soccer game during this period.

The United Club has the appearance of a simple recreational facility which binds individuals, castes, and communities not otherwise brought together. In fact, however, the club is a thinly disguised front for the political ambitions of a Thakur family resident in a village one mile from Tezibazar. Although the membership of the club is multi-caste, it is uni-political. One of my informants described it as a "political stable" for the Thakurs' lackeys. This is not to deny that the club performs an integrating function, but it is a function defined by the political ambitions of a definite caste and family and rural area. Many people who would join a purely recreational club do not take membership in the United from political or caste opposition to the Thakurs. Several years before, another (now defunct) club had existed for the other political group within the town. For the most part, then, the voluntary associations of Tezibazar are really only extensions of ascriptive organizations such as castes and communities, or of political oppositions.

The conflict of castes and their competition in politics is another aspect of town life unconducive to community cohesion. Undoubtedly, this antagonism existed in the past, but its most flagrant aspects were mitigated by the authority of the zamindars as overlords of the town. Caste conflict has diminished somewhat as the internal organization of the various local caste groups has deteriorated. But even as this form of conflict has lessened, Muslim-Hindu antagonisms have grown up. Personal conflict and the perception and state of public morality are other negative factors in town cohesion. The popular perception of social relations in Tezibazar is of a universe governed by an unruled and immoral desire for personal advancement and aggrandizement. Friendship, ethical judgments, and social responsibilities are all felt by townspeople to have disappeared in the modern age. The few ritual observances which are communal and the even fewer voluntary associations suffer from the divisive effects of caste, communal, and personal rivalries and do little to establish the town as a coordinated entity.

Tezibazar people look back on the time before World War II as a period when definite brakes existed on the hostile or negative behavior which is now so prevalent in the town. They do not identify this change with the downfall of the zamindars and zamindari, but we have seen that the last throes of the paternalistic system based on such individuals and institutions occurred about a decade before the Second World War. These men furnished Tezibazar with the sense of community and integration which the traditional caste, commensal, and ritual structure failed to supply. Once the zamindars had gone, only the machinery of the modern state was left to fulfill the same function.

An important reason the town could not readapt its traditional social usages to the loss of the zamindars can be found in the organization of the economic activities and the traditional merchant castes which defined Tezibazar as a market center. The following chapters will consider this point.

CHAPTER 7

Town Commerce

The orientation of the Tezibazar market has undergone a significant transformation in the last half-century. Sixty years ago the town was a major entrepôt for long-distance trade in a number of commodities as well as a primary processor of several items, most importantly *gur* and sugar. At that time Tezibazar was intimately involved in grain and *ghi* shipment and in large-scale transportation of other goods to and from the Punjab and western U.P. and Calcutta. The approximately half-dozen sugar factories then present in the town produced such famous *desi* ("country") sugar that it was desired and therefore shipped throughout northern India. Informants at present testify to its fame and value for the town by exaggerated praise of its impossibly excellent qualities—for example, they say that it was so fine, a handful would slip completely from a man's clenched fist.

The emphasis of the town economy at the turn of the century was not on providing commercial services to the surrounding rural area; rather, its existence was predicated on its position as a local station in trans-India trade as well as its production of *gur* and sugar for equally long-distance commerce. Those men who could remember what their grandfathers did mentioned either sugar and *gur* sales or grain, oilseeds, and *ghi* speculation. The fundamental function of the Tezibazar business community vis à vis the nearby rural area at that time was seemingly the supplying of capital for agriculture or of cash for taxes through money lending and the purchase of surplus subsistence crops and sugar cane. Aside from these activities, the town merely extracted commodities from the countryside. Whereas it is now almost totally dependent for sales on the surrounding villages, in those days these villages were primarily dependent on the town for capital and as a market for excess subsistence produce as well as the cash sugar cane crop.

The coming of the railroad at the end of the last century ended all this for Tezibazar as well as for many other similar small-town markets.[1] No longer was the function of entrepôt necessary—and what activity of this sort remained shifted to the rail hubs and now easily accessible cities. Further, the construction of modern sugar mills, more efficient and cheaper than their less mechanized predecessors, destroyed the town's indigenous productions. Such undertakings soon located in cities or other advantageous locales, not in an increasingly marginal town such as Tezibazar. I was told that vegetable shortening (*dalda*) was introduced at this time, and its cheapness and therefore popular acceptance put an end to any large-scale *ghi* business. Then, too, the rise in population of U.P. and particularly Jaunpur district from 1921 onward turned this region into a grain deficit area. Although this development benefited Tezibazar trade, it meant a complete shift in emphasis: away from long-distance trade with other regions of India toward supply of the local rural populace. This revolution in the grain trade was paralleled in the commercial movement of other commodities. *Gur*, sugar, oilseeds, and *ghi* businesses to a large extent died and were replaced by purely service concerns such as cloth, ornaments, groceries, and hardware shops. The change in commodity type and commercial direction also altered the spatial aspects of the Tezibazar market. Because of the railroad and metaled highway as well as the paternalism of Udai Baks, Sahibganj began to replace Old Town as the primary commercial nexus. The old grain market in Anjahi gave way to Gola Mandi. The market surrounding the Jama mosque in Naiganj was reduced to a specialty locale for leather

[1] Kashi Nath Singh, "Barhaj: A Study in the Changing Pattern of a Market Town," *National Geographical Journal of India*, VII (1961), *passim*.

goods, and the sale of many commodities moved to Sabzi Mandi. Importantly, the new business center in Sahibganj grew up around the same kind of religious and political edifices (the *rani kothi* and Udai Baks' temple) as had the old commercial district of Old Town (the Jama mosque and the family house of the Khans in Sipah *mohalla*). Both cases illustrate the entrepreneurial function of the political authority. But the days of the zamindars are gone, and the last thirty years have witnessed a proliferation of shops in Naibazar, in lower Sahibganj, and along the Jaunpur and Pratabgarh roads. These business developments testify to commercial growth apart from the subsidy of an all-powerful overlord. These shops arose because they proved profitable and were in good *commercial* locations, not because they were nourished and protected by the authority of a local big man.

COMMERCIAL ORGANIZATION

Types and Number of Businesses

My business survey lists 567 concerns in Tezibazar: 57 wholesale, 373 retail, 21 mills and factories, and 116 services. They form 10, 66, 4, and 20 percent respectively of the town's commercial ventures. In all there are a total of 67 types of firms: 9 wholesale, 42 retail, 4 mill and factory, and 12 service. Table 10 lists the kinds of business done in Tezibazar.

There are indeed a profusion of shops and a large number of types of business in Tezibazar. The individual merchant limits the amounts and types of goods he carries to minimize potential loss, and this is one reason for the multiplicity and duplication of shops in the market. When the businessman does carry many products (usually a larger-scale merchant), he has no feeling that they should be in any way related. Such practice indicates a non-Western deployment of business energies. Thus *ghi*, cement, and hardware may all be sold from the same shop by the same merchant, who regards them each as a separate business rather than as different lines of merchandise. In counting the number of concerns, I have superimposed my own categories

Table 10. Types and numbers of permanent businesses

Business type	No.	Description
A. Wholesale		
Mustard oil, *dalda*, *ghi*	13	Goods often sold from same shop
Grain and/or salt	13	
Jarda tobacco	7	Tobacco used in *pan*
Chewing tobacco	7	
Ornaments	5	Of pure or alloyed silver and gold
Cloth	5	
Hardware	3	
Grocers	3	
Leather goods (hides)	1	
Total	57	
B. Retail		
Grocers	52	Spices, salt, grains, matches, etc.
Hotel, tea shop, sweetmeats	37	"Hotel" meaning restaurant
Cloth	35	
Pan and cigarettes	34	
Grain	24	
Parched grain	21	Snack foods made of rice, wheat
"Very small"	19	Businesses handling numerous goods on very small scale
Provisions	15	Soap, candies, tea, packaged goods generally, separate from grocery
Vegetables and potatoes	13	
Trinkets	13	Shoelaces, locks, beads, etc.
Hawkers	13	Hawk food, cold drinks, etc.
Ornaments	12	
Dry goods	9	Flashlights, lanterns, ready-made clothing, umbrellas, etc.
Utensils	9	Of brass, nickel, aluminum
Shoe shop	5	
Government fair price store	5	Grain, sugar sold at regulated prices
Stationery and books	4	
Bicycle	4	
Bangle	4	
Druggist	4	
Mustard oil, *dalda*, kerosene	4	
Hardware	4	
Betel leaf	3	
Rope and cord	3	
Cement	3	
Hair oil	2	

Table 10 (cont.)

Business type	No.	Description
Silver pounders	2	Make silver leaf to put into tobacco and on sweetmeats
Loud speaker rental	2	
Watches and clocks	2	
Chewing tobacco	2	
Ghi	2	
Trucking	2	
Miscellaneous	10	(Gas station; opium husks; electrical goods, *bhang* and wine; electric fans; *hukkas;* life insurance; leather skins; printing press; meat shop)
Total	373	
C. Mills and Factories		
Flour, etc.	15	Grind wheat, husk rice, press oil
Saw mill	2	
Soap factory	2	
Miscellaneous	2	Machine shops, etc.
Total	21	
D. Services		
Tailor	35	
Shoe repair	16	
Bicycle repair	15	
Barber	14	
Doctor/*hakim*	10	Traditional and scientific medical care
Ornament making	7	
Utensil repairing	5	
Carpentering	5	
Miscellaneous	9	Electrical repair; washerman; etc.
Total	116	
Grand total	567	

upon the local classification. A man who sold hardware and cement from the same shop and with the same account books was classified as the owner of a single business, even though he maintained that they were separate enterprises. If a merchant vended one or more commodities in different shops or with separate accounts, or under different supervision (for example, a son), he was enumerated as the owner of two or more businesses. However, if two highly dissimilar enterprises (such as *ghi* and hardware) requiring distinctive knowledge, techniques, and capital were carried on in the same shop, they were counted as separate businesses. Still, it was sometimes difficult to decide whether an item was a new business or only a new line of merchandise because of the often bizarre combination of salables in the same shop.

The multiplication of the most common types of shop is one reason for the intense competition which I shall note below.

The Areal Distribution of Business

Table 11 below further substantiates the overriding impor-

Table 11. Areal distribution of businesses

Area	No. of types	No. of concerns	%
Sahibganj proper	52	240	
Sahibganj, Jaunpur rd.	20	33	
Sahibganj, Pratabgarh rd.	12	36	
Sahibganj *phatak* (south of railway tracks)	9	13	
Gola Mandi	7	24	
Sabzi Mandi	8	25	
(Sahibganj total)		(371)	65.43
Naiganj (including Darziana and Suthatti)	37	97	17.11
Anjahi and Katra	22	45	7.94
Gurhai	14	26	4.59
Naibazar	10	28	4.93
Grand total		567	100.00

tance of Sahibganj as the market center for the town. Not only are businesses overwhelmingly massed in this area in gross terms, but also most of the wholesale and larger concerns congregate here.

Immigrants and Commuters

Eighteen percent of the present Tezibazar business population has migrated to the town within their or their fathers' generation. Well over 50 percent of these people have come in the last twenty years, and 81 percent have arrived from nearby villages and small towns. The reasons for migration are undoubtedly many, but the kinship factor is an unusually strong conditioner: 16 percent of the migrants came for purely kinship reasons—to inherit property, usually from their father-in-law (*sasur*). Another 27 percent, having decided upon migration, chose Teziba-zar as their new home because it was their mother's or wife's natal residence—*nanihal* and *sasural* respectively (women refer to their father's house as *maeka*). In both the above cases the migration was circumscribed or defined by kinship considerations. From this point of view 43 percent of the immigrants came within a kinship framework, whereas 57 percent chose the area for purely business considerations (see Table 12A). This is not to say that the former are less rational in their migration, since in many cases businesses are easier to start when one has previous connections. This point adds a quantitative backdrop to a situation I shall mark later: the Baniya as merchant (77.41 percent of the immigrants are of Baniya castes) is fearful of uprooting and moving to new areas unless he can be almost totally sure it will offer him better opportunities. This fear of residential change is a strong example of the lack of an entrepreneurial discipline. It is part and parcel of the fact that almost half the immigrants come with the surety of an inheritance or a close affinal or consanguineal relative to call upon. A few Tezibazaris in the same fashion use consanguineal or affinal connections to form new business structures outside the town, such as the founding of a branch office for a large firm. Once we pass outside this close kinship range, the choice is made purely on rational economic grounds. Either a man migrates to his *nanihal* or *sasural* or in a few cases to other "relational" areas (such as a married sister's residence), or he chooses and comes to a locale for purely business considerations. In the same way within the town, a man can depend on his family and close affinals or consanguineals, but beyond this limited kinship range no structured community relations or group cooperation exists.

Table 12A. Immigrants doing business in Tezibazar

Migration distance (miles)	No.	To inherit from		To live/do business in			For business purposes only	Per-cent-age
		sasur	other rel.	nanihal	sasural	other		
1–5	7	1 †		1	1		4	7.53
6–10	16		2 §‖		3	1 ‡	10	17.20
11–25	21	3		2 #	5	2 ‡**	9	22.58
26–50	20	3 ††	1 ††	2	3		11	21.51
51–100	9	1	1 ††				7	9.68
101–200	6	1				1 ‡‡	4	6.44
201	5	1	1 §§				3	5.38
Unknown *	9			2	2		5	9.68
Total	93	10	5	7	14	4	53	100.00
Percentage	100	16.13		26.88			56.99	

* Informants either did not know birthplace, refused to tell, or names and distances given were contradictory and could not be effectively checked—probably from close-by villages.

† Father inherited from his *sasur* (father-in-law).

‡ To live with *mausa* (mother's sister's husband).

§ Father inherited from *nana* (mother's father).

‖ To inherit from non-joint brother's widow.

In this case due to Muslim marriage, man married into same family in the same town from which his mother came; thus *sasural* and *nanihal* are the same for him.

** To live with father's sister's husband (*phupha*).

†† To inherit from *phupha*.

‡‡ To live with widowed sister.

§§ To inherit from *nana*.

Note: This table does not include (1) widows or women who are now shop-owners but who came to Tezibazar originally in marriage; (2) absentee owners—that is, people not actually resident in the town; (3) persons born outside of Tezibazar or who were living so but who ultimately returned to inherit from or to claim the property of their fathers or grandfathers.

Sixty-eight men, or 12.84 percent of the family sample, commute to Tezibazar from their home areas for business purposes. Such people are not only typically of certain castes but do in general only a certain type of business and primarily in a certain

Table 12B. Migration times

Years ago	No. of migrants
0–5	17
6–10	15
11–15	12
16–20	14
21–25	10
26–30	6
31–35	3
36–40	8
41–45	1
46–50	3
51–55	—
56–60	2
61–65	1
Unknown	1
Total	93

Prewar migration   = 25.80%
Postwar migration = 73.11%
Total (known)   98.91%

Table 12C. Origin of migration

Origin	No.	%
Village *	56	60.22
Town †	20	21.51
City ‡	17	18.27

* Under 3,000
† 3,000 to 30,000
‡ Above 30,000

area of the town (see Table 13). They have moved into the newly developing market areas in Tezibazar peripheral to the old commercial centers and the residential nucleus of the town. They generally perform low capital and low profit services such as selling *pan*, tailoring, cycle repairing. They are totally of such non-Baniya, agricultural, or traditionally rural-based status cate-

Table 13A. Commuters doing business in Tezibazar

Distance commuted	No.	Village	Town
1 mile or less	27	27	
2–3	16	16	
4–5	13	13	
6–10	5	4	1
11–25	4	4	
Unidentified	3	3	
Total	68	67	1

Table 13B. Types of businesses done by commuters

Business	No.
Pan	17
Tailor	11
Cycle repair	8
Cloth	5
Shoe repair	5
Other	22
Total	68

Table 13C. Location of commuter businesses

Locale	No.
Sahibganj Main Street	35
Sahibganj Jaunpur rd.	4
Sahibganj Pratabgarh rd.	17
Sahibganj *phatak*	1
Sabzi Mandi	2
Naiganj	5
Anjahi	1
Naibazar	3
Total	68

Table 13D. Castes of commuters

Caste	No.
Brahmin	13
Thakur	6
Camar	7
Shekh	6
Barai	5
Yadav	5
Bari	4
Hindu Nau	4
Others	18
Total	68

Note: Tables 13A–D do not list the four
absentee owners of businesses in Tezibazar.

gories as Brahmin, Kisan, Sudra, and Thakur. These commuters have moved into the interstices of the town's economy and, although adding little to the essential commercial nature of the urban area, nevertheless provide it with usable services.

Economic Stratification

A quantitative measure of the obvious concentration of wealth in Tezibazar can be obtained through data on the extent of multi-businesses and real estate holdings of town businessmen. I use real estate here to refer to town property only—generally houses.

Of the business families, 8.96 percent own 18.58 percent of the concerns (see Table 14). This figure does not show an extensive concentration of business activity in the hands of a few. In real estate this latter situation is much more effectively expressed: 7.58 percent of the business families own 23.83 percent of Tezibazar houses (after nonresident commuters who do not own a residence or shop in the town have been deducted; see Table 15). This figure shows a fairly high degree of real estate concentration. One of the reasons for the disparity in the amount of wealth concentration mirrored by multi-businesses and that

Table 14. Families owning multi-businesses

No. of multi-businesses owned	Kinds *				Total businesses owned	Total no. of owning families	Caste
	w	r	m	s			
4	1	4	2	1	8	2	Umar Halvai
3	3	11	5	2	21	7	Umar 3 Kesarvani 2 Others 2
2½ †	1	4 ‡			5	2	Umar Kalvar
2	12	39½ ‡	2½	14	68	34	Umar 9 Kalvar 3 Halvai 3 Others 19
1½	1	2			3	2	Umar Kalvar
Grand total	18	60½	9½	17	105	47	18 castes §

* w = wholesale; r = retail; m = mill; s = service.
† Fractions refer to partial ownership of firm.
‡ Includes a retail brickkiln outside the N.A. limits.
§ Castes' total: Umar 15; Kesarvani 4; Kalvar 5; Halvai 4; other Baniya 6 (5 castes); Muslims 8 (5 castes); others 5 (4 castes).

Table 15. Tezibazar houses owned by businessmen

	No. of houses per family									Total
	0	½, ⅓, and ⅔ *	1	1½ and 1⅓ *	2	3	4	5	6 †	
Families	29	16	293	11	78	20	8	2	5	462
Houses	0	8⅓	293	15⅚	156	60	32	10	46	621⅙
Totals		427 families, 473⅙ houses				35 families, 148 houses				

* Fractions indicate partial ownership as, for example, between brothers.
† Indicates ownership of six *or more* houses.
Note: This table does not include 59 commuters and three absentee proprietors who own neither house nor shop in Tezibazar.

shown by town real estate holdings is the physical limitations placed on business expansion, given the size of families and a commercial system where there is extreme distaste for supra-familial partnerships and/or joint stock companies. The number of a man's adult sons or brothers is limited by social and biological factors, and these also impede new business formation in a commercial order where partnerships and stock companies are feared and avoided.[2]

Such limitations in family size exercise no restraint on investment in real estate, however. The latter, then, is a quite important "commodity" both for the allocation of business profits or savings and also as an additional source of income through rental. One hundred eighty-two shops are so rented out (primarily by Baniyas), and the financial return from those in good commercial locations is excellent because of the high rentals charged. One Thakur earns at least Rs. 300 monthly from shop rental alone. Urban real estate and houses have perhaps become a more favorable investment since zamindari abolition made speculation in agricultural land illegal and insecure unless worked or supervised by the owner himself.

Even though the figures for total business concentration are low, nevertheless 9 percent of families who have multi-businesses own 31.58 percent of all wholesale firms and 45.24 percent of all mills and factories. The former businesses are, of course, the largest both in capital and income, whereas the latter require a heavy initial investment (for machinery and equipment). Looked at in this way, even the business data show a large concentration of wealth. Expectably, the families who own multi-businesses are in most cases the same ones who own many houses: 12 families own 67 houses and have 31 multi-businesses

[2] Some quantitative support for this assertion can be given. Among families owning either large retail or wholesale firms, the average number of adult males in families owning *only one business* was 2.21 (43 families, 95 adult males). However, the average number of males in families owning *multiple businesses* was 3.17 (23 families, 73 adult males). This difference highlights the importance of family size in determining new business formation—that is, family size in its most relevant commercial aspect, the number of adult males available. (Only wholesale and large retail concerns were counted in an effort to keep wealth constant. It was assumed that with sufficient wealth the merchant would either enlarge his existing business or, in the presence of sufficient family labor, start new ones.)

in the town. Almost every important public figure comes or derives his support from one of only a few dozen families.

SOCIAL ASPECTS OF COMMERCE

Caste and Business Occupation

Fifteen castes constitute 73.89 percent of the families in the business survey and own 78.86 percent of the businesses in the town. A complete listing of these castes and their total commercial concerns is given in Table 23 in Appendix I. It will be seen that a great variation exists in the number of business types done by each caste, a differential only partially explicable by the different size business populations of the castes. This situation indicates the persistence of various castes in their traditional business or service callings. Thus the Bhuj almost monopolize parched grain sales, and the Hindu Halvai to a lesser extent tea shops and sweetmeats sales. The Barai caste is well represented in *pan* shops. The Camars are almost entirely found in shoe repair. The Muslim Kunjra caste has complete control over vegetable and potato sales. The Kasodhan and Thather handle over two-thirds of all utensil businesses. Only Muslim Curihars sell bangles; almost all carpenters are Lohar by caste; and the Sonar *biradari* makes up a high proportion of ornament makers. In all these cases, the specific caste maintains a traditional occupation where it is an overwhelming majority. The preponderance of a group in one special business category explains their relative scarcity in other types. But note that the persistence of a caste in its traditional occupation means the continuance of a particular caste's members in it, not its monopoly over the specific activity: many Sonar caste individuals are ornament makers, but also many other people who are not Sonar make ornaments.

The Dominance of the Umar

In Tezibazar the predominant caste in population, wealth, and consequently influence is the Umar. Ninety-eight families (18.70 percent) of Umar appear in the business sample, almost three times the number of the next largest caste in the survey. They own over 20 percent of the businesses in Tezibazar, particularly wholesale ones (36 percent approximately). In ownership of multi-businesses, 15 out of 47 families or almost 32 percent are owned by this one caste (see Table 14). The Umar control slightly more than 25 per cent of the town real estate held by Tezibazar businessmen. Thus, the overwhelming dominance of the Umar in commercial population and most profitable businesses as well as in local real estate accounts for their control over all aspects of the town's public existence.

Communal Effects upon Employment

Hindus do not like to employ Muslims in their businesses because they do not feel that anyone of alien religion could be good for the luck of their shops. Then too, at the time of *divali* or other festivals, a Hindu employer could not allow his Muslim help to sit on the *gaddi*. A Muslim servant would also suffer grave social disabilities in the discharge of his duties. He could never bring his employer water or handle cooked food, and these are services often performed by *munim*s (clerks) for their shop owners.

For the other side, many Hindus do not like to work for Muslims because in addition to the constant danger of pollution through food, they feel that such labor demeans them. In any case, Muslim merchants prefer to hire other Muslims as an aspect and inducement to communal homogeneity. Since restricted commensality or food pollution among Muslim castes is absent (although interdining with Bhangi and Shah low castes is avoided), caste within this status category does not condition in any great fashion feelings of identity or job performance in the shop (see Table 16).

Caste Factors in the Employment of Servants and Clerks

There is a definite status category patterning in the employment of servants (generally unskilled manual laborers) and *munim*s, or clerks (who keep the accounts and are usually also

empowered to sell goods). Most of the manual laborers in Tezibazar are either Kisan or Sudra and come into town daily from
residences in the nearby rural area. These two status categories
account for 78.35 percent of all servants employed in Tezibazar.
On the other hand, such superior jobs as *munims* or credit
collectors (where salaries range from Rs. 60 to 130 monthly,
whereas servants receive only Rs. 20 to 40 a month) go in large
proportion to the Baniya groups. Of thirty-five *munims* and
credit collectors employed in the town, twenty-two, or over 60
percent, are Baniya by caste.

Table 16. Number of business employees by status category and community
employed by Tezibazar merchants

	Caste						
	Servants				Clerks/credit collectors		
No. of merchants	Caste Hindu	Sudra	Muslim	Total	Caste Hindu	Muslim	Total
Hindu 84	141	50	10	201	30	2 *	32
Muslim 19	11	0	19	30	2	1	3
Total 103	152	50	29	231	32	3	35

* In one case a Muslim clerk was employed by a Hindu absentee owner, and,
in such a situation, much of the disability in employing Muslim help was irrelevant.

The kinship factor was slight in determining servant or *munim*
status. In only two cases was an employee related to the firm
owners. In one, a partnership between *saru* "brothers" (two men
whose wives are real or classificatory sisters and who therefore
call each other *bhai*, or brother), the servant was the *mama*'s *sala*
or mother's brother's wife's brother of one of the partners. In the
other case, a man's non-joint brother acted as the concern's
munim. Both these cases had to do with Brahmins.

Thus status category or community does play a direct role in
conditioning access to employment in the town. Muslims and to
a smaller extent Sudras are denied job opportunities open to caste

Hindus. In both these cases the limitations stem from traditional inferiorities in commensality which condition the working ability and usefulness of the individual. Where such traditional disabilities are lacking, as, for instance, among caste Hindus, there seems to be little if any tendency to employ persons on the basis of caste. There is, however, a definite unconscious patterning to the castes which become servants, but this is due to economic factors: the poor rural Kisan and Sudra categories are forced into the lowest rungs of the labor market. Those who become *munim*s also show a marked uniformity of caste and status level, but again this is because of the indirect selection for which castes enter this field, rather than of purposeful selection on the part of the employer. Once beyond the communal aspect, kin or caste plays little role in the determination of employment opportunities. As my informants maintained, neither of these traditional phenomena took precedence over the simple criterion of how industrious and profitable an employee any specific individual would make. In these cases, commercial skill pre-empts kinship and caste and indicates the impersonal quality of the Tezibazar market—a point which will be brought out in more detail in the following chapter.

CHAPTER 8

Business Style

The commercial organization of Tezibazar contains a striking anomaly. On the one hand, the structure of enterprise is primarily defined by the market economy in its specific local manifestations. As the preceding chapter has indicated, the nature of the commodities sold, employment, market location, and caste occupational distribution are in large part aspects of the monetized and depersonalized economy of the district and nation. This chapter will show the same situation to apply to credit and competition. On the other hand, the social organization of businesses is exceedingly "conservative." In an earlier section I noted that Baniya or traditional merchant castes retain the majority of business concerns. Further, a great proportion of all shops are familial both in business organization—that is, by whom and how the business is carried on—and capitalization or financing. The more sophisticated and larger commercial concerns can no longer afford to retain a purely familial organization of the enterprise, but with few exceptions, they remain familial in capitalization. Partnerships are frowned upon and "joint stock" companies are considered commercially suicidal. Indeed, in almost every aspect, the financing as well as supervision of business in the town is done on a family basis. Again, in profit policies and depreciation allowances Tezibazar merchants fail to distinguish household from business. Most of them are totally unaware that a commercial accounting can be made separately for business and household.

In the context of the peculiar economics of an underdeveloped

country this retention of business as an adjunct of family—in
Tezibazar there are "business families," not "family businesses"—
leads to a general commercial orientation that perhaps is best
styled "subsistence-type." That is, people are chary of investment and risk taking. They seem to be content to accept a
smaller profit so long as it covers their subsistence needs rather
than to venture their capital in a potentially profitable but possibly losing investment. Such an orientation directs the highly
developed profit motive of town merchants not into large-scale
entrepreneurial channels but into the less risky but equally profitable realms of adulteration, cheating, and black marketeering.

In opposition to this greatly restrained, conservative familial
and subsistence orientation of individual businesses and merchants is the highly competitive, anarchic nature of town business in general. There is in fact no regulation of business practices in Tezibazar. Neither a traditional town organization nor
individual caste structures exist to impede the heated competition for customers which is such a large part of local commerce.

"SUBSISTENCE" PROFIT AND INVESTMENT IDEOLOGY

The figures given in Table 10 indicate an important aspect of
business in the town: the profusion of commercial ventures both
in absolute numbers and types and the lack of any form of
"general store." Every possible and minimally profitable commercial niche is exploited. Three types of shops exist which in
the kinds of goods carried, capitalization, and size could well be
combined into one: the grocery, the provisions shop, and the dry
goods concern. In fact, many times the goods carried in each of
these store types greatly overlap, but their distinctiveness is
maintained in the mind and purse of the owner as well as in the
minds of his customers. This proliferation of business ventures
highlights the heavy "subsistence" bias of much of the trade
done. That is, stores and commercial concerns provide and need
only provide a rather low return to the merchant for him to be
willing to undertake their operation. The attitude of the merchant matches his business practice: he is for the most part

willing to content himself with a small yearly return on his invested capital. Because of lack of literacy or business knowledge, he often has no idea of the profits he makes or business expenses he incurs. Almost half the Baniya merchants interviewed (fifteen of thirty-three) did not keep any form of accounts, and these merchants represent the more sophisticated traders. If his family is fed and his desire for savings appeased, the typical merchant is satisfied and neither asks nor expects any more from his business. Because most shops are small and capital is limited, the businessman is extremely wary of further investment.

At the same time, he is fearful of fully committing his capital in a single large enterprise and prefers a small but highly varied inventory. Although nearly every respondent in my Baniya castes survey said he would like to start a new business, very few wanted to risk the capital that such an undertaking would require. Of thirty-one Baniya merchant respondents, slightly over half (sixteen, or 51.61 percent) said they were satisfied with the earnings of their businesses. The reasons for their satisfaction indicate the subsistence-type thinking that forms their business procedure. One man explained, "I get my daily bread from [the shop], and that's all I need. Why should I think of more when I meet my expenses from it." Another respondent declared, "Whatever I have, I am satisfied with, and whatever the future will bring, will be all right, too. When I earn little, I spend little." Most other people said they were content with their income because it met their outlay, but later in the interview were forced to admit that they tailored their consumption to their business profits. Even those merchants who said they were dissatisfied with their earnings—generally they controlled the larger, more profitable concerns—did not manifest a great desire to leap into new fields of enterprise. They all complained of lack of investment capital, whereas their neighbors (and they concerning *their* neighbors) always accused them of having thousands of rupees merely hoarded. Indeed, when these businessmen complained of lack of capital, they were speaking of "risk" capital—as judged from the relatively inhibited risk-taking attitude created by a "subsistence" syndrome concerning commercial venture. Not one of the many Baniyas or other merchants I informally interviewed named risk taking as one of the fundamental aspects of successful enterprise, although some admitted its importance upon prompting. Their concern was put primarily upon owner-buyer relations: the necessity for "sweet and gentle" behavior on the shop owner's part and the ability to gain the confidence of the customer in order to exact an even greater profit on second-rate goods. In answer to a question, one informant summed up in this fashion:

Risk taking is very important in business. For example, I must take some loss to convince people that I sell at a cheap rate. Thus, when a man enters my shop for the first time I would sell him something that usually goes for 8 annas [one-half rupee] for 6 annas. Then after I had obtained his confidence by this method, I would sell him something that normally is Rs. 2 for 3.

Thus the "profit motive" among the local merchants and particularly Baniyas takes an involuted form in a high rate of savings and business chicanery rather than an outward manifestation in large business investment and expansion. This does not mean that given a black market situation, the merchant will not maximize his profit, will not charge "all the market will bear." Indeed, it is precisely only this sort of situation which the merchant anticipates as a source of profit and toward which he channels his business energies. He views his daily business profit as providing for his bare subsistence in between times of black market or scarcity. He therefore is satisfied with a profit set at a minimal level.

The great multiplicity of businesses in the town and the filling of almost every possible economic niche—both aspects of the subsistence business attitude—impart two distinctive qualities to the market place. First, they introduce an excessive price and credit competition to attract customers which is abetted by the nature of the rural economy on which town business depends.

Second, they open wide the doors to all forms of adulteration and sharp dealing by the merchants, who use these techniques as ploys to meet the price and credit competition of their fellows. In a more direct form, the subsistence motif clamps a strong brake on new investment and the formation of new commercial ventures.

Wealth and Prestige: The Baniya Attitude

Politics and social power have their firm bases in wealth: "A rich man has many friends." However, the converse of the above statement is not true. All wealthy individuals do not wish to become important public figures. This retreat from, or unwillingness to accept, the public status which their wealth could confer is a rather common attribute among wealthy Baniyas—particularly the Umar caste. It is so characteristic of many individuals to a greater or lesser degree that it cannot be only a matter of personal disposition, but is in fact a cultural stereotyping. "He puts money before his prestige" is very commonly said of any one of a number of men in Tezibazar. Yet, these men are in a way given a status system unto themselves, and even though they are rebuked as misers—"He is a man of *lakhs* yet he has never worn wool"—at least other Baniyas sympathize with their positions and accord them the honor, deference, and status of rich men. In my survey of Baniya merchants, almost all respondents mentioned the same individual as the most successful businessman in the town. Yet, when asked about his prestige, the same people opined that he had none. Concerning their own desires, these merchants invariably preferred honor to wealth—but for typically "Baniya" reasons. They felt that wealth was transitory. If there is one bad year or a black market does not materialize, riches can disappear; prestige, however, is constant. A man who enjoys it can always get a loan to start up business again should he suffer a grave loss, whereas such is not the case for the merely wealthy man without prestige. Thus the "prestige" which is rated so highly here is a peculiarly pragmatic and economic one. In fact, preference for this sort of prestige over wealth is an indication of the conservative, "play-safe" investment attitude of the Baniya merchant. One must "bank" a certain amount of public acceptance and honor just as one saves money for emergencies. As the merchant grows richer and becomes less fearful of such contingencies, he is content with the prestige of riches alone and the public acclaim which such possession guarantees among the Baniya community.

This prestige system exists aside from the general ranking people profess (although some individuals do think that prestige is conterminous with wealth). Rather than on the possession of public charisma—which the social personalities of Baniyas often negate—it is based on the mere possession of wealth and ownership of shops and houses. As such this system reinforces the basic acquisitive interests which form so much a part of the Baniya interaction with the world.

SALES, PROFIT, AND LOSS

It was often difficult during the business survey to draw information on houses from merchants, yet I nearly always obtained a good estimate, although one which tended toward understatement. The businessmen felt I could easily check their urban property holdings. But when it came to statements about their wealth, business capital, turnover, and so forth—which they never correctly told to anyone, so they said—it was impossible to get figures with any assurance of accuracy. Fear of tax collectors and government "exactions" are uppermost in the minds of the merchants in their refusal to answer such questions. As sophisticated Baniya merchants say, they keep two sets of financial books; "ek khane-ke-lIye, ek dIkhane-ke-lIye" (literally, "One to eat from, one to show [the tax collector]").

Checking business data with neighbors was always dangerous because political opposition and economic envy or even respect on their part often led them to give answers as false as those of the original respondent. I also found that neighbors respected each other's right to fabricate information, particularly if they felt that in doing so they formed part of a united front against some new government conspiracy "in restraint of trade." Anyone acquainted with the economic situation of this part of India in 1964—when many Tezibazar merchants were hoarding food grains, sugar, and oilseeds and manipulating them on the black market—will understand why my informants were so secretive. Thus, in the following section I am forced to rely primarily on statements from a few fairly trustworthy informants.

The largest wholesale businesses in Tezibazar do an annual gross business of about four to six *lakh*s of rupees (one *lakh* = Rs. 100,000). There are no more than ten such concerns in the town. Most shops fall into the great middle range of from Rs. 6,000 to Rs. 40,000 in annual sales. Below them come the small, marginal enterprises engaged in by women or the very poor. Such shops may have a yearly turnover lower than Rs. 1,000, although this is difficult to estimate since their owners have no idea of this measure themselves.

As we shall see, a shop's rate of profit is not fixed in a clearly discernible manner, and it is therefore impossible for most merchants really to ascertain their markups. Generally wholesale businesses use an 8 to 10 percent markup; the same figure for retail concerns is about 20 percent. These figures refer, of course, to an unadulterated, fairly weighed commodity. When one considers the various possibilities for chicanery, the markup can be fantastically high: upwards of 100 percent. Some businesses have less opportunity to practice deception than others, and the markups quoted above apply to such relatively "sure" businesses as cloth, dry goods, and provisions. They are less valid for trade in food grains, oilseeds, oils, and sugar.

In the main market of Sahibganj and Old Town all transactions are based on money either at hand or in credit. However, a very minimal amount of barter is practiced in the Naibazar commercial area. Here, at the entrance to the main market, various merchants have set up small "general stores" (this is the only place where they are found in the town) which primarily stock food grains, kerosene, *dalda*, and other immediately required consumer goods. These items are directly bartered to the rural population coming to the town without cash or unwilling to go into debt. These people bring mainly surplus food grains such as wheat and rice or occasionally a home-manufactured item such as *gur*.

The richest men in Tezibazar are worth about Rs. 200,000 (2 *lakh*s) individually, and net at most Rs. 50,000 a year. There are probably no more than five such men. These are the biggest wholesalers—generally in grain and oilseeds but also in cloth. More commonly, business earnings amount to Rs. 5,000–15,000 a year for better shops, whereas the smallest can bring a return of hardly Rs. 50–75 a month or even less. The great majority of enterprises run between Rs. 2,000–5,000 yearly. The supposedly richest man in the town, Beni Madho, was said to earn no less than Rs. 3,000–4,000 monthly, while his *cacera bhai* (father's brother's son), Manik Chand, ekes out about Rs. 50 in the same space of time. A strikingly large gap exists in the relative economic positions of rich and poor, even though the wealthiest residents refer to themselves as "middle-class" and to their less fortunate fellow townsmen as "third-class." There is, indeed, great variation in income, even in so small a market place as Tezibazar.

The small Baniya merchant tries to save at least something—even the most negligible amount—from his income, even though it may mean personal deprivation. The steady accumulation of money over the years, although a significant method of capital formation in a poor economy, is not the way individuals become wealthy. Instead most *"lakhpatti"* (worth *lakh*s) men achieved their riches through windfalls: black markets, price speculations, or illegal commercial dealings. Often this change from poverty to great wealth is dramatic. Paras Nath Umar Chiniha (so named for his sugar—*cini*—business) was in terrible economic straits ten years ago. At one point he was on the verge of selling his home. From an old friend he managed to borrow Rs. 10,000 with which to get started. In one year he regained all his former wealth and more: a dearth of sugar allowed him to earn Rs. 10 on a sack whereas the usual rate was Rs. 3–4. Another man,

Raghu Das Kalvar, made all his present money in one year because of a scarcity of pulse. Almost all Tezibazar's rich or well-to-do residents have much the same history of wealth accumulation.

On the other side of the coin, people can lose their money as quickly as they made it. In one year Kamta Prasad Umar lost Rs. 70,000 on speculation in a *gur* black market which never developed. Other causes of sudden loss besides unprofitable speculation are the drain of litigation and court actions and, more important, the fraudulent practices of servants and clerks or business partners. In the first instance, thirteen out of thirty-two Baniya merchants, or more than one-third, were or had been involved in some court action within the last ten years. Mata Din, a medium-sized retail merchant, spent Rs. 500 yearly on legal suits out of a total annual household expenditure of approximately Rs. 2,800. The present reduced economic position of the town Chairman's family was said to stem from the expenditure of thousands of rupees in losing court cases. The effects of employee larceny are even more pronounced: one year Nokhai Ram Kalvar began a type of business (*jarda* tobacco) with which he was not well acquainted, and through the manipulation of credit, his two *munim*s defrauded him of nearly a *lakh* of rupees. They then set up as businessmen in their own right and now carry on legitimate and accepted enterprises of the same sort as that their unwilling "benefactor" had attempted to start. Two of the most successful merchants in the town are said to owe their present affluence to their dishonesty as former *munim*s in a wholesale cloth house. Usually such illegal activities are never reported for fear of government reprisals against the injured merchant himself. When Sitla Prasad lost Rs. 20,000 to a fraudulent *munim*, he never retrieved it. If he had set the authorities to work on this case, he would have had to admit to this much income. To absorb the loss quietly was less expensive and less damaging to his reputation with the tax collector.

Business operations in the town show a relative lack of permanency. Many commercial concerns are less than five years old, and most were started no more than fifteen years ago. Some few commercial ventures are over fifty years old. These are various caste hereditary professions such as grain parching, barbering, or tailoring, where the family has been engaged in that activity in the same location as far back as can be remembered. In general, Tezibazar businesses enjoy relatively short lives. Even in the case of the old-time Baniya merchant families, a man is rarely found in the same business as was his father and most businessmen have conducted two, three, or more different kinds of businesses in their lifetimes. This kind of commercial mortality and constant business transformation indicates the great massing of small marginal firms in the market. It is also an insight into the toll exacted by severe commercial competition. In the case of the larger concerns, which are no more permanent than the smaller ones, this mortality shows the ups and downs of major profit making and large-scale loss, of business dissolution and reformation. For, if a Baniya merchant fails either by suffering heavy loss or expenditure of capital, he does not leave Tezibazar for hopefully greener pastures; he merely liquidates or retrieves what capital he can and begins again on a smaller scale or in a new line.

Large profit and loss then are both conditioned by one business activity: speculation based on scarcity and resultant black market prices. The expectation of profit by the merchant is often the expectation of a windfall, not of a fair or good return on his investment. The latter concept as a conditioner of behavior does not exist in Tezibazar, either in the minds of the customers who might provide it or of the merchants who might claim it. The businessman lives in anticipation of a scarcity or, what since World War II has become even better, a governmentally regulated or licensed commodity; then he takes full advantage of the situation. His expectations, his business acumen, his capital allocation are all geared to this form of profit taking. To be sure, this kind of speculation is entrepreneurial; but it is enterprising in terms of social speculation (black markets, scarcities) rather than commodity speculation (the creation of new businesses, increased turnover, and so forth). Undoubtedly, the antecedent and present conditioners of this form of business activity lie in the impoverished condition of the local countryside and the fact that under such circumstances the profit of merchants is usually extracted from the subsistence of the peasant. This factor in interaction with the still predominantly traditional caste determination of commercial groupings and the social and business traits which such genesis entails produces the local market situation. Thus, the economic activities of Tezibazar merchants are basically of two sorts: a normal, conservative, capital-retentive "subsistence"-oriented business which periodically flares up into a dynamic, highly speculative and capitalized venture, set off by a regional or national scarcity or commodity regulation.

CREDIT, CAPITAL, AND MONEY LENDING

Any merchant, whether he be a wholesale cloth dealer or a very small grocer, who has enough capital will give credit to his customers. In fact, no man can contemplate doing business on a large scale without sufficient funds to finance huge credit advances, often running as high as Rs. 1,000–2,000 per customer (see Table 17). Credit of this magnitude is one of the few ways a trader can insure return sales. The Baniya merchant, particularly, feels that a definite correlation exists between the amount of his credit sales and his percentage of steady customers. Also, a man in need of an article but without money is more likely to settle for a shopworn or actually adulterated product, whereas a man with money in his pocket usually spends a great deal of time in comparison shopping. The situation obtains in retail businesses especially. In the wholesale houses, credit is also used to bind customers—but in these concerns it is the rural shop owners who are attracted and attached by credit policy. Generally wholesale firms do not do business with rural dealers who refuse to contract with them more or less permanently, although such a rule cannot be too vigorously enforced because of fear of large-scale desertion.

Credit sales among the Baniyas interviewed accounted for from 10 to 40 percent of total sales in general, depending on the size of the shop and type of business. Usually the larger the shop

Table 17. Amount of credit given by Baniya merchants

No.*	% of credit sales	Largest amount of credit given (Rs.)	Distance (miles) to which given
1	30	15	4
2	20	200	1
3	0	0	–
4	5	22	2
5	25	20	4
6	40	1,000	8
7	0	0	–
8	10	2,000	60
9	10	10	2
10	25	200	20
11	12	50	10
12	10	400	32
13	20	10	6
14	40	5	(in town)
15	5	200	2
16	85	5,000	30
17	4	50	10
18	75	100	6
19	10	30	10
20	20	50	5
21	0	0	–
22	(Does not apply) †		
23	0	0	–
24	0	0	–
25	0	0	–
26	(Refused to respond)		
27	40	2,000	25
28	20	200	3
29	20	20	5
30	25	50	20
31	10	200	10
32	10	50	2
33	30	10	6
Average	24% ‡ per firm giving credit	432 ‡	13 ‡

25 firms or 80.65% allow credit
6 or 16.12% do not allow
1 or 3.23% does not apply

* Numbers indicate respondents in the survey of Baniya businessmen.
† This shop is a government fair price store and legally cannot give credit.
‡ These figures are rounded to nearest whole unit.

and the greater the cost of its merchandise, the higher was the percentage of credit sales. Most larger firms offer a discount of from 3 to 5 percent for cash purchases. Generally, the merchant sustains a loss of from 2 to 5 percent on the total credit given, although this figure may rise to alarming proportions when, for example, a silversmith absconds with a large amount of precious metal. For the most part, however, no great difficulty is met in collecting money given in credit, although in retail sales it may be many months before the return is made. If a villager does not pay back credit extended, the merchant first tries to retrieve it from the debtor directly; failing this, he goes through the village *mukhiya* or *panc* (formal village leader). Should the merchant see his debtor in the market, he will by public embarrassment and shame make the defaulter sit in his shop until he or his family pay up the debt. Generally, the merchant tries to secure from the debtor some personal article or purchase which he refuses to return until after he has publicly denounced at length the bad faith of the defaulter. The *mukhiya* or *panc* is usually approached for the first time in the market, also. If the debtor refuses to repay after an informal request from this leader, the businessman will go to the village personally and publicly complain before the *panc* and, if necessary, the whole *pancayat* (meaning either the statutory board or the informally recognized village leaders). Once the *pancayat* has taken action, if the man still refuses to pay, the merchant usually then requests legal permission to attach and auction the debtor's property.

Wholesale concerns have a much more rigorous system of credit repayments. Wholesale cloth shops generally expect repayment or partial repayment of credit within two to three months. In the chewing tobacco business repayment is desired within six to eight months. One *jarda* tobacco firm does not require credit returns until three years after the initial purchase, although it demands periodic partial returns, and does not let a dealer exceed a specified amount (in this case, at most Rs. 20,000). After the expiration of the time allowed by the individual concern, the owner usually enters a court action against the debtor. No interest is charged on credit returned within the proper time, for to do so would be to alienate all one's customers. These big houses do, however, employ full-time credit collectors who tour the countryside by bus or bicycle every week or two and try to coax at least token amounts out of the rural shop owners (who are the main customers of the wholesale houses). These men are paid a certain percentage of what they collect, although there is an informal minimum—as was quickly pointed out to me by one agent who had gathered only 1½ rupees in a day's work.

Baniya merchants feel that some caste groupings are better credit risks or preferred debtors than others. The merchants like to lend to Camars and other Sudras or Kisan castes because these people are considered "simple," honest, and more easily intimidated by the Baniya. These traits are supposedly a result of their lack of education and relative poverty. Brahmins and Thakurs, on the other hand, are regarded as poor credit risks because they are arrogant and demanding and refuse to repay what they owe. "The man who lends to Brahmins and Thakurs will be repaid with beatings" is a common expression of the apprehension felt by Baniya merchants in credit dealings with these two status groupings.

In a commercial system which depends on the relatively impoverished peasant as prime consumer, price rather than quality is the main sales point. In Tezibazar, merchants do not and cannot compete over quality or location or service, but only over price, and even the smallest differences will attract customers. Since profit cannot be lowered below a certain point and still give a reasonable return and since in their own way merchants are unwilling to settle for a small profit, adulteration is widely practiced in order to provide a commodity with a tantalizing low price. As I shall note later, quarrels occur periodically among businessmen dealing in the same line of goods wherein one accuses the other of underselling him by adulteration. But this does little to stem the tide of customers to the underseller's shop.

Why the peasants continue to buy what they must know are

adulterated goods or to patronize dishonest shopkeepers is connected with the preponderance of credit buying. The Baniyas
only say that the peasants are simple folk and ignorant and thus
are easily beguiled. Perhaps a more likely explanation is the
pressure of small and seasonal money incomes—the self-same
pressure that drives the merchant to debase his product. A man
who must buy on credit can ill afford to be overly selective in
picking his item since either he cannot, in fact, go elsewhere or
"elsewhere" as a market choice rather than just a locational
change does not exist. Naturally, the merchants who adulterate
most offer the most liberal credit policy, and wherever credit is
given equally freely, adulteration is equally great. One jeweler
boasted that even though he sold a two-rupee item with one
rupee as credit, he still profited because the real price of the item
was only three-quarters of a rupee.

Capital makes the world of Tezibazar business go round. Not
only are large amounts of it required for credit, but it also
determines who can afford to set up in business. Generally at
least Rs. 5,000–20,000 is needed to set up a good-sized retail
business in the town. Rs. 50,000 to one lakh is necessary for
beginning a wholesale venture, and an enterprise such as a *jarda*
tobacco manufactory would entail outlay of over Rs. 100,000.

Large capital allows a merchant much more freedom in the
style of trade as well as a much greater potential profit. The
expenditure of capital in credit allowances helps bind customers
to a particular merchant. It also permits him to make the most
advantageous use of seasonal price fluctuations in his commodity
market. One young man, Gaya Prasad, owns a large ornament
business (*srafa*) where he sells silver and gold jewelry mainly to
the rural populace and to small town and village merchants.
Gaya Prasad has been quite successful and in the four years since
the inception of his shop has been able to double his capital
(from Rs. 15,000 to Rs. 30,000). Most of his profit comes from
buying large quantities of silver in the cold season, when the
prices are low, and reselling it in the marriage season, when
increased demand raises the rate. He also supplies local small

ornament dealers with amounts of silver and gold. Because he has a large capital, Gaya Prasad can afford to *deal* in pure silver ornaments for his retail trade. The small dealers to whom he allows silver on credit, however, must have the metal melted down and alloyed, for their capital is not enough to stand so high an investment as pure silver.

People are willing to allocate capital to credit dealings and stockpiling, but they do not care to lend it out. Many of the Tezibazar merchants complain of inability to find someone who is willing to lend money for business purposes. Those who have sufficient capital prefer to keep and invest it themselves. What often happens is that unused capital mounts up steadily over a few years until the merchant sees a chance for a large profit through a black market or other scarcity-produced situation:

The big men do not give loans to people to start new businesses. This is because they think that people will get wealthy and then go into competition with them. Makhundi Lal lent a man Rs. 5,000 and in a matter of months this man became almost as wealthy as Makhundi Lal. So, instead, people just keep all their money around, ready to buy something up if they see a good deal and without having to pay taxes.

The possession of capital, then, gives great advantages in business. It allows large credit financing; it means ability to take advantage of seasonal market fluctuations. But the usefulness of capital is not exploited fully. The individual merchant would rather keep it in his own possession and wait for an economic opening than risk it by financing other businessmen. This retention also has a competitive aspect: it cuts off possibilities for economic growth of potentially rival merchants.

Some men do lend money, however. In Tezibazar these individuals are few; they are also old, the remnants of the Baniya zamindar class, who have retained the formerly adjunct enterprise of money lending as their present prime income source. Baniya businessmen now consider the times unprofitable for money lending because of government restrictions. Up until the last World War, money lending was a large part of Tezibazar capital investment. Now, however, moneylenders are scarce, and they are loath to risk their own capital. In fact, they use the modern commercial machinery of bank loans to finance much of their money lending. Beni Prasad Umar, a sixty-five-year-old ex-zamindar who carried on a money lending business (although he was not registered as such with the government) stated:

Many people come to me to pawn their ornaments to get small loans [a few hundred rupees at most] that would require a great deal of time and very good security to get from the bank. Actually only the very big businessmen go to banks for borrowing, and they can put down stock such as cloth or oilseeds, and so forth, as security for the money they borrow. Beni Madhu, the richest man in Tezibazar, borrows Rs. 4,000–5,000 per year in this way.

In this fashion the bank does good service for businessmen in the town, and the big merchants support the little ones. I borrow money from the bank on my own good credit, and then lend it out to people who do not have security to get such money from the bank. If the bank lends me the money on 12 annas interest per month per Rs. 100 [¾ percent], then I lend it out at 20 annas per month per hundred [1¼ percent]. This margin of ½ percent [or more than 6 percent a year] makes it profitable for me. I borrow on the basis of my bank account. But small people do not have credit in this way and do not have any access to the bank.

Beni Prasad and most other moneylenders do not tie up their own capital, but utilize the bank's and still make a substantial profit. Note, too, that not only does he lend to cover contingency expenses such as marriages and funerals, but he also helps finance small businessmen. *Srafs* (ornament dealers) also perform this function when they accept personal jewelry in pawn for cash. Their charge for this service is stated as 1 or 1½ percent monthly although it is actually higher, since the interest is discounted for a specified time when the money is handed over.

Even though some individuals engage in money lending, the sums they are willing to outlay are small, and the total capital allocated to such activities is limited. For these reasons, loans for financing commercial ventures are scarce at best in Tezibazar. A man faced with the problem of insufficient capitalization rarely turns to partnership (although this is the main cause for those partnerships which exist) and never to a joint stock company: to do either would mean a loosening of familial control on the enterprise—a development which no merchant accepts with equanimity. Rarely, however, can he obtain a loan for the required amount. So, even had he a desire to expand his business or innovate commercially, he is by lack of resources often forced to remain content with his present status.

BUSINESS INNOVATION

The preceding discussion has indicated a number of business habits which impede the formation of novel enterprises. Indeed, in Tezibazar, most of the new types of businesses have been started by non-Baniya residents or by recent immigrants and the commuters from the rural area.

There is, however, a fairly common manner in which new style firms come into existence among the settled Baniya merchants in the town. This method also says something about the transfer of commercial and family control from father to son. A man who is reasonably successful in business will continue as head of his family and shop until he dies or becomes aged and incapacitated. If, however, he happens to suffer a serious setback commercially during his lifetime and his sons are mature and enterprising, it often happens that the old firm is liquidated and a new concern in a different sort of business is established with the son or sons at its head.

Laksman Das Umar and Kamta Prasad Umar were both separately engaged in the *gur* business a decade ago, and both had grown affluent from it. In 1951 these two men, independently, became involved in an abortive black market in *gur*. A scarcity of *gur* existed in that year, and the government fixed a ceiling price of Rs. 19 a *man* (40 *ser* = 1 *man*, or approximately 80 pounds) on it. Many merchants began to stockpile *gur* in the expectation of a large and profitable black market. Generally they bought this product from the surrounding rural areas. But the expected demand in neighboring states did not develop, and they could only unload their stocks, if at all, at a meager price. Laksman Das had bought *gur* at Rs. 23 a *man*, and sold it at Rs. 7 a *man*. He estimated his loss at Rs. 50,000—which totally impoverished him. Kamta Prasad, who tried to store his *gur* during the rainy season and consequently let most of his stock rot, sold very little, and his loss was close to Rs. 70,000. He, too, became a poor man as a result of this speculation.

In 1951, Kamta Prasad was thirty-seven and his eldest son was only nine. In the same year, Laksman Das was forty-seven and his eldest son, Ram Sakal, was twenty-three. This difference in age was highly significant for the future of these families. Unlike Kamta Prasad, who was a fairly young man in 1951 and had no adult son to take over for him when he lost everything, Laksman Das was old enough to have an enterprising son who was quick to assume control once his father had shown himself finished commercially. As Ram Sakal tells it, "I started out completely on my own in *jarda* (tobacco) whereas before my father had run the *gur* business alone. My father had no interest in the business and tried to dissuade me from starting out in this pauperlike [small] way, when we had been such big merchants before. But I did anyway, and now our family is wealthier than it was before the loss in *gur*." Ram Sakal was one of the richest men in the town, was one of the five men who owned an automobile, and had sufficient capital to send Rs. 23,000 to the national government for the purchase of specially imported scents used in the *jarda* business. Note that Laksman Das deprecated his son's business and would never have taken the risk or embarrassment of beginning afresh onto himself. What might have been the outcome had Laksman Das been a younger man is shown by the subsequent history of Kamta Prasad and his family. Kamta weathered the loss of 1951 and remained in a small-scale *gur* and grain business which still continues at the present. He has never come near to recouping the loss in *gur*, and his sons, who were too young in 1951 to take over command, have now entered adult-hood with poor future commercial prospects. Nor has Kamta Prasad himself recovered from the loss, for as he says, "It is hard to accept poverty once you have been rich."

Another point at which business innovation becomes likely is upon partition of a joint estate (including the business) by a group of brothers. Often the eldest brother is left in possession of the family business intact, and the younger brothers take their shares in cash, ornaments, or household articles. They often use these as capital with which to begin new businesses in different lines from that of their former family enterprise.

COMPETITION, DISHONESTY, AND SOCIAL CONTROL

The wiles of the merchant, and particularly the Baniya mer-chant, in techniques of deception and adulteration are notorious. The simpler accusations are that jewelers sell alloys for pure precious metals, or that grain merchants mix barley and other so-called "inferior" grains with wheat. More cunning is the puncturing of a filled *dalda* (vegetable shortening) can with a needle and extracting some of its contents; or the use of mercury in scale beams. Whatever be the quality of inventiveness, wa-tered milk, chalky flour, false weights, and a hundred other debased commodities and deceptive practices are all considered expectable behavior of the Baniya trader in action. The preced-ing discussion of capital and credit should have somewhat tem-pered too exacting a distaste for this commercial chicanery. An impoverished consuming class not willing to accept the necessity of a merchant's profit, plus the similarly caused "subsistence" attitude of the merchants themselves toward their ventures and capital all condition such illegal and antisocial aspects of the commercial structure. Nevertheless, it is true as both a statement of behavioral reality and as a psychological perception of the business community that, as one Baniya informant put it, "No-body can be rich by honesty; nor is any rich man honest. If an individual is not a crook, then someone else in his family must be." Another commonly heard remark, although said in a humorous vein, is that all town businessmen are "Four-Twenty." This is the English title of a very popular Hindi film in which the leading character is a man of total malevolence and corruption. To be "Four-Twenty" is to be deceptive or dishonest in commercial dealings. These sentiments are constantly expressed in Tezibazar, and they parallel and accompany the statements about the absence of public morality and ethics cited in Chapter 6.

No point is served by a dull recital of the numerous accusations and conflicts about cheating and dishonesty. More relevant at this point are the social aspects of this tendency to cheat and adulterate; the economic background to such practices has been sufficiently covered in the preceding sections.

In the face of the overwhelming fact and reputation for sharp dealing and dishonesty, the merchants of Tezibazar do not contradict it. They do, however, advance reasons for its prevalence. It is described either as the consequence of government restrictions and taxes that cut profits to the bone; or as an innate quality in Baniyas to want more and more money because wealth is an end in itself; or as the result of a new consumption desire spurred on by the beneficial economic aftermath of the Second World War.

Whatever may be the popularly accepted cause for what most people consider a degeneration in business standards (although the practice is probably not a new phenomenon), there is no generally enunciated cure for it. No agencies, either traditional or otherwise, exist at the moment in Tezibazar which can control or contain the sharp dealings of merchants with each other or with customers from outside the town. In this sense the market is completely unhampered and unhindered in its impersonal operation. A businessman wishing to retrieve credit given to a villager can resort to the informal village leader and *pancayat* for help in regaining his money. In Tezibazar no such office and no such aid exist. When asked who in the town beside himself was against dishonesty and corruption, Yogendra Nath, leader of the local Jana Sangh party and self-styled opponent of corruption in government and business (he held several meetings in 1964 to condemn such behavior), replied, "No one. Since all the people here are Baniyas, they would hardly at heart want to change a situation in which they might begin to profit at any time, even if they do not happen to be doing so at the moment."

Similarly Tribeni Lal Umar said that neither his own Baniya caste nor any other tried to regulate in any fashion the business practices of caste members. This is true at present and was the case in the past: "I feel very much that it is unfortunate my caste brothers have not laid down rules for proper business behavior and honesty. But the reason is that all rich men in my caste as in all others are completely dishonest, and that is why they are rich. So who will hear any plea for reform?"

One incident illustrating the lack of town control over dishonest business practices had to do with a dispute concerning silver ornaments. Cunni Lal, a large-scale *sraf* (jeweler), had some dealings with a *sonar* (an ornament maker, who in this case happened also to be Sonar by caste) in Varanasi city. He commissioned him to make an ornament of pure silver worth Rs. 200. As is the usual procedure in such transactions, Cunni Lal did not give the *sonar* the required amount of silver to make the ornament. When he received the finished product, the *sraf* returned to the *sonar* equal weight of the raw silver which had been expended in the manufacture plus the labor charge previously agreed upon. On this particular occasion Cunni Lal gave the *sonar* old and broken ornaments instead of a block of silver. These were to be melted down and made into new ornaments. However, shortly after returning home and putting the old ornaments into a fire, the *sonar* allegedly discovered that instead of being of pure silver they were nickel alloy. He immediately brought them back to Cunni Lal and asked him to exchange them for real silver. The jeweler refused, and the dispute began.

The *sonar* had no place to turn to for succor. In this case he could not complain to the police because all dealings between him and Cunni Lal were on a barter basis as described above. (People were always amused when I suggested seeing the police.

Merchants have no faith in police powers unless it be at a price which makes the original injury seem slight.) The *sonar* was in a desperate situation. He had handed over an ornament containing Rs. 200 of silver and received only Rs. 50 of metal in return. He had thus lost much of his capital.

Distraught, the *sonar* first went to one leading jeweler and afterward to another, trying to get them to intercede with Cunni Lal on his behalf. The first merchant said there was no point in trying since Cunni Lal was such a big "Four-Twenty"; the second man refused because he thought the *sonar* should have known better and should now have to accept the consequences of his failure to distinguish silver from alloy. No one doubted that Cunni Lal was responsible and thoroughly unscrupulous, but also no one thought anything could be done. Cunni Lal and his brother were infamous in the market because of such underhanded dealings, and people listed many previous swindles, yet said nothing could be done but to accept them and to be personally cautious. Some individuals expressed disgruntlement regarding the success of these brothers in competition with other, allegedly more honest, jewelers. Yet, even such envy did not motivate any sort of retaliatory or restrictive behavior. Finally, a good friend of Cunni Lal happened along Main Street, and the *sonar* persuaded him to discuss the matter with Cunni Lal. Nobody thought he would be successful or that the *sonar* would get his silver or capital back, and indeed he did not.

This conflict concerned an outsider in Tezibazar, but business squabbles within the town are in no way different. Laksmi Narain Umar and Ram Svarup Agrahari were both provisioners in Naiganj and their shops were only a few doors apart. One morning Ram Svarup's wife (who was, for a woman, unusually involved in business) began to lambast Laksmi Narain from the public vantage of the stoop in front of her shop. She informed all her neighbors that Laksmi Narain was underselling her by cheating his customers. She added in explanation that he drilled holes in factory-sealed *dalda* cans and extracted a minute amount of the shortening, which he then sold loose. Thus, by giving false weight he could afford to retail his *dalda* a bit cheaper than she could. Her customers were being attracted to the cheaper price, and they did not know about Laksmi Narain's deception. Afterward, she told me the reason she had made this vilification a public matter was that "when a dispute like this breaks out, there is no influential man or group that people can go to in order to have their dispute settled since no one listens or is concerned." But, she added, she would never join with her competitor to fix a price because each one of them wanted more of the market (even though she admitted there was enough business to fill both their pockets). When asked how she would compete with Laksmi Narain's lower price, she said she would continue to publicize his chicanery while she herself remained honest. I later asked a number of people whether her public denunciation of the fraudulent practices of her neighbor would have any effect. They doubted this and concluded that in any case most people would assume they were both dishonest; not even a public display of one's grievances brings relief or even sympathy.

The matter of price fixing which I raised with Ram Svarup's wife is another indication of the lack of controls in the Tezibazar market, in this case of controls conducive to the merchants' increased profit. I was told that in the large cities the *sonar*s had associations to supervise their business dealings and guarantee them a good price.[1] Thus the dispute between Cunni Lal and the *sonar* would have taken a different turn had it been in Varanasi. In Tezibazar, however, as one informant said, "Everybody is out for his own gain alone, and no one wants to join with anyone else in matters of business."

The one existing internal regulation of the Tezibazar market has to do with the periodic (and infrequent) calling of *hartals*. These are days on which, out of reverence to some recently departed national figure or as a political protest, all shops close their doors and refuse to transact business. Two such occasions took

[1] D. R. Gadgil reports the existence in Poona of associations of brass and copper utensil merchants; *Poona: A Socio-Economic Study, Part 1, Economic* (1945), pp. 138–139.

place in Tezibazar during my stay. The first, on Friday, March 20, 1964, was called by the Jana Sangh party to protest both the high price of food grains and other basic commodities and a recently instituted property tax (the *bhumi-bhavan kar*) in Uttar Pradesh. By about 10 A.M. almost every shop in the town was closed, even food stores, and those which had not actually shut their doors were not doing any business. The enforcement of the *hartal* was accomplished by roving bands of young men who saw to it that all business was halted. They met little opposition. People said that not even at the time of Gandhi's death had such a complete *hartal* been observed in Tezibazar. They also suggested that the Jana Sangh had chosen an exceedingly favorable day for the *hartal*. It was a Friday, one day after the big market of Thursday, when business was always quite slack and particularly at this season. Most businessmen saw no reason to disobey the Jana Sangh's ultimatum; it would not have been especially profitable to stay open.

The second *hartal* was called out of deference for Prime Minister Jawaharlal Nehru. On Thursday, May 28—the usual market day in the middle of the best business season—a total *hartal* was announced by the Notified Area committee in honor of Nehru's memory. A gang of adolescents, some young men, and an occasional adult roamed the streets to enforce the closing. Several unfortunate incidents such as beatings and even stock damage occurred to recalcitrant merchants who did not want to miss the business opportunity. At one point the "vigilantes" seemed to have become a completely unrestrained body and went howling and brandishing staves up and down Main Street. Still, people complained that business was being done surreptitiously. A shopkeeper would invite a customer into the back of his shop and sell him goods there. Those who did not sell merchandise thought it perfectly correct to accept payment from creditors who had come in from the villages—although they also did so secretly. Even in the face of the strongest group enforcement of desired business practices, some of the Tezibazar merchants chose not to acknowledge it as binding upon them. It should be mentioned, however, that at 1:30 P.M., when Nehru's funeral began and in the heat of midday, all business did stop.

These examples illuminate the lack of any traditional regulation—either by caste or town—of the market in Tezibazar, whether in its dishonest or, what amounts to the same thing, competitive aspects. It also exemplifies another aspect of the lack in the town of community and cohesion: the fact that the economic order disperses group interests into trade competition, that the market structure of the town leaves little room for sentiment or behavior aside from personal or family aggrandizement.

CHAPTER 9

Commerce and Family

Clearly, then, in Tezibazar the conduct of the market proceeds without inhibition and quite impersonally, defined and channeled only by special conditions peculiar to the Indian and local economy. Such organization contrasts sharply with the structure of *individual* businesses. Just as the Baniya castes have retained their pre-eminent commercial positions in a modernizing market situation, so, too, trading concerns have maintained an overwhelmingly familial bias in capitalization and organization, in profit taking and cost setting.

BUSINESS FAMILIES

Slightly more than 53 percent of the total business families and slightly more than 36 percent of the business population are organized in nuclear families or as individuals living alone (single man or woman, or man or woman with immature children). About 46 percent of the families and slightly less than 64 percent of the population live in joint or extended families (two or more males above 18 years of age).[1] However, only about 53 percent of the joint families are anything more than simple stem ones— that is, father and mature son, a very minimal form of jointness. The average family size is 6.68 persons. (For these and other figures see Table 18 and Chart 1.) The family size of the average town resident is 6.48. This figure corresponds closely to the 1951

[1] I have used Mayer's definition of joint family: a household wherein there are two or more adult males (males over 18 years old); Adrian Mayer, *Caste and Kinship in Central India* (1960), p. 181.

Table 18A. Family organization of businessmen

	No.	%	Population	%
Nuclear families	277	53.37	1,255	36.21
Joint families	242	46.63	2,210	63.79
Total	519	100	3,465	100

Table 18B. Number of adult males in joint families (males over 18)

	No. of adult males					Total
	2	3	4	5	6	
No. of families	141(28) *	71	24	3	3	242

* Figure in parentheses indicates the number of two-adult joint families which are not stem, that is, which consist of two brothers or similar organization.

Note: This table is of families of residence only. Individuals considered joint family members but permanently or semi-permanently removed from the actual household were not tabulated.

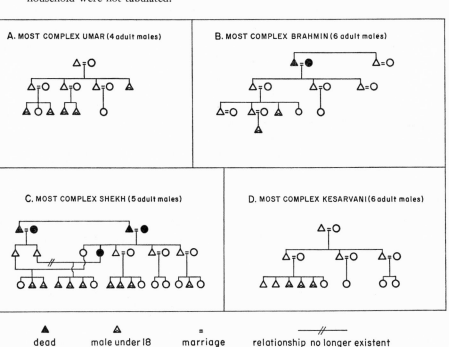

Chart 1. Examples of complex joint families

census figure of 6.4 for urban families in Jaunpur district.[2] The same source, however, lists the average rural family size as 5.5—a figure in strong contradiction to my average of 7.96 for the nonresident business population (which is almost entirely from the surrounding rural area). This discrepancy points to an important economic aspect of the business done by rural commuters in Tezibazar. They are not motivated or forced to start concerns in the town because of poverty but, instead, because their above-average wealth allows them to branch out into a new economic sphere even though their businesses tend to be small and marginal (see Chapter 7, the section on "Immigrants and Commuters"). Thus, the Camars in this group are wealthy enough to perform their traditional services of shoe repairing and leather working. Those who are not so well placed are forced into the lowest economic stratum of the town as unskilled manual laborers. Similarly, many of the smaller ex-zamindars in the rural area have transferred wealth in land to commercial enterprises in town. The above-average size of the nonresident families is therefore an indication of the greater than average wealth of the rural families involved in town business.

Of the thirty-three Umar, Kesarvani, and Kalvar merchants interviewed in the second survey, there were twenty individuals who could possibly be joint with their fathers or brothers: that is, either their fathers or one or more brothers were still alive. The actual organization of these twenty was: joint with father or father and brothers, 5; joint with brothers (father dead), 3; separate from father or father and brothers, 4; separate from brothers (father dead), 8. Twelve men who were not joint with their fathers or brothers or where this was not a possibility had one or more adult sons. Of these men, eleven were joint with their adult son or sons, and one man was separated from his adult son. These figures indicate the greater persistence of the joint family structure based on father-son organization over that based on a community of brothers. This fact is also demonstrated by

[2] Census of India 1951, *District Population Statistics, Uttar Pradesh: No. 29 Jaunpur District.*

the preponderance of stem families (based on father and adult son) over any other form of two-adult-males joint family organization, 113 families to 28 (see Table 18B and Chart 1).

FAMILY BUSINESSES

The business survey indicated that no major proportion of commercial activity in Tezibazar is supra-familial. There was only one case of a joint stock company (of shoemakers), and it was owned by nonresidents. Only thirty-five cases, or 6.17 percent of the total concerns in the sample, were partnerships (see Table 19). This figure is deceptive, however, because 40 percent of these partnerships are pseudo-partnerships in the social sense. That is, they are legally organized as partnerships even though all members belong to the same joint family.[3] Such a measure tends to save the family from high taxes since the partners pay as individuals, each with his own exemptions. Since the total profits are thus divided into a number of shares, each individual usually falls into a lower income bracket.[4] This device is used almost entirely by large wholesale or retail firms. Discounting this sort of pseudo-partnership, one finds that only 3.70 percent of the total businesses in the town are real partnerships—a significant indication of the overwhelmingly familial locus of commercial concerns. In my survey of Baniya merchants, of thirty-two respondents only nine, or 28.12 percent, had ever been involved in partnerships in the course of their business careers, and of these partnerships all but two lasted less than five years.

This avoidance of partnerships in favor of family is neither limited to Tezibazar nor new to India. Gadgil writing about the organization of trade in 1750 reports, "The unit of establishment was ordinarily everywhere the family. It was also usually the

[3] Official or legal recognition of a business comes from paying sales tax or from income tax. The latter is levied on any individual earning more than Rs. 3,000 yearly, or any joint family whose income exceeds Rs. 6,000 annually. See I. S. Gulati and K. S. Gulati, *The Undivided Hindu Family: Its Tax Privileges*, p. 9.

[4] *Ibid.*, pp. 32–33.

Table 19. Business partnerships

Organization	No. of firms	No. of partners per firm					Type of business *			Caste of partners and relationship, if any
		2	3	4	5	6	w	r	m	
1. By same joint family	14	5	5	1	2†	1	12	1	1	Umar 7, Brahmin 2, others 3
2. By brothers or fathers/sons not in same joint family	8	2	2	4†			2	5	1	Umar 2, others 3 (all brothers) Kalvar (father & sons)
3. By other relatives, non-joint	3	3					1		2	Umar (sons of real sisters) Shekh (sons of real brothers) Ahir (men whose wives were real sisters)
4. By non-related members of the same caste	1		1					1		Umar
5. By members of different caste but same status category	3		3				2		1	Umar-Kalvar, Pal-Kurmi, Julaha-Curihar
6. By members of different status categories	6	5†	1				1	3	2	Muslim-Thakur, Vaisya-Thakur, Vaisya-Kisan
Total	35	19	8	5	2	1	18	12	5	28 families or sets of partners

* w = wholesale, r = rental, m = mill.

† In these cases, there is multi-firm ownership by one or more families or partnerships.

traditional Hindu joint family. . . . No forms like that of a continuous joint stock venture appear to have emerged, though *ad hoc* or short-period partnerships . . . were common." [5]

Table 19 indicates that partnerships formed between caste mates other than relatives are quite limited and seems to substantiate informants' statements that business acumen rather than caste membership is primary in forming partnerships. The same is true for the kinship factor outside the joint family, even though 31 percent of the partnerships are formed between non-joint relatives. Most of these cases result from the dissolution of formerly joint families without division of business interests (because the total capital was not sufficient to allow all to set up independently). Only 8.57 percent of the partnerships link parties who have kin ties but who were never members of the same joint family or even related patrilineally. Only 28.77 percent of the partnerships occur among partners who are not kin.

Although partnerships may be entered into for other reasons, most such firms are formed because of lack of capital. People think of them as unfortunate but necessary ventures, by which no matter who the partner (partners) may be—kinsman or not—the individual commits himself to a great deal of potential trouble. No one outside the joint family can be expected to suppress his own interests in favor of another's, and this credo applies as much or even more to business partners as to anyone else. The degree to which Tezibazar businessmen avoid partnerships is clearly demonstrated by the survey figures.

Another method of tax evasion similar to that of the pseudo-partnership is the establishment of two or more legally separate firms within the multi-businesses of a single joint family. Again, only large, sophisticated businesses use this device. In Tezibazar twelve families controlling twenty-six firms resort to this practice. Sometimes the devices of pseudo-partnership and pseudo-firm are combined, and two firms organized and recorded in different names are owned by the same joint family, with mem-

---

[5] Gadgil, *op. cit.* (1959), p. 34.

bers of the joint family as partners in both. An example of such a business organization is given in Chart 2. Firm 1's official name is Makhundi Lal (*a*)–Gaya Prasad (*b*) and consists of a partnership of a man (*a*) and his four sons (*b, c, d, e*). Firm 2 is legally known as Gaya Prasad (*b*)–Suraj Lal (*c*) and consists of partners *b* and *c*, the two adult sons of *a*.

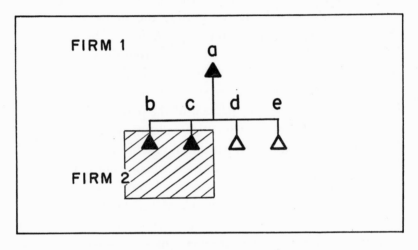

▲ over 18
△ under 18

Chart 2. A form of multi-firm partnership organization. Firm 1 consists of a man and his four sons as partners. Firm 2 consists of this man's two eldest sons as partners. All individuals are members of the same joint family.

Business and Household

If a Tezibazar merchant is asked what his business profit is, even an unfalsified reply would not be a correct answer to the question, because profit is usually conceived of in two ways: (1) the amount or percentage added on to any one item above its wholesale or dealer cost, that is, markup, or (2) the amount of money remaining after all business and household expenses are paid, that is, savings. Divergence from "Western" definitions results primarily from lack of differentiation between business and household. It is foreign to the business and social thinking of most merchants in Tezibazar to distinguish business expenses from household outlay and business profit from savings. Even when a trader maintains several businesses, he does not compute the net profit from each—if, indeed, he bothers to compute anything. When he pays household expenses or even some business costs (such as building repair, travel, and so forth), he treats household and business as a unit and subtracts his financial needs from the combined gross profit of the several businesses.[6] Given a system of familially organized businesses, the occasional partnership where such computation may be made is the exception rather than the norm. Even in partnerships, for the most part, profit is not calculated as if the business were a separate entity from its owners; rather the procedure is simply to divide all income in half and to disburse funds to meet bills equally from the individually maintained capital stocks of the partners.

Two factors contribute to this lack of separation of household from business. One is the way income and sales taxes are computed. Instead of filling in his income, a merchant in India is asked only the amount of his total sales, and the income tax officer computes the correct tax from this figure. Another conditioning factor is that many businessmen—particularly the smaller ones—do not keep books.

The nature of capitalization is further proof of the primarily familial organization of Tezibazar business. Of thirty-two Baniya merchants, twenty-six (81.25 percent) indicated they had received their starting capital from their fathers (21), mothers (3), or brothers (2). Only six men began their concerns in other than direct transfers of capital from family members, and of these only three started on the basis of loans.

[6] In this sense, one might argue that multiple businesses cannot exist by definition. But this technical point ignores the fact that some merchants control larger parts of the market than others; that separate accounts are often kept; that a dispersion of family labor is usually required to handle such multi-businesses, and that they are so looked upon by the local populace.

Price and Depreciation

There are other important familial dimensions to town business. Profit setting is in large measure influenced by a merchant's subsistence expectations and his desired amount of savings. Business depreciation is also absorbed in the savings of the family rather than taken out as an expense of the firm.

A large wholesale cloth dealer (whose procedure is undoubtedly more consciously rationalized than would be characteristic of the majority of Tezibazar businessmen) described the common technique for deciding at what profit to sell his goods. First he adds up the cost of a bale of cloth, its transportation charges, taxes, and so forth, and then adds a set amount—for instance, one anna in the rupee—to cover his other expenses (which include those of both household and business). This means a gross profit of 6.25 percent, probably an underestimate. In determining the markup, no accounting is made for buildings or shops, either their construction or repair. These expenses are thought to come out of the "profit" (savings), and thus this and other equipment are not depreciated through direct markup on goods.

Of course, few businesses in Tezibazar require high capital investment goods whose financing is difficult or whose economic burden for the purchaser is large. The biggest debt among thirty-three Baniya merchants was one *lakh* owed by a large wholesaler as inventory advances rather than nonsalable equipment. No other debts were equally high: 53.13 percent of the sample respondents said they had no debts; 18.75 percent were in debt for Rs. 1,000 or less; 15.62 percent owed Rs. 1,001–5,000; 12.50 percent owed over 5,000.

The manner in which the profit percentage for a business is computed is, thus, not completely rationalized. It is set in terms of the merchants' past experience regarding how much they sell in a year and what their total household and business expenses are, plus what they want to end up with as savings. In other words, under normal conditions the profit margin largely mirrors an individual family's demands in relation to consumption and savings and is controlled by the consumption demands of its competitors and the general economic state of the area. Naturally in black-market times the only conditioner of profit is what the market will bear, but in other periods the consumption and savings expectation of the businessmen condition their expectations of profit. Such a situation is no doubt similar in type to the practices of small businessmen in many other areas.

Some people—those with larger families or more expensive business property—need a greater rate of savings or profit to cover their overhead, however. Given the extreme price competition, these people are faced with one of two choices: either to lower their subsistence requirements and family expenses or to adulterate, to chicane, and to grant large amounts of credit to overcome perception of dishonesty by the customers. Many smaller merchants who lack such capital lower their subsistence requirements—another facet of the complex I have delineated previously. The larger merchants, however, can often successfully overcome this limitation by the second method. Naturally, too, wholesalers are more immune than retailers to excessive price competition because of their style of business and the scarcity of numbers.

CITY, TOWN, AND VILLAGE

After all that has been said about the limitations and difficulties of the town market, it may be well, at this point, to summarize the Baniya merchant's attitude toward other locales and his reasons for remaining in Tezibazar, overcrowded and overcompetitive though it may be.

The Baniya merchants' appreciation of the differences between cities, towns, and villages and their evaluation of these different areas represent a combination of realistic and idealized notions. Idealization particularly works toward shaping their conception of the village. In their description of villages and in direct statements, the Baniyas surveyed made it clear that they thought of Tezibazar as much closer to the city than to the village both in terms of physical amenities and social relations.

Some respondents did not even bother to differentiate city and town in reference to Tezibazar. Their concept was a simple dualism of the *dihat*, or rural countryside, as against the *sahr*, which subsumed both cities and towns.

Baniyas preferred villages to cities for health reasons: the "air" is good in villages, whereas in cities poor sanitation and over-crowding breed mosquitoes and disease. Although they recognized the benefits of such physical facilities in the city as electricity, they did not rate these higher than the more "natural" aspects of village health conditions. They prefer to incur the extra expense for such facilities only in connection with businesses or actual income-earning activities. One man said, "Electricity only allows you to keep your shop open longer." The Tezibazar Baniya merchants often see the village and the peasantry as the only remaining haven of honesty and "simple" qualities in India. They impute to the rural area all the idealized notions and misconceptions that one often hears in India in a much more urbanized atmosphere. They use a different set of valuations, ones which upgrade the ignorance and gullibility of the rural populace, when involved in business dealings with the *dihat*. However, the notions of peasant simplicity and honesty were important in the merchants' positive feelings toward the village and its social framework. The major drawback of the *dihat* in the opinion of the Baniya merchant was that business was poor there because of the limited number of consumers. This consideration outweighed any of the advantages of the village.

The city was primarily admired for its wealth of facilities and entertainments: "All things are found there." People mention better educational media, better medical care, cinemas, and more choice of shops. Most of the respondents characterized the social relations of the city as similar to those which hold in Tezibazar, where every man was interested solely in his own and his immediate family's profit. They also considered the city a good locale for business. As was the case of the village, however, the city had one damning fault which removed it from consideration: besides being overcrowded and bad for health, it was too expensive.

Most people said they preferred to live in a town environment, meaning Tezibazar. In fact, the distinction between Tezibazar and "town" as a type was difficult to communicate, because the merchants themselves rarely make the distinction. My respondents (all but two) wished to live in Tezibazar because it was their "birthplace" or "natal land." This expression of attachment to the town itself is quite strong, and along with it goes an equally powerful hesitancy about leaving the town forever. Very few men of Baniya castes leave Tezibazar for Calcutta or Bombay, whereas eastern Uttar Pradesh is famous for supplying much of the labor force in these cities (the *"bhaiya log"* in Bombay).[7] However, the customary phrasing of this hesitancy as love of one's natal area simply hides a fear of starting afresh in a new locale. The Baniya reply to any suggestion that their business might be better in a new locality is: "We have a shop here and an income from it. Who knows what will be in a new area." For many people it is this fear of moving to a new, unknown location rather than any strong attachment to Tezibazar which promotes adherence to the town and its market. What the Baniyas fear is the economic uncertainty of change, and when they say they prefer to live in Tezibazar because it is their birthplace, they primarily mean it is where their father's business was, and thus where they themselves find security. One man who had come to Tezibazar in a very impoverished condition and at an early age once told me that he preferred to live here because it was his birthplace. When I reminded him of the contradiction, he replied that I had misunderstood, and that what he had really meant was that since his home and shop were now in Tezibazar, it was like his birthplace. The conservative, status quo attitude which motivates men to remain in known Tezibazar rather than

[7] I refer here only to migration for commercial reasons. Many more town Baniyas emigrate to take up civil service posts than to change their business location. Even here, the number is probably small compared with other status categories (particularly Kisan and Sudra).

to risk the uncertainties of the outside parallels the subsistence orientation to their business and its profits.

This conservatism does not rest on fear of the outside or ignorance of it nor on any pronounced distaste for the city and its ways (since for economic reasons, potential migration would be toward the cities). Most businessmen left Tezibazar at least six times a year and some as often as sixty or a hundred times, primarily to replenish inventory. Then, too, three people in my survey had traveled either to Rameshwarum, at the very southern tip of the subcontinent, or to Kashmir in the north, and almost all had visited on numerous occasions the pilgrimage centers of Allahabad and Banaras. During the rainy season's slack period, the more adventurous young men organize small outings of a few days to nearby sites. There is no lack of interest in seeing new places or in the adventure of travel. The conservatism that keeps men in Tezibazar or that makes them return there is economic and of a piece with the style in which many of them conceive of and conduct their businesses.

The structure of business in Tezibazar is conditioned primarily by three factors: a large degree of "subsistence" thinking and procedure in capital allocation and investment; a highly competitive market situation based mainly on price, which leads to wide-scale adulteration; a fundamentally familial capitalization of commercial ventures, and a familial conditioning of profit margin and attitudes and definitions of profit. For reasons stemming from the familial aspect of business and its subsistence bias as well as the impoverished and untutored nature of the consuming public, the Tezibazar businessman shows his commercial skill in how effectively he dupes or overcharges his customers, not in how much he risks capital or moves into new lines. The concept of sizing up consumer demand to make a profit is only entertained in the form of the socially illegal charges made in a black market operation or during a time of scarcity. To vantage but not to venture is the motto of the Baniyas of Tezibazar.

The commercial process provides a set of social and economic conditions which at present as well as in the past set sharp limits on town social cohesion. The lack of any restraint upon the excesses of a competitive market and the perception by the individual of a total absence of regulative norms in the economic order indicate the traditionally amorphous condition of the town. This situation is heightened by the containment of most businesses within the joint family and the debilitating effect on larger commercial associations that this naturally implies. As long as the overlords existed, the economic autonomy and unbridled competition of the town merchant castes could be mollified and even subdued. The zamindars were the traditional agencies for the resolution of commercial disputes, the spatial allocation of business concerns, and the bestowal of social status. They were the single institution which bridged the natural anarchy of the town's commercial sphere.

CHAPTER 10

The Role of Politics

Politics, both local and national, looms large in Tezibazar. Most people in the town take special pleasure in narrating the history of political alignments and feuds and of the triumphs and indiscretions of particular figures. Whenever a small group collects in a tea shop or a number of men sit together on the white sheeting of a shop floor, the invariable topic of conversation is politics. As an activity and intrigue politics is also important to many in the town. Some individuals through fear and extremely careful balancing do not become aligned with any group, but their position is highly precarious. If they should need some favor or require help from higher officials, they are forced to seek out one of the big men of the town. This act automatically aligns them with that party—if not in fact, at least in the eyes of the other townsmen. Then, too, if even a distant lineage mate of an uncommitted man is strongly involved in politics or merely an active member of a faction, other people assume this individual to be either his kinsman's advocate or opponent. Where caste or community is the organizational structure of a political group, then mere membership in this large but politically active body can stereotype an individual's role in the town: "He's a Muslim, so naturally he belongs to X's party." Usually only very small men of small families whose allegiance is worth little, or very important men willing to use their wealth to placate both sides, can successfully avoid full-hearted commitment to one or another political group.

Tezibazar people show no distaste for the modern political

process through fear lest it rend the community and replace town cooperation with party fractiousness. Indeed, because the power structure of the town is so completely intertwined with formal political structure at the state level, in contrast to the situation in many Indian villages, people in Tezibazar welcome the contest for political power. No leaders exist in Tezibazar who do not also hold formal political office or aspire to it. No town decision-making body holds sway other than the elected one (although non-office-holding party cronies help). No artificial do-nothing statutory *pancayat* functions in opposition to an operative traditional one. Modern political machinery has filled the vacuum left by the demise of the traditional political structure based on the personal fiat of the large zamindars who controlled the town or surrounding areas.[1] As a result of Tezibazar's necessary acceptance of modern politics and the democratic state has come a concomitant direct merger of town and region in the political realm. This merger, however, has not forced the town to lose its identity but merely to move into a system of complex and multiple political reciprocities and "favors" with district and state party apparatus or political organization.

THE NOTIFIED AREA AND THE HISTORY OF POLITICAL POWER

From its inception in 1907 until 1922, members of the Notified Area committee were appointed by the Jaunpur district magistrate, and the local (Baragaon) *tehsildar* was ex officio Chairman of the council. Both these officials were, of course, civil service appointees of the British colonial government. Throughout these years official selection of townsmen to fill the N.A. seats reflected the actualities of power within Tezibazar. The zamindars —particularly the Muslim ones—held all the reins of authority.

---

[1] In the succeeding discussion I analyze Tezibazar politics as if the political unit was coterminous with the town. Of course, the Notified Area is the official sphere of political jurisdiction. In terms both of population and wealth and also of leadership and of the groups defining local politics, however, the town in effect is the political unit.

In 1922 for the first time the N.A. committee was elected by limited adult franchise and secret ballot. Four seats were to be filled, and a Chairman (who need not have stood for public election) was to be chosen by a majority of council members. This particular election signaled the end of one form of political organization and contest in the town and the start of another. Two major transformations took place: (1) 1922 was the last year when the old (Muslim) zamindars—that is, the Khan and Shah families—were powerful enough to challenge the rising number of Baniya small zamindars and thus signaled the end to town supervision by these overlord families; and (2) in this year intra-caste and lineage disputes began to move into the town political arena under the impetus of the electoral system. A similar process has recently been noted in Indian villages where the breakdown of institutions of traditional caste and village control leads to a re-emergence of feuds and caste conflict within the formal machinery of the state.[2] In Tezibazar this process dates back to 1922 and goes hand in hand with the growing impotency of the zamindar-overlords.

The previous twenty years had seen a gradual deterioration in the status of the Muslim zamindars and the rise to power of the Baniya merchants who had recently purchased extensive land-holdings. By 1922 the erstwhile leader of the Muslim cause, Ahmad Ullah Khan, had succeeded in decimating his family fortune as well as in debilitating the political position of the Muslim zamindars.

Nowadays people say that forty years ago Muslim-Baniya or Hindu conflict was of the same type as at present. At times, violent conflicts did break out between the two communal segments. These were short-lived riots, however, brought on by the sentiment of communalism implicit in separate religious faiths. Indeed, for the most part in Tezibazar when people speak of

[2] See Ralph H. Retzlaff, *Village Government in India*, pp. 114–125, *passim*; Mildred Stroop Luschinsky, "Problems of Culture Change in the Indian Village," *Human Organization*, XXII (1963), pp. 73–74; Kusum Nair, *Blossoms in the Dust*, pp. 93–97.

Muslim-Baniya conflict in the past, they are referring to contests between various Muslim and Umar Baniya zamindars. Neither of these two groups was organized communally at this time, nor did they resort to this type of entity for power or support.

The noncommunal nature of these groups forty years ago is indicated by the other development of the 1922 election: the entrance into the town political sphere of lineage and caste disputes. In that year a member of one Umar lineage opposed the leader of another, and the enmity between these two *khandan,* or maximal lineages, continues today. In 1922 a purely internal caste conflict spread into the political field, an event prototypical of much of present-day town political behavior as well as a first indication of weakening intracaste social control and political structure. One of the Umar lineages involved in this conflict consisted of the Umar zamindars who opposed their Muslim counterparts. On either political side, lineages and castes in opposition to one group or the other gathered with little concern for community. The Umar lineage which opposed the Umar zamindar lineage sided with the Muslim landowners; Muslims, on a caste and lineage or individual basis, who disliked the Muslim zamindars joined ranks with the Umar Baniya zamindars. Even in 1922, however, the Muslims tended to be more unified than the Baniyas, perhaps because they had fewer such social impediments as limited commensality to remind them of their separateness. Nevertheless, the strong internal unity and communal organization of the Muslim group seen in Tezibazar today did not exist, nor was there any leadership of the Muslim whole based on the ideological utilization of such a unity. Religious alignment had not yet crystallized into a politically significant form.

During the succeeding years, as the powers and prestige of the Muslim landowners declined, the formal political machinery came increasingly under Baniya control, particularly that of Umar zamindars. At the same time, intracaste and lineage feuds increasingly ramified into the political sphere. This progression was accompanied by the rising influence of the moneyed but propertyless big merchants. By the beginning of World War II, there were four elected members on the municipal council and three nominated by the government. The chairman was still chosen by vote of the entire council rather than by popular election. From 1943–1947 the N.A. committee in Tezibazar consisted of two Srivastavas (Kayasths) one of whom was Chairman; two Umar; two Muslims and one Camar (all nominated). The two nominated Muslims were members of the old zamindar families. The British were subsidizing these Muslims' power claims as a counter to Hindu independence sentiments, even though Muslim influence was at its lowest ebb in the town at this time.

With independence in 1947 came many changes, the most important of which was the broadening of the electorate to include all adults. Even more than in prewar times, caste and lineage conflicts continued to play a major role in determining electoral allegiances and enmities. More important, the political realities of population now became meaningful, and a structured Muslim communal apparatus emerged to meet the challenge of a Hindu majority. Communal rather than caste or lineage political group formation on the local level came from persecution of Muslims and to a much smaller extent of Harijans, or in the very recent case of the Baniyas, a "backlash" fear of Muslim incursions due to the supposed liberality of the Congress government. These communal groupings in Tezibazar mirror in a smaller and differently organized fashion what has been recognized as characterizing Indian district and state political groups. Tezibazar comprises a midway point between village political organization involving caste or caste factions and that of the district or state based on large "caste-like" communal voting bodies such as Thakur or Baniya which are based on sentiment rather than group organization. Many politicians in the town interpret their own role and that of Tezibazar politics in the district and state as an interplay of communal factors. Other equally astute and sophisticated individuals describe town politics only in terms of caste and Umar intracaste lineage hostilities. That both these interpretations fit the Tezibazar political scene indicates its position straddling localized caste and regional communal politics.

Perhaps the most significant change brought by Independence was the creation of an entire and complete structure of government—from national level through state and district, *tehsil*, town, and village strata—wherein Tezibazar was given a definite (if limited) position. Under the British hegemony, to be sure, district boards and legislative councils had been established, but in powers, appeal, and backing these bodies were legally and by the nature of their acceptance limited to the more colonially bound and anglophile members of his Britannic Majesty's Indian territories. The democratic, universal adult suffrage format introduced by the independent government of India also brought with it the phenomenon of national or regional political parties —for the most part in the early days, the Congress party. National independence, because of those economic changes brought on by the Second World War delineated earlier, saw the complete replacement of the old Baniya zamindar class by the big Baniya merchants. It also introduced a new type of political figure or desirable political quality: individuals having contact with outside regional party apparatus and leaders.

Since Independence, the articulation of local politics with regional and even national politics has become an increasingly close one, wherein leaders on both levels look up or down the organizational ladder to gain their ends. In Tezibazar some men become powerful in large measure because they have entree into the inner circles of the Congress party on a district level or because they have contact with various U.P. state legislators. Town political groups form and dissolve in accordance with the permutations of faction within the Congress party or the U.P. government. Increasingly, too, higher level political and party leaders must be receptive to the wishes of their associates in the town. Their powers are often called upon to settle purely local tussles or to remove a disliked government official assigned to the town.

In the years 1948–1953, eleven elected and three nominated

members constituted the Notified Area committee. Although the 1948 election was held on a non-party basis, the Chairman as well as many of the council members were known as Congress party sympathizers. The Chairman was Sita Ram Dube, a Brahmin; six Umars were on the council, one Kalvar, two Muslims, one Thakur, one Kurmi, one Camar, and one Srivastava (the latter a woman who never attended meetings; she is the only woman ever to sit, in this case figuratively only, on the council). The last three individuals were government appointees.

In October, 1953, a new election was held, the first and last one in which the electorate directly chose the N.A. Chairman. The voting public picked Tribeni Lal Umar, an ex-zamindar who had been Chairman and had served on the committee many times between 1914–1930, and whose prestige in the town was and is very high. Tribeni Lal as an independent contested the election with Dube, who this time ran on the Congress ticket, and also with a Muslim independent. The election of this leading Umar as Chairman unleashed a great amount of political activity and maneuvering, and the ensuing events of this period which I shall note later have left an extreme bitterness that still partially conditions town politics. It was at this time that the powers of outside political groups were utilized to revoke an internal decision of the town populace or at least a sizable segment of it. Since then the employment of such external devices has gained ascendancy and no longer do these only impede and activate local politics; now these outside contacts condition and define internal groupings. The N.A. council under the chairmanship of Tribeni Lal consisted of eleven members, all elected: four Umar, two Muslim, one Kesarvani, one Teli, one Kalvar, one Kurmi, and one Camar. This year marked the absence of all traditional Muslim leaders even as nominated members, and their replacement by a new sort of man: the aggressive communal representative who owed his position to wealth rather than to family antecedents. The committee members in 1953 were not all of the same political opinion as the Chairman, since the latter's election in this year had been completely independent of the election of members. There was great dissension in the council, and in April, 1956, one group carried a vote of no-confidence against the Chairman. The latter was replaced in an interim capacity by the council's Vice-Chairman, and a by-election in 1956 brought back into power the Brahmin Dube who had governed the council from 1948–1953. The by-election was on a formally nonparty basis. Dube stayed in office until late 1957, when new general elections were held which raised to power the committee that controlled the town during my stay.

In the elections of 1957 another formal political party, the Praja Socialists, entered town politics and contested with the Congress party led by Moti Lal Umar, the present Chairman. The Congress was overwhelmingly successful, and the eleven members of the council as well as their chosen Chairman were all Congressmen. When I reached Tezibazar, one committee member, a Muslim Julaha, had died, and no replacement had been made for him. The council then consisted of Moti Lal, Chairman, and five others, all Umar; one Kalvar; one Bhuj; one Muslim Halvai; one Kurmi; and one Camar.

This committee had tenure for only four years, but twice their term had been extended, once for the Chinese emergency and another time for no reason I could discover. Even in 1964 the announced municipal elections were postponed twice. In April, 1964, they were indefinitely canceled because of an open factional split in the ruling Congress party of Uttar Pradesh. These decisions were, of course, those of the state legislature, and the town had little say in the matter. Finally, in November, 1964, after I had left Tezibazar, the Notified Area elections were held. Three groups competed for seats: the Jana Sangh party, whose membership in this year was almost the same as that of the Praja Socialists of 1958 and therefore might better be called the party of opposition or "political brand X"; the Congress party; and a number of self-declared independents who, in fact, were bound by loyalty to one political personage. The Congress party again swept the field, and the incumbent Chairman was retained. The present committee consists of five Umar, one Kesarvani, one

Kalvar, two Muslim, one Kurmi, one Camar. The total council membership was reduced to ten, not counting the Chairman, who again was chosen indirectly. In 1964 there were only four town wards: Sahibganj and Naiganj were formally combined (in Chapter 2 I have retained the previous organization as it more clearly set apart Sahibganj from Old Town). The merger of these two wards was beneficial to the Congress party and detrimental to the Jana Sangh. As we shall see, the Kesarvani and small Baniya castes back the latter party in general, and they are primarily resident in Sahibganj. The Muslim population which usually votes Congress, however, is massed in Naiganj. Thus, the merger of these two wards canceled out any advantage the Jana Sangh might have received because of Kesarvani support and gave the Congress the opportunity to use Muslim electoral weight to good advantage in both areas.

It should not be thought that because a man is elected to the N.A. council, he automatically gains a voice in town affairs or is influential even in his own caste or community. The present Camar member, who has been on the committee since 1957 and who sells vegetables in the dirt road before the current Chairman's house, is hardly more than a figurehead in his own grouping. He does not take part in the activities of the N.A.; he is only pointed to as an example of the new spirit of India. His lack of power is easily contrasted with the ability of equally low Muslim leaders to gain their own ends. The unity and organization of the communal political base in either case determines to a large extent the effectiveness of an elected representative: in the case of the Camar, it is minimal; in the Muslim case, it is exceedingly strong.

The listing of castes shows a similarity of appointment over many years, with the Umar holding a consistent and preponderant plurality. There is also often a continuity of family and individual membership. Since 1943, sixty-six individual seats, counting the Chairman's place, have been open on the Notified Area council. Only twenty-eight different individuals or families have filled these posts. Every year since 1948 has seen at least one place occupied by each of the two leading Umar lineages, and sometimes they have been joined by a third. For the same length of time, one or the other or even both of the factions within the leading Umar lineage of the town have gained a voice in the council. Every year since 1948 has seen a Kalvar on the committee, and each time it has been a different member of the same joint family. On a different plane, a Muslim elected on the basis of communal backing has held office in the town every year since 1953. This continued and repetitive arrangement or allocation of seats by intralineage faction, lineage, caste, and finally community gives a strong insight into the more or less corporate groups from which politicians and town leaders derive their support. Chapter 11 analyzes the organization of these groups in detail.

FRUITS OF VICTORY

In this account no consideration has been given to the motivations or personal qualities of the town leadership. Such matters are not really germane to my argument. In one sense, however, individual motivation is important to an understanding of what is so attractive about town politics. The question then is: Why does a man want to be a politician, and what does he gain from political victory?

An individual elected to the N.A. council acquires a certain prestige from his office. There is, of course, the formal recognition of his new status by appropriate titles of deference, a point of etiquette meticulously followed in Tezibazar. To his name is attached the term "member," and he is addressed as "Member-Sahab." The more tangible aspects of this prestige, however, have their basis in fear of the powers this man wields as a N.A. committee representative. In this sense, then, the discussion of prestige is only an aspect of a consideration of the punitive and permissive powers of the elected officeholder.

Taxation

Individuals want to be elected to the N.A. committee because through it they gain powers, foremost among which is that of municipal taxation. A man whose political group has been elected to the N.A. expects his municipal impost to be discounted according to the value and extent of his political services. Similarly, losing a political battle or enmity with committee members brings on a substantial financial loss in the sense that higher taxes are levied on defeated political candidates and their allies. It was said that one council member's brother who was a very wealthy man paid only Rs. 12 a year, whereas a Bhuj whose actual earnings were only Rs. 1,000 annually paid Rs. 100 because he belonged to the opposite party. Technically, the N.A. committee members themselves cannot benefit their own purses in this fashion because their assessment is made by the *tehsildar*, a government official, but it would be foolish to imagine that this officer would jeopardize his relations with the committee and especially the Chairman by an overly heavy levy. Of the eight men who now pay the highest tax allowed (Rs. 200 per annum), three are declared opponents of the present committee and only one is an avowed advocate.

The political basis of tax assessment and payment has profound effect on the public attitude toward the municipal impost. Even were town Baniya and other merchants willing to allocate part of their income to urban improvement, the political nature of the tax would deter them. As the Chairman noted, "Once people give their tax money, they think of it as lost and useless. They do not expect to derive any benefits from it." Another man said, "No one is willing to give to civic improvement when the tax burden is so uneven."

Another aspect of this situation is the use of taxation as a political football by the "loyal opposition." Any opponent of the current ruling clique in the town refuses to pay his assessment, whether fair or unfair, as a protest and embarrassment to the committee. In the most undisguised fashion the municipal tax is made a means of political retribution or reward. In 1962, Tribeni Lal refused to pay his municipal levy until the arrears of the N.A. members and their political friends were removed. His cow was finally confiscated and auctioned under official auspices to retrieve the amount of the taxes. The collection of town duties for civic improvement is the last reason for the municipal tax. The cause of town progress is further hindered by the reluctance of almost all Baniyas to contribute to any project beyond their respective joint families and businesses.

The fact that any house, shop, or other construction contemplated in the town must be cleared through the N.A. committee offers another avenue for exercise of retribution against local political adversaries or for benefit toward one's own followers. There have been a number of cases over the last few years where house construction has been halted or delayed by politically motivated opposition from one or another council member. And just as in the matter of municipal taxes, the political "outs" attempt to embarrass the current administration in this realm, too. For example, when a site was selected for a public construction project and compensation offered its owner, Sita Ram Dube began a legal suit against the Notified Area's "encroachment" even though he had no connection with the property. To be sure, some people said that this spot had been originally selected especially to embarrass and, through low compensation, to hurt financially one of Dube's followers.

Perhaps the most significant advantage accruing to an N.A. incumbent is access to government officials and to political favoritism from the regional party machinery, especially if the latter happens to control state administration. Local people claim that members of the N.A. council have used their position to grab pieces of land or to validate a hazy claim for one of their friends or themselves. The committee members have first access to the *tehsildar* and other lower-level officials who often rule in such matters and who are equally frequently under the control of the N.A. Chairman. The *tehsildar* usually bows to the will of the Chairman, who can make it uncomfortable for a civil servant by appealing to the sitting M.L.A. (Member of the Legislative Assembly) of the *tehsil* or, if this man is of a different party, to other M.L.A.'s on the state level. Thus *tehsil* decisions and awards usually favor the group currently ruling in the town. In 1964 all the government-appointed fair price shops were managed by individuals who were part of the local Congress organization. In an economy becoming increasingly circumscribed by official licenses and regulations, it is to the merchant's advantage to be able to influence those who oversee the distribution and enforcement of such curtailments on free trade.

There are many allegations concerning the misconduct of the present town leaders and their use of government contacts to gain economic advantages. It is said that, besides controlling all the fair price shops, local Congressmen also circumvent them by selling governmentally supplied goods at the prevailing market rate rather than at the lower prices set by the administration. Such accusations reflect the obvious shortage of food grains in the fair price shops in summer, 1964. At the same time they voice the expectations of the Tezibazar public regarding why a man becomes a politician. One ex-Congressite stated it succinctly: "The Congress party is the thieves' party. In any town the biggest crooks are also the leading Congressmen." Even were another party's name to be substituted and even were the party imbued with equal powers, the equation of politics with dishonesty and illegal privilege would remain intact, for such statements reflect the attitudes of the general populace and, accordingly, the actual behavior of those who can achieve political position. As Mahavir Prasad, a leader of the opposition for many years, opined:

If the Jana Sangh were to gain power [now], they would follow their principles for three or four years, but after that they, too, would fall into the same corruption, although not as much as the Congress since they would not be as all-powerful. The only solution is to start educating India's youth in spirituality and honesty. A whole new frame of mind has to come over the country.

CHAPTER 11

The Organization of
Political Groups

All my informants agreed that really only two parties existed in Tezibazar—regardless of the number of national parties represented, or the number of leaders, or the number of caste and communal groups. In respect to the normal and striven for political situation, there are indeed only two parties, but it is often difficult to tell what their composition will be from year to year and, in election times, from month to month. They are a mélange of lineage feuds, caste conflicts, communal oppositions, and outside contacts with all the resultant disputing groups coalescing and changing allegiance *ad hoc*. How they will combine at any particular time is a subtle mixture of all the motivations behind the respective groups, dominated by a bare quality of opposition. The parties themselves are almost totally amorphous.

In the succeeding sections my interest lies in the delimiting of these groups, their origin and organization, their composition and political control. When I speak about lineage and caste bases to politics, I will not be concerned with all lineages or all castes but only with those which are meaningful entities upon the political scene. Almost every lineage or caste in Tezibazar has maverick members who from feud or frustration oppose their natal group. The important point is that such individuals or even small bodies of discontents must attach themselves, albeit in a tangential way, to one or the other of the active political groups —which in turn are not transformed in any significant fashion by the addition of this new membership. Thus the groups I discuss below do not characterize all the elements to be found in Tezibazar politics, but they are the entities which govern the *expression* in group terms of all the elements in the town; and in and of themselves, they directly organize the great majority of politically active individuals.

LINEAGE AND CASTE

In describing the Hari Har Prasad Lohia–Moti Lal dispute, I noted how commentators saw different groups in opposition, and how their judgment was colored by the unit in which they themselves were involved. A man who is on one side of an intracaste lineage feud sees an opponent of another caste merely as an ally or potential ally of the opponent lineage of his own caste. However, the "other-caste" man may view the conflict not as a matter of lineages but of caste versus caste. Thus, the Umar see most disputes as one lineage with its other caste allies arrayed against another lineage and caste allies. The Kesarvani would phrase this as the Kesarvani with the help of a few rebellious Umar (the "other" lineage) against all Umar. The Muslims, were they to take sides in this dispute, would see it as basically a communal conflict between, on the one hand, the Muslims and a few disloyal Baniyas (one Umar faction) versus the Baniya community (the Kesarvani, maverick Umar, and other Baniya groups). This complex superimposition of groups and the changing perception by individuals regarding the intrinsic groups and their organization characterize the political sphere of Tezibazar. It should also be noted that these differential perceptions do not merely represent idiosyncratic divisions of a unified political reality according to individual sensibilities concerning what the organization of politics is or should be. What is really true is that at one and the same time, independently and together, sometimes with, sometimes without, mutual effect or repercussions, all these integral units work to create a unity of action which in Tezibazar is called "politics." These units are not just nebulous categories of ascriptively prejudiced local minds which must see all existence in terms of caste or lineage or community. Tezibazar politics is carried on by groups with more or less corporate electoral and (insofar as they are successful) judicial functions, from which the tenuous image of "party"—whether called "local," "Congress," or nothing—can be deduced by the democratically inclined individual or the liberally educated Indian statesman. Symptomatic of this important distinction is the fact that in its primary meaning the word "party" (the English word is used in Tezibazar) denotes any political grouping based on faction, caste, lineage, or community, and only secondarily the amorphous entities entitled Congress, P.S.P., or Jana Sangh.

Intralineage Political Dispute

In the subsequent discussion of intra- and interlineage political groups, I am referring to a patrilineal exogamous descent group, of maximal generational depth; Chart 4 affords an example. The terms for lineage of whatever dimension commonly heard are *"khandan"* or, rarely, *"parivar"* (which generally refers to the joint or nuclear family). The word *"khandan"* may also be applied to joint family. Consequently, this one term is able to cover both the generational depth and the structural range between minimal and maximal lineages. In the intralineage disputes discussed below, however, both disputant units represent various orders of lineages, but they are rarely called *khandan* by local people, since this term is used only of the complete maximal lineage. In the case of intralineage disputes people refer to the component groups as the "party" of the particular (submaximal) lineage leader. "Party" thus indicates a structure of political conflict and, as such, outweighs or replaces the use of other, kinship terms. Neither minimal nor maximal lineages are named in Tezibazar save by the employment of a leading individual's name. This practice is often confusing, for there may be more than one leading figure in any group. To expedite identification I have chosen names for them.

The "Chairman" *khandan* is the leading maximal lineage among the Umars of Tezibazar and constitutes a powerful entity in town life (see Chart 3). Although it is not the Umar lineage of largest population, it has supplied the Chairman for the N.A. committee for most of the years since its inception. In every year for which I found a listing of the N.A. members, at least one individual and sometimes three came from this *khandan*. Their history is that of large landowners, and they were the Hindu group which assumed on a smaller scale the social control duties

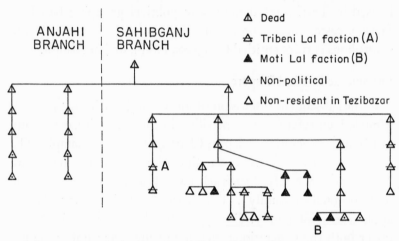

Chart 3: The Chairman lineage. The Chairman lineage is divided into two politically opposed factions led by Tribeni Lal (A) and Moti Lal (B). Only the richer branch of this lineage—resident in Sahibganj—is politically active; the poorer, Anjahi branch is non-political.

of Udai Baks after the latter's death. At the end of the last century the family moved from Anjahi ward to its present location in Sahibganj near the *ram lila* ground. Some members of this lineage still reside in Old Town, but they are poor and relatively unimportant politically. When the ancestors of the present Chairman *khandan* moved, they constructed large, imposing *pakka* buildings on either side of Main Street in central Sahibganj. These still stand, and are presently occupied by the groups in political opposition within the lineage. The lineage factions joked that they merely had to step outside their doors to gaze upon their opponents across the street—that is, until one man on the other side of the road switched allegiance and upset the geographical balance.

In an earlier chapter, I quoted Tribeni Lal, a leading member of the lineage, on the powers and responsibilities of his family in town affairs during the early decades of the present century. Generally speaking, this *khandan* remained unified, at least in a political sense, until Independence, not so much from lack of internal conflicts but because lineage leaders were usually powerful enough to suppress them. From 1948 onward, however, an open split appeared in their ranks. This quarrel quickly entered the town political arena and converted a significant part of political behavior into merely lineage factionalism.

The public split resulted from the eruption of a long-standing, hitherto suppressed enmity between two branches within the lineage. When his father—a man characterized as being quiet to the point of passivity—died, Moti Lal, the present Chairman, evidenced much more aggressively a long-standing distaste for his lineage-mate (*pattidar*), Tribeni Lal. The conflict began when a court case ensued about repayment of a sum of money which Tribeni Lal had lent to Moti Lal's father. Moti Lal's group contends that Tribeni Lal lied about the principal, and Tribeni Lal's side declares that they were not being properly repaid. In any case, in an immediate sense this event precipitated the present lineage discord. More indirect but just as important are the effects of family partition and the creation of units with differential wealth within the lineage. People in Tezibazar assume that in most cases only enmity and hatred can characterize the relations of formerly joint brothers or brothers' sons and so on over several generations. It is no surprise to the local populace that, given the differential fragmentation of wealth in the Chairman *khandan* (as a result of separate life and reproductive histories consequent upon partition), envy and political opposition should exist between the lineage "haves" and "have-nots." The segment led by Moti Lal has generally fallen to an economic condition which, although still usually above the average, is well below the level of its former prestige and family fortunes.

Tribeni Lal and his followers, although also victims of a decrease in family position from that it enjoyed before the Second World War, are still considered to be among the richest men in town. They have also been quicker to move into profitable forms of modern business.

In 1948 the Moti Lal group either did not exist or had only a weak voice in politics. In 1953, when Tribeni Lal defeated Dube (in direct election for the chairmanship), he also defeated his lineage rivals, although because of the nature of the voting, one lineage opponent was elected. This man as well as other Moti Lal supporters constituted part of the group which successfully passed the vote of no confidence against the Chairman in 1956. Since 1957, the Moti Lal lineage faction has been on the ascendant and, indeed, the leader of this group has been Chairman. Since 1957, also, Moti Lal and his followers have been identified with the local Congress party.

Intracaste Lineage Groups

The predominance of the Umar economically, numerically, and thus politically has been noted several times. Part of the organization of political groups within Tezibazar is analogous to the internal structure of the Umar caste.

Since the 1920's opposition between two Umar maximal lineages has been almost continuous. These lineages are the Chairman *khandan* and another which I shall here call the "Leader" lineage. The latter is the largest single lineage of any caste in Tezibazar (see Chart 4), but its economic situation has been much inferior to that of the Chairman *khandan* and therefore its voice in town politics, although authoritative and decisive in terms of votes, has been limited to secondary status. Since 1948, every N.A. council has had one man from this lineage as a member, but never has anyone from it sat as Chairman. In recent years, however, its members have played a significant role in determining who the chairman would be.

The Chairman *khandan* clusters along either side of Main Street in the midst of Sahibganj, whereas the Leader lineage is located in somewhat spotty distribution along the main road between Anjahi and Gurhai.

The conflict between the Chairman and Leader *khandans* stems from the natural antagonism between two local groups within a caste which have markedly different wealth and therefore status levels. At the present the Leader people claim they

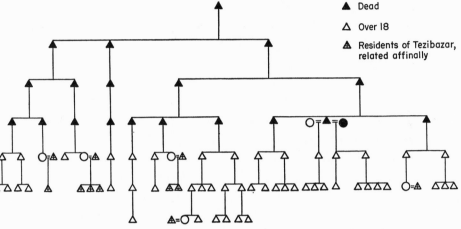

Chart 4: The Leader lineage.

were treated disparagingly by the Chairman lineage because of their relative poverty. The alleged incident which set off the original squabble had to do with an insult suffered by the informal leader of the lineage about forty years ago when he was attending a *ram lila* celebration at the present-day home of Tribeni Lal. This event is advanced in explanation of why the Leader lineage holds its own independent *ram lila* celebration in Gurhai *mohalla*.

It was the Leader *khandan* which opposed the Chairman lineage in the first N.A. elections in 1922. This group sided with the Muslims in opposition to the Umar zamindars, who were, in fact, members of the Chairman *khandan*. Since 1948, the Leader lineage has been consistent in its continual opposition to the Tribeni Lal faction of the Chairman lineage—which, of course, is heir to the wealth and reputation of the Chairman *khandan*.

Expectedly, the Moti Lal lineage segment and the Leader *khandan*, since they share a political rival, have for the most part joined forces and influence in the last few elections. This cooperation has united most of the Umar caste on this level as well as in higher organizational frameworks, whereas the Tribeni Lal group, looked upon from a caste vantage, appears as a maverick entity. The Leader *khandan* regards its opposition to Tribeni Lal as a matter of lineage against lineage. They see the addition of Moti Lal to their forces as a fortunate result of intralineage enmity which does not change significantly, however, the structuring of the conflict as one between lineages.

Caste Political Groupings

The extent of caste oppositions in Tezibazar and their primary locus in the Kesarvani and Umar has already been noted. In this case, the "Kesarvani" political unit consists of most of the other small Baniya castes in town (Kalvar, Teli, Halvai), whereas the Umar group with which they contest is for the most part and in a structured sense entirely composed of the Leader lineage and the Moti Lal segment of the Chairman *khandan*. The Tribeni Lal group aligns itself in nearly all questions against the other Umar and with the Kesarvani. The latter caste regards this conflict as *biradari* against *biradari*, and the fact that Tribeni Lal's lineage section is their ally is only seen devoid of its social structural meaning. Thus Tribeni and his people are "honest" Umar—somehow benevolence entered the hearts of a few of an otherwise totally miscreant caste. In no sense does the defection change the popular phrasing of this feud as caste against caste. It is not that such an idea is incorrect, for, in fact, most Kesarvani just as most Umar line up in the same corner. What is lacking in such a statement is an appreciation of the structural aspects— which cover both internal lineage segments and lineages themselves and make the formation of dissidents more than a mere whim of personality or an individual attitude of Tribeni Lal and his followers.

I have already noted conflicts between the Kesarvani group and the Umar in the Hari Har Prasad Lohia dispute and the Ram Svarup episode. In 1964 this caste conflict was moving into a new organizational realm. Under the urgings and propaganda of the Jana Sangh political party, the Kesarvani, their allied Baniya castes, and the Tribeni Lal lineage segment, plus diverse smaller and scattered groups, were forming a single entity whose structure, although minimal and amorphous, was approaching that of a community—that is, a Baniya communal grouping.

Thus, in the cases of intralineage and intracaste oppositions the present section has indicated the movement of previous or current internal disputes into the modern political arena, yet with a retention of basically kinship or kin-factional organization. In the case of caste political oppositions, splits which were once based on economic competition have now taken on a political cast and press for political solutions. Decisions within the political sphere now determine not only power in the town but also within the caste, lineage, and lineage segment. The political machinery of the modern state is the arbiter of social and power relations within caste and lineage, and in recognition of this fact, these various groups avidly compete for access to the official political positions.

Many local people picture Tezibazar politics solely in terms of the political interaction and antagonism of lineages and castes. For them the political world is subsumed by Umar and Kesarvani, by the Chairman and Leader lineages. The following section will indicate how decidedly limited such an interpretation is.

COMMUNAL ASPECTS

The Muslims of Tezibazar are the group most threatened by minority status, and they first developed a communal aspect. However, the self-conscious and vocal section of this community is but a small part of the total. Other Muslims are considered part of the community as a result of reflex groupism, a unanimity of sentiment which is consciously exploited by leaders seeking support. Communalism has two aspects which have already been explained: (1) an organizational aspect where the semblance of a group structure is approached; and (2) an ideological aspect which rests only upon a diffuse common sentiment among various castes. Tezibazar communities have both these qualities to varying degrees. To have strength, a local community must have organization; weaker communities have little but common sentiment. The Muslims are much more self-consciously communal and better organized than, for example, the Sudras who accordingly *as a group* exert hardly any force in local politics. Among Baniyas, the Jana Sangh party cadres have supplied the self-conscious element and organization. They have based their appeals for Baniya unity on the fear of other communal organizations.

As communal sentiments become organized and as these organizations take on political functions similar to those performed by caste and lineage bodies, they become local embodiments of the strong ideological and electoral bias which since Independence has characterized state and district politics. As such, they represent local readjustments of political group formation to conform to voting and lobbying practices of the region and even the nation. In Tezibazar, the Muslim is the only community which competes as a *de facto* group—mainly as a result of the powerful, repressive, anti-Muslim feelings of the Hindu majority. However, in the summer of 1964, rising food prices, increased government regulations, and a variety of measures oppressive to town merchants were encouraging the formation of a Baniya communal group.

The History of Muslim-Hindu Relations

In the early years of the present century, Hindu-Muslim conflict was little more than a struggle for power between Baniya zamindars and their Muslim counterparts. It had few, if any, communal implications. But Tribeni Lal, the present leader of the dissident Umars, decided not only to combat his Muslim opponents as individuals but also to attack them in religious terms. In 1915 he and a few English-educated Hindu (small-scale) zamindars formed the "Hindu Sabha [council]" which endured until 1940.[1] The Sabha succeeded in broadening the purely economic appeal of these Hindu landowners to include religion and gave a formal basis to much of the communal hatred which now exists in the town. It also dramatized the weakness of the Muslim minority and the potential power held by the Hindu majority. Still, strong communal political organizations did not emerge until after Independence, even though Hindu-Muslim animosity steadily increased throughout the last days of British rule. Periodically riots or violent disputes flared up, and men rallied to defend their religion, or social values, or whatever was the battle cry of the day. These violent occasions were, however, short-lived and relatively infrequent, and once passed, individuals soon reverted to an unorganized, merely passive resentment or distaste for the other community. The "community," then, was based on sentiment, which under unusual circumstances could bring concerted action but brought no consistent or forceful group behavior. Yet, even before communities crystallized into competitive political groups, the creation of the Hindu Sabha helped polarize the two categories. It intensified the antagonistic feelings and religious or social hatreds which would later stimulate the growth of true communal groups in Tezibazar.

The Hindu Sabha from its inception had an office in the town, carried on an annual function, maintained a library, engaged in social work, and subsidized a cowshed for the protection of sick and weak animals. Its anti-Muslim activities proceeded on two fronts: discouragement of Hindu participation in Muslim festivals, and unbending opposition to all Muslim "encroachments" of Hindu preserves or privileges. Tribeni Lal recalls the events of the period, 1916–1920:

[1] This Sabha was informally connected to the Hindu Mahasabha founded by Madan Mohan Malaviya (who also began Banaras Hindu University); see Paul R. Brass, *Factional Politics in an Indian State: The Congress Party in Uttar Pradesh*, p. 20.

In 1918–1919 *dasehra* and *muharram* coincided. The Muslims wanted the Hindus to stop the celebration of the *ram lila* that day. But we organized the Hindus and opposed the demands of the Muslims; then we approached the district leaders and were successful in getting the Muslims pacified. But in Anjahi ward, the Hindus did not perform *ram lila* out of respect for Muslims. At that time even Hindus used to carry the Muslim banners [at *muharram*], and did them homage just as did the Muslims, and took large part in Muslim festivals. I opposed this practice and got the Hindus to change and give up their contacts with the Muslims.

There were several instances of open conflict during this period. Once in the early 1920's *muharram* and *gurva mangal*, a local Hindu festival, coincided, and the Muslims did not wish the Hindus to carry out the procession usually held on this occasion. But Tribeni Lal and his associates organized a public protest, and the Hindu procession was allowed. At about the same time, a Muslim threatened to slaughter cows in the town in retaliation for the performance of *gurva mangal*. Again, the Hindu Sabha was successful in preventing a Muslim activity—in this case the slaughter of the holy cow. Finally, in 1925 several people were badly beaten in an extensive Hindu-Muslim riot in Tezibazar.[2] A court case was filed, and three members of the Umar Chairman lineage including Tribeni Lal were accused of instigating the outbreak. The ensuing litigation required a large financial outlay which was provided by these zamindars and the Hindu public, but finally the case was settled out of court.

From about 1910 to the early 1920's, Muslim power as exemplified in the role of the old overlord-zamindars declined, and Hindu merchants or merchant-zamindars became ascendant. From this time to the end of World War II and the coming of Independence, Muslim influence in Tezibazar reached its ebb. When this influence re-emerged, it was no longer in the garb of the zamindar, but in that of a minority community, fearful of its

[2] The outbreak of communal riots in Tezibazar during the early 1920's coincides with communal violence on an all-U.P. basis; Brass, *op. cit.*, p. 22.

position in a democratic voting situation where individuals chose mainly on the ascriptive basis of caste and community. Muslim fear nowadays is real and pervasive and grows out of their being considered pariah by the majority element of the society and of their own impotent resentment of this relegation to inferiority.

The temporary, violent Hindu-Muslim conflicts continued and perhaps worsened after Independence. Ten years ago a dispute erupted over the performance of *holi* near a Muslim burial ground in Sipah *mohalla*, and this same conflict flared up again just a few years ago. Whereas the Hindus—primarily Baniyas—who took part in these excursions of hate immediately thereafter returned to their caste and individual conflicts, the Muslim combatants were strengthened as a corporate entity by each incursion of the majority. Even now Muslims look back on prewar days as good times for Hindu-Muslim relations, and they attribute the present rancor to the democratic electoral system introduced by an independent government of India. This attitude is part of a larger tendency to turn to the zamindari past for finding an esteemed opposite to a distasteful present. These statements also note a significant change which has occurred since Independence and to some extent as a result of democratic elections: the formation of a Muslim communal group as an important competitive political entity.

The Muslim Community

As a political *group* the Muslim community can be illustrated in four main ways. The first concerns a case of communal violence barely avoided during my stay in Tezibazar. Sipah *mohalla* contains the tomb or *mazar* of a locally famous (legendary) Muslim martyr, Sayid Mansur. Muslims decorate this monument with flowers every year about one week after the celebration of *id ul fitr*. However, in 1964 under the instigation of Mohammad Akbar, the Muslims decided to make this small ceremony into a grandiose one—in fact, an assemblage and public acknowledgment of the entire Muslim community. Mohammad Akbar was head of the Muslims not by virtue of a zamindar background or as heritor of a long family tradition of leadership. His antecedents were of the poorest and, as even his followers admitted, much of his appeal came from his great wealth—a fact, as well as his dedication to the Congress party, which he emphasized by wearing even in the hottest times several layers of *khadi* wools. Akbar was an example of the new style Muslim leader, a political fighter without the *noblesse oblige* of zamindari days, exacting in his determination for personal gain and influence, and believing that the natural concomitant of his own aggrandizement would be benefit to his community.

The Hindus—particularly Baniyas—accused the Muslims of making preparations for their celebration in secret. A broadside had been published giving details of the coming event and appealing to a sense of Islamic brotherhood to get people to turn out, but since it was in Arabic script, for most Hindus it was a closed book. It is also true that the distribution of this sheet was highly selective and not publicized. When the news did leak out shortly before the event, people were greatly agitated and fearful of violence. Baniya merchants especially claimed that homage to the tomb had never been performed on such scale before nor should it be begun now. The local leader of the Jana Sangh protested loudly and called upon the Jaunpur and even Lucknow police as well as upon all types and levels of government officials in an effort to have it stopped. The Muslims, meanwhile, claimed that they had performed such festivities before and that the present plan was no great departure from normal. It was known, however, that several Muslims at least quietly sent their wives away in anticipation of communal conflict. Significantly, none of the leading politicians of Tezibazar save the Jana Sanghi leadership opposed the celebration: in fact, they argued strenuously in its favor. Akbar had made his own and his community's influence felt in local politics. To ignore or to stop this communal festival would be to be blind to the political importance of the Muslim community. This event took place at a time when Akbar's stock was low with both the Muslims and Hindus because of public embarrassment over his treatment of his brother Ali and other social acts judged immoral. By engineering this coup, Akbar temporarily reestablished himself as the intercessor and mediator between Hindus and Muslims. He knew that once the battle was joined, the Muslim communal sentiment and structure would not desert him and would suppress the growing movement within the community to find a replacement for him.

The Sayid Mansur-ka-mazar episode clearly demonstrates the fundamental organizational difference of Hindus and Muslims. The match to the communal fires was a premeditated, effectively supervised, and dramatically staged attempt by Muslims acting as a unit under a unified leadership to impress their structure upon the Hindus and particularly the Baniya leaders of the town. This event occurred in mid-February: the Notified Area elections were scheduled for early May. It was not an insignificant way to impress the town with the potential political power and unity of the Muslim community. Once this goal had been accomplished by the coming of all politicians except the Jana Sangh to his side, Akbar gave in to the pleas of the local police and officials, and the ceremony was staged as in former years on a relatively limited basis.

The way the Muslims view their position in the political system is another proof of their being organized on the basis of community. Just as the Umar see the political realm as consisting mainly of lineages and their allies, or the Kesarvanis look on electoral conflict as between castes, so, too, Muslims see the political world as conforming in type to their own communal structure. In the following statement Mohammad Akbar clearly demonstrates this attitude as well as a belief that local communal organization is linked with that on a regional level. Akbar interprets the politics of the town as a sideline of the communal politics of the district:

The Thakurs of this area have been trying to suppress the Brahmins and want to establish their own political monopoly of the town. In order to get Sita Ram Dube [former Brahmin N.A. chairman] and other Brahmins out of power, the Thakurs persuaded the Muslims to side with them. They said the Muslims were a minority, and that they would protect our rights, and that the Brahmins were Jana Sanghi and encouraged communal conflict. The Thakurs [to defeat the Brahmins] wanted the votes of the Baniyas, so they set up Moti Lal [present N.A. Chairman] as their frontman. . . . The Thakurs schemed in this manner because almost all the important positions in Jaunpur politics are occupied by them, and they are powerful in the whole of Uttar Pradesh as well.

Another indication that the Muslim community exists as a group is the fact that it is implicitly recognized as such by those who wish to destroy it. The Jana Sanghis in Tezibazar have tried to create dissent in *Muslim* ranks, not in Muslim *caste* ranks or Muslim *lineage* ranks. Their technique has been to champion the cause of any sufficiently unfortunate Muslim who must resort to their good offices and to entertain legal suits and general town sentiment against this man's opponent, if he be a leading Muslim. In a dispute over a parcel of land in front of the Jama mosque in Naiganj a poor Muslim of Julaha caste opposed a respected Muslim ex-zamindar. The Jana Sangh pursued the Julaha's case to embarrass the high-status Muslim and to highlight for the rest of the community the internal dissensions within it. The most famous example of the Jana Sangh's politically-motivated intercession concerned the brothers Ali and Akbar which I discussed earlier. Akbar at that time was the openly acknowledged leader of the Muslim community and the prime target for the Jana Sangh's vilification. In most cases, the Jana Sangh has failed to split the Muslim community, because it has been unable to win a significant number of Muslims over to the side of its political puppet. The very fact of Jana Sangh aid taints the chances of a Muslim's finding acceptance in his own community.

But in the case of Ali, Akbar's brother, the violation of society's standards was so flamboyant, Ali as an individual was so well-liked, and his brother Akbar's other social acts so outrageous that willingly or not in 1964 the majority of Muslims found themselves favoring Ali in spite of Jana Sangh help. It had taken three years for this sentiment to prevail because the Muslims were fearful of forcibly removing Akbar as leader and thus initiating an internal power struggle. Until 1964, the unity of the community prevailed. By then, Akbar's reputation had sunk so low and his political friends on the regional level had so admonished him that of his own accord he decided to step down from public leadership in favor of a man whom he had handpicked as his replacement on the N.A. Committee. Thus, even when the Jana Sangh came closest to sowing discord in Muslim ranks, the cohesiveness of the group successfully survived the challenge by a formal change of leadership without internal disunity.

The final way in which the Muslim community manifests itself is, of course, the most important: in political maneuvering. Other caste and lineage groups are only committed to opposition —either to their lineage segment or to another caste—and therefore can and do amalgamate, align, disconnect, and realign themselves within different national parties or different local political groupings. However, by its very nature a community introduces an ideological commitment into the random, opportunistic shiftings of the caste and lineage groups. If, for the moment, the advantages to be derived from membership in a party which controls the regional political machinery are ignored, it makes little difference to the Kesarvani whether they are segments of the Congress party or the Jana Sangh on the local level. Their only necessity is for maintenance of a proper opposition to the Umar—therefore they must be in one party and the Umar in the other. In contrast, the ideological commitment of such communal groups as the Muslim limits their political mobility as a whole and also that of their leaders. No Muslim leader can advocate merger with Jana Sangh party constituents nor with any group or individual possessing Jana Sanghi sentiments. On the other hand, a man whose political following is not ideologically defined has much freedom to align himself and his group wherever his acquisitive fancy leads him. For example, in 1957, Sita Ram Dube, who in the two previous elections had built his strength on the support of Muslims and Sudras and others, failed to receive the Congress party nomination and so jumped to the

Praja Socialist party, which in that year represented those Baniya elements that in 1964 formed the Jana Sangh. In the early months of 1964, Sita Ram Dube was again continually linked with communal Baniya interests which would have led to a Jana Sangh ticket. However, as the hot season began, it seemed that the Muslim communal group had wooed him into the nascent "party" in which it was contained. As it turned out, for various reasons Dube was forced to contest the elections without the support of either of these two groups. I shall discuss the ideological implications of communities further below.

Generally Muslim political and electoral behavior has been to ally with whoever received the Congress ticket—a point which the following section on outside influences will consider. Knowing this, politicians have made a concerted effort to get such supralocal party recognition even though they would have given it little thought were it only a matter of official title. Then, too, the Muslims have not merely passively accepted whatever leader emerged from the fray for Congress party support. In the 1964 elections, for example, the Muslim communal leadership fought vigorously to install its own choice for town chairman. Often such preliminary maneuverings are more competitive than the actual elections—if in their course enough of the larger groups can be welded together and then be satisfied that they will have fair representation on the N.A. committee. But as the case of the 1964 election also illustrates, even when the Muslim communal choice did not prevail, the group could not break away from the local Congress organization as a political entity based on caste or lineage might have done in its stead. Their only alternative lay in the groups forming the Jana Sangh. Yet such an ideological contradiction would not have been tolerated by the Muslim electorate, even had it been considered politically sound by the communal leadership. Further, Muslims identified with the Congress goals of a secular state and of the protection of minorities, and so since Independence the Muslims have been on the Congress side. In Tezibazar this has generally meant that they have joined with Moti Lal against Tribeni Lal, with the Leader *khandan* against the Chairman lineage, with the Umar against the Kesarvani.

Community: Ideology and Political Leadership

The ideological stereotyping of communal groups has two important effects on the whole structure of town politics including the place in it of the groups themselves. One is that leadership in a town-wide capacity (the office of chairman) is for all intents not open to heads of communal groups because of overly close identification with ideological matters. Thus, when Moti Lal becomes Chairman, everyone knows that he will favor his own lineage segment and will try to even the score in the old family enmity with Tribeni Lal; but no one equates this activity with the reordering of society that the rise of, for example, an Akbar to power would entail. The Akbars do not simply represent individuals out for their own profit or for the benefit of their followers. Akbar is indeed such an individual, but at the same time he is something more, because he is the leader of a communal group and so must uphold and symbolize the ideological commitment of the unit. In this case, he must stand for Muslim acceptability as citizens of India on an equal basis with the Hindus, for a secular state with fair opportunity for all religious and ethnic entities, and for the end of majority oppression of the minority. Such identification with a communal ideology or party preference greatly hinders the communal leader's mobility in gathering allegiance from other groups. He is overly-stereotyped in a political structure which is not yet entirely polarized between competing communities, each possessed of its own competitive ideology.

For this reason, most of the town-wide leaders necessarily come from the lineage-caste stratum of local politics. The continuance of political activity at this level and of the various kinship or caste-bound disputes which give these groups life is functional in the present political organization of the town and will continue to remain so until the local society is totally divided into communities. The present Tezibazar political structure is a halfway house, in which relatively meaningless lineage and caste disputes condition the groups from which the main town leaders emerge, although the locally and regionally significant phenomenon of community has still not inherited the full reins of political control. In this sense, too, Tezibazar stands midway in political development between village and district or region.

The ideological commitment of a communal group and leadership makes regional or national party allegiance a reality and necessity. Lineages or castes can first organize themselves into a politically tenable unit and then solicit aid or recognition from any national or regional party. A community has by default a much more permanent and binding attachment to a particular party and its philosophy. Thus, everyone in India as well as in Tezibazar associates the Muslim vote with the Congress. No one, however, can make an equally positive declaration about the party affiliation of an individual from the non-communal levels of political activity. I have indicated this point in the description of Sita Ram Dube's multiple party transformations.

As Tezibazar becomes more and more polarized into communities by the strengthening of the Muslims and the continued growth of the nascent Baniya grouping described below, the town's direct amalgamation with regional and national society proceeds apace. For growth of community means the political commitment of communal ideology, and this in turn requires more or less binding alignment with one or another national state party. The present trend in Tezibazar is not only toward emulating on a structured basis (of groups) the tenuous communal organization of the district and state levels; it is also toward forming alliances ideologically and physically with other organizations on those levels.

Ideological dependency of communities, however, is two-way. The major political parties, by providing ideological justification for pre-existing communal groupings, are playing an important role in the town's emerging political set-up. The Congress party's espousal of a secular state and of the ending of ascriptive bars is exploited in Tezibazar to justify the formation of Muslim and (less forcefully) of Sudra communal groups. The Jana Sangh's advocacy of an anti-Pakistan, anti-Congress government policy is being used to justify the creation of a Baniya communal group fearful of Muslims and of government regulations on commerce. Because this influence is indirect does not mean that local leaders are not conscious of the effect or twist that particular ideologies will be given by specific communities. Indeed, the Congress in its propaganda of equality openly courts Sudra and Muslim votes based on communal sentiment (notice, not necessarily communal *group*), whereas the Jana Sangh relies on its anti-Pakistan, anti-Muslim stance to capture the Baniya communal vote. As these communal bodies become more organized, the ideological messages of the Congress or the Jana Sangh will become permanently attached to them. As particular regional parties and philosophies come to represent the special viewpoints of specific communal *groups* on the local level, a complete transformation of town politics and of town political integration with the larger society will be accomplished.[3]

The Formation of a Baniya Community

A Baniya communal group based on the merger of traditional merchant castes was fast becoming a political reality in Tezibazar during 1964. For the most part this development depended on shared sentiment and fear, but the Jana Sangh party did provide a definite and well-organized if limited hard-core structure. In 1964 merchants felt a growing concern over what they

[3] This is not to say that the Muslims could not switch allegiance to a party other than the Congress—as, for example, the Communist Party—if it existed at the local level. Such change in allegiance, however, would only be possible if that party's ideology reflected the particular point of view which now draws the Muslims to the Congress. The Muslims would be committed for fundamentally ideological reasons to this regional or national political party, whereas the attachment of a caste or lineage-based political group would be basically anomalous and opportunistically defined. The communal group is thus more forcibly absorbed in larger political entities in contrast to the ad hoc allegiance of caste and lineage political bodies.

thought were the ever-increasing exactions of the Congress national and state governments. Official corruption, new taxes, trade limitations and duties all increased their alienation from the Congress party and its administrative measures. These people also put the blame for what they saw as the humiliating Chinese episode on the Congress government and its overly friendly attitude towards the "unpatriotic and untrustworthy" Muslims. The events of *id* and the Sayid Mansur-ka-mazar affair intensified their hatred of Muslims, and now fear played a role in such feelings. The political necessity for town Congress leaders to recognize at least in token form the status and commensal claims of the Muslims, and more fundamentally, the latter's electoral power all exasperated many Baniyas and other Hindus. The final blow came in the summer of 1964 when the government began to drastically curtail hoarding of food grains, sugar, and other basic commodities. When Nehru died in late May, amid all the genuine feeling of remorse at his passing many sophisticated Baniyas made sharp remarks regarding the extent of corruption under his government and the weakened international reputation of India because of the Chinese debacle:

The Congress is extremely corrupt, and some of this must be put to Gandhi and Nehru although they are to blame only indirectly. Gandhi and Nehru were such inspired and great leaders that no other groups opposed to them and the Congress could ever arise. This is one of the reasons and the main one that the Congress is so powerful at the present, and this is why it is so corrupt. [Govind Ram Umar.]

Nehru believed that only through the Congress party could India remain united, and therefore he put uppermost the victory of the party at all costs, even if it meant shutting his eyes to corruption and dishonesty in government. Nehru probably thought that these unethical practices would pass in time, but I believe these are the really basic problems of India at the present time. [Bajrang Lal Umar (interview in English).]

The formation of this Baniya group has had little effect on the Umar of the Moti Lal faction, the Leader lineage, and several smaller Umar *khandan*, but it has gathered most of the other Baniyas into its fold. These Umar groups have not become involved because of their present political "entente" with the Muslim communal group. Given the abstention of these Umar, it was only natural that the Tribeni Lal Umar lineage segment and the Kesarvani caste would enter even more intimately into the Baniya movement. This combination had run on much the same platform in 1957 under the banner of the Praja Socialist party. In 1964 the nascent Baniya community came under the aegis of the Jana Sangh, with its organizational base in the Jana Sangh cadres (a point I discuss in the following section), the Tribeni Lal lineage segment, and Kesarvani and allied castes. But it was more than this, for the dissatisfaction of the Baniyas in the town pushed many disparate groups into the still nebulous new community: Umar representing the smaller, uncommitted lineages, Teli, Bhuj, and Kalvar. Brahmins with strong anti-Muslim anti-Congress feelings, and many Kisan with similar views also joined. Because their number in the town was small, their proportion in the communal entity was not highly significant. There were also a large number of Camar who had been alienated from the Congress party because of a lawsuit involving the Notified Area and one of their brethren.

Wealth and Town Politics

Before leaving the discussion of internal politics in Tezibazar, I should comment about one aspect of politics whose absence the reader may already have been led to question. Wealth as a conditioner of political groupings does not exist in Tezibazar, nor do the wealthy or rich as a political class contend in town elections. This situation is not caused by lack of significantly large wealth differentials and concentrations; rather it is due to the fact that ascriptive and (to a lesser extent) territorial determinants of political grouping and leadership are so great that there is no room for the separate development of a body based solely on the accumulation of wealth. Treasure is primarily important as an adjunct of political power within each ascriptively-based group and in some cases as a significant reinforcement of political group structures founded on other than ascriptive criteria.

Of ten political leaders in the town, five depend on a combinaton of lineage, caste, or communal backing plus wealth. Two rely on such ascriptive support with help from regional parties and officials. One depends on the combined support of a territory (*mohalla*) and a lineage group. Another relies on wealth, territorial backing, and contact with district party leaders; and the last depends on wealth and territorial support. (The territorial backing of the last two individuals comes from outside the town and is therefore appropriately discussed in the subsequent section.) Although wealth is not a primary determinant for any of the political leaders mentioned above, it should be noted that all have incomes much above the average in Tezibazar. From the individual's viewpoint wealth is one of the most decisive factors regarding who becomes a leader and who does not. In the larger sense, however, wealth in most cases is a factor in selecting which individual from a particular lineage, caste, or communal group will become a big man. That is, if a group is large enough to give adequate support to a leader, then wealth will only be a factor much the same as (although of greater importance than) personality, group recognition, or social service. Wealth plays a more positive role in establishing politicians whose support is based on territorial bodies. The latter in Tezibazar are formed from those parts of the urban area inhabited by minority groups that by themselves cannot effectively support their own leaders within the town. Their leaders must depend on such other sources of power as wealth or external political connection and support in the rural area (including the rural sections of the Notified Area). Such minority groups can usually be successfully courted by a local big man.

EXTERNAL INFLUENCES

The caste, lineage, and communal units which form the basic internal structure of Tezibazar politics are not the total of political activity in the town, nor can they be considered a full listing

of political groups. There is also an important external component to Tezibazar political organization, a component of two
sorts. One is the obvious concomitant of the amalgamation of the
town into a regional and national political structure. A large part
of the power base of some town politicos stems almost entirely
from their contacts with the district and state elective machinery
and parties. Another even larger segment use such opportunistic
acquaintances to reinforce and solidify their local positions.
These techniques will be elucidated in the following chapter and
illustrated by an actual example of local and regional political
interaction.

Another facet of external influence is the intrusion of nonresident political groupings or personalities whose power in the
town results in large degree from non-local sources. There are
three examples of this situation in Tezibazar: (1) the influence
of the Jana Sangh party in the form of a nonresident, professional organizer; (2) a resident Brahmin politician who derives
much of his urban political influence from a power base in the
surrounding rural area; and (3) similarly, a nonresident Thakur
family which takes great part in town politics by virtue of its
ownership of urban properties and its power position and political contacts in the district and state governmental machinery.

The Jana Sangh

The leader of the Jana Sangh in Tezibazar was Yogendra
Nath, a young man who was said to be a paid political servant of
the former Raja of Jaunpur, a well-known Jana Sangh leader in
the area. Much of the organization of this party, at least on a
local level, is subtle and secretive. Yogendra Nath marched in the
organized protest demonstrations of the Jana Sangh, but none of
the leading townsmen known to be sympathizers took part.
Whether Yogendra was indeed a paid agent or not I never
discovered, but the fact is immaterial since he was treated as one
and was considered an outsider who had come expressly to
strengthen the local Jana Sangh.

The Jana Sangh party in Tezibazar, or at least the nucleus of

sympathizers now in it, seems to have been created in 1952.⁴
Several years thereafter—probably about 1958 although no one
could or would tell me the exact date—Yogendra Nath took
charge and began an extensive protest program against the local
Congress group. Four years ago, Akbar, the Muslim leader, with
the help of the N.A. Chairman filed reports of alleged miscon-
duct on the part of Yogendra and compelled him to leave town.
Akbar, of course, opposed the anti-Muslim nature of the Jana
Sangh ideology, and with the help of the then sitting Congress
M.L.A. (member of the Uttar Pradesh Legislative Assembly)
from Baragaon *tehsil* (who was a Muslim), he was able to expel
Yogendra. Two years ago, after the 1961 elections returned a
Brahmin Praja Socialist to the Legislative Assembly, Yogendra
came back to town in comparative safety. The Praja Socialist
M.L.A. was highly receptive to Yogendra's cause because his
own electorate was for all purposes the same which backed the
Jana Sangh, and party name, at least in this local case and with
this individual, was merely an option of convenience.

The protest program of Yogendra and the Jana Sangh in
Tezibazar was extensive and well organized. In 1964 there was
one *hartal* and hunger strike, at least five public meetings against
corruption or high prices, and several communal incidents, the
most potentially volatile being the confrontation with the Muslims over the *mazar* festivity. Each morning at about 6:00 A.M.
and on special occasions, such as Independence Day in the after-
noon, the Hindu youth of the town organized and led by Yogendra would march up and down the Pratabgarh road or along
Main Street singing and chanting highly patriotic and Hindu
communal phrases (such as "hInd, *mata*-ki" or "jai hInd").
They also performed exercises and military-type formations
under the supervision of the Jana Sangh.

The work of the party or at least its popularly recognized
local representative went on in another fashion as well. One

⁴ The Jana Sangh was formed on a national basis on the eve of the
1951–1952 general elections; see Myron Weiner, *Party Politics in India*,
pp. 165–222.

night in December, 1963, the Muslim leader Akbar was beaten along Main Street by several young men whom everyone acknowledged to be Yogendra's disciples. A number of such incidents occurred in one of the intermediate colleges as well—a young boy was quite severely injured in one case—again at the universally-acknowledged instigation of the Jana Sangh leadership. These occurrences highlight an important facet of Jana Sangh influence in Tezibazar: the party aims its propaganda and organization at the young men of the town, in a way which the Congress leaders are quick to note as the antithesis of their own democratic style. The Jana Sangh's manner is authoritarian and regimental, but its strength of purpose matches the force of its enunciated, overriding desire: in Yogendra's words, "To make India a world power and independent of foreign domination."

Town Politicians with Rural Power Sources

Pandit Sita Ram Dube has been Chairman of Tezibazar several times and was in the past one of the most influential men in the town, yet his power base in Tezibazar itself is small. At best it consists of the small urban Brahmin population, and many of the Camars of the town. Dube's influence in the urban locale bears no relation to his actual following therein because his real power stems from his contacts with outside political forces. He has been a Congress leader for many years (he was imprisoned by the British during the "Quit India" movement), and his associates in district and state government are many. Further, he enjoys a reputation as a leader of the many Brahmins who reside in the rural sections of Sarai *pargana* and Baragaon *tehsil* (including the villages within the Tezibazar N.A.). Dube is said to control many of the rural villages surrounding the town where Brahmin residents out of respect and deference to him follow his leadership in voting, or so is the manner in which his power was explained in Tezibazar.

The circumstances surrounding the election in 1961 of the present Brahmin M.L.A. from Baragaon *tehsil* seem to indicate that some truth exists in these popular conceptions. In any case it is clear that Sita Ram's power source is mainly external to Tezi-bazar.

Within Tezibazar, besides the allegiance of the small Brahmin populace, Dube's political prowess depends heavily on wealth. This man owns one of the largest wholesale concerns and is regarded as among the wealthiest men of the town.

Because of the absence of a large local political following, Dube is even more free than are other politicians to choose any side in the political scene he desires. His position is not at all stereotyped in the sense of lineage, caste, or ideological alle-giance. At the same time he is heavily dependent on external backing. When, in the years since 1957, the particular political unit to which he trusts his influence failed to hold power region-ally, Dube's fortunes in town politics have also suffered. His present eclipse belies the considerable influence he exercised over the town in the years shortly after Independence. For an exam-ple of this extensive control on the basis of external groups, I turn to the Thakurs of Rampur.

Rampur is a small village about a half-mile away from Teziba-zar along the Janghai road. It is hardly visible from the main road, and once seen, its smallness and abject quality give no indication of the stature some of its inhabitants enjoy in the nearby town. Three brothers from one Thakur joint family in Rampur are often termed the "kingmakers of Tezibazar politics" —particularly in the public figure of one brother, Bhanu Pratap. In Akbar's interpretation of politics in the town given above, he describes the present town Chairman as a mere front for Bhanu and his brothers. Indeed, their power in the town is highly sig-nificant, and in one sense they are able to intercede in internal town affairs; by the nature of their political backing, they can virtually decide which one of a number of contestants will re-ceive the Congress ticket. They enjoy this power through the advantageous placement of a relative in the district's administra-tion as well as their excellent reputation and influence with district and state Congress party leaders. Their control over the allocation of the Congress ticket gives them a strong hold over any politician in the town, for the Muslim and Sudra vote—a sizeable segment of the town electorate—is generally considered for ideological reasons to follow the Congress banner.

The Thakurs of Rampur, through contacts with higher-level administrative machinery, can also apply positive and heavy sanctions against a recalcitrant ally or an entrenched foe. The following discussion of their role in the school dispute with Tribeni Lal Umar will make this point quite clear.

Such facts may explain the powers of the Rampur Thakurs in the town, but the question why they enjoy such high repute with the regional Congress political organization remains. As in the case of Sita Ram Dube, town residents trace the Thakurs' influence to their leadership of a significant rural area close by the town. Tezibazaris claim that the present prestige of these Thakurs stems from their former position as locally-important zamindars, and the favor of the Congress government which they now enjoy is an acknowledgment of their ability to muster the rural (especially Thakur) vote. This picture of the Rampur Thakurs is very similar in basis and extent to that of Dube, except that the one is said to solicit Brahmin support and the other, the backing of Thakurs.

Again like Dube's, the Thakur influence in Tezibazar has a firm basis in wealth and control of large and significant business enterprises. They own and rent out thirteen small shops in southern Sahibganj and along the Pratabgarh road. They have extensive business interests in the town as well: partial ownership of a saw mill and of a brick kiln; full control over a trucking business. The political consequences of the Rampur Thakurs' considerable economic investment in Tezibazar is great, as they have many people directly under their economic control and even more who know the potential value of business favors from them. These Thakurs also operate the "United Club" as a recreational meeting hall for themselves and their town followers.

A final reason for the Thakur influence in Tezibazar is tenuous, yet it was a most commonly offered explanation for their prowess: many townsmen, particularly Baniyas—whether for or against the Thakurs—claim that fear of physical reprisal is the reason why the Thakurs enjoy such unchallenged power in the town. Since they are ex-zamindars with many close attachments to the rural area, and since the Thakurs and their followers are considered inherently "pugnacious" castes (Thakur, Kisan), they can on short notice assemble a gang of "*gundas*" (toughs) to wreak revenge against any challenger of their authority. During my stay in the town, no one provided an instance of such activity, although the several murders which took place in the surrounding villages were in each instance put to the Bhanu Pratap camp or its opponent group. Of course, these accusations were merely interpretations of internal village struggles in terms of larger political personalities and did not imply any direct or even knowing involvement of the Rampur Thakurs in these misdeeds. The one possible occurrence in the town of such physical reprisal was the assault upon the Jana Sangh's Yogendra Nath the night after the 1964 election results were announced. This assault was alleged to be the work of the Thakur group.

Considering the diverse and multiple bases of their political status in Tezibazar, it might appear that, like the Brahmin Dube, the Rampur Thakurs would be totally mobile and freewheeling in their allegiance and interaction with town political groups. Such, however, is not the case because of an overriding grudge and long-standing feud with the Umar Chairman lineage. This dispute is at least fifty years old and stems from the former zamindari days of both this Umar lineage and the Thakurs of Rampur. The first property bought by the ancestors of Tribeni Lal was purchased from a Thakur belonging to the same patrilineage as Bhanu Pratap and his brothers—a sale which impoverished the Thakurs to the extent that it profited the Baniyas. This event goes so far back in their mutual family histories and the accompanying circumstances have grown so vague that the present feudists have only amorphous recollections of the genesis of what they only know is an old family hatred. The Rampur people do remember, however, the many years before Independence that Tribeni Lal of the Umar Chairman lineage worked for the election of various Brahmin candidates to the district board of the state legislative councils in opposition to Thakurs and even relatives of the Thakur brothers. As Akbar noted in his statement quoted earlier, politics in Jaunpur district has involved in an electoral sense (though not as organized groups) the communal voting patterns of Brahmins and Thakurs, because both represent unusually large population segments of the area. This fact is indicated by pre-Independence elections for district board and legislative councils where when one candidate was a Thakur, the other was a Brahmin. Tribeni Lal and his lineage followers joined the Brahmins because of their local feud with the Thakurs. The career of this man as an officeholder in his own right and as a campaigner for others shows continual opposition to the Thakurs of all localities but particularly to his close rivals from Rampur. Similarly, the kinder sentiments of these Thakurs are not wasted on Tribeni Lal, and the event which of all others has created the bitterness that now characterizes Tezibazar politics was a move by these same Thakurs to discredit thoroughly their Umar rival (see Chapter 12). Far from the unstereotyped hand they might play in local politics, the Rampur Thakurs have been motivated to play a game of personal vengeance.

Naturally this interest brought them into political fellowship with the Umar Leader *khandan*. When after his father's death Moti Lal became family head and began to carry on his family's enmity with Tribeni Lal in a more aggressive and retributive fashion, he logically fell in with the Leader lineage. It was only a short step further to alliance with the Thakurs, the long-standing foes of Moti Lal's lineage but who in the present circumstances were willing to advance the affairs of Moti Lal as a further embarrassment to the personification of their dislike, Tribeni Lal.

Such is the multi-structured and multi-leveled ordering of political groups in Tezibazar. Much of the political organization is built upon oppositions between family and family, lineage and lineage, caste and caste, and although these groups maintain above all their respective oppositions, they freely switch allegiances to national political parties and ideologies. Still other political entities, unrestricted by such constant caste or lineage oppositions, are even freer to move about, to ally, or to dissolve as the winds of fortune for themselves and their leaders dictate. Such an entity is the political individual symbolized by Sita Ram Dube and the smaller caste and territorial groups within the town which he represents. Such, also, are the Muslims, although they are restricted in an altogether different way by the ideo-

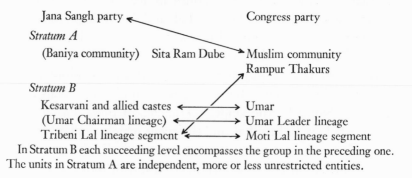

In Stratum B each succeeding level encompasses the group in the preceding one. The units in Stratum A are independent, more or less unrestricted entities.

⟷ = opposition
( ) = non-group or nascent group

Chart 5. Major political groups as of early 1964

logical content to their communal existence. This ideology forces them to support the local Congress party, but who or what this party may consist of in any election year is the outcome of a system of free political enterprise, of opportunistic group merger and dissolution, in which the Muslims can and do play a large part. The same holds true for the nascent Baniya community, although its interaction is restricted by the previous existence and political choices of the more developed Muslim community. As the Baniya unit develops further, it will create the same sort of opposition vis à vis the Muslims as exists in the case of caste versus caste or lineage against lineage. At that time the political mobility of the Muslim community will be severely reduced—to the same level of intransigence as now characterizes the caste and lineage strata—and its power as a shifting factor in

Tezibazar politics will be sorely restricted. The evolution of a
Baniya community can be seen as a development *sui generis* from
the fear of government suppression of business, from distaste for
Muslims, and from disgust with administrative corruption. However, it can also be viewed as the political development of an
effective balance (in terms of opposition) to the Muslim community.

Thus, a distinctive duality exists in Tezibazar political activity: on the one hand, the important role of old lineage and caste
disputes, and on the other, the emerging power of communal
blocs. The former groups define a more internalized and localized style of political expression; the latter point toward ideological and structural merger with political developments on the
district and state levels.

CHAPTER 12

The Modern Political Arena

In 1953, Tribeni Lal Umar was elected to the chairmanship of the N.A. committee by direct and popular vote, the first and last time such an experiment was tried either in Tezibazar or in the rest of Uttar Pradesh. One opponent of Tribeni Lal, Sita Ram Dube, ran on the Congress ticket, and another, a young Muslim, stood as an Independent, as did Tribeni Lal himself. The electoral votes were split, and the membership of the council was about equally divided between Congressmen and sympathizers of Tribeni Lal. The ensuing factionalism and political infighting in the council caused the then district magistrate to complain bitterly in his annual review about "party feelings" which so hindered the committee in the execution of its duties. The Congress group accused Tribeni Lal of setting up the Muslim candidate as a front to split the Muslim vote and therefore defeat the Congress. They started a formal legal protest in the courts against this alleged misconduct. Tribeni Lal complained that Sita Ram Dube and the Congress organization were only trying to make trouble for his administration and that he had inherited an impoverished treasury from his predecessor, Dube. In 1956, fifty-eight assignees, claiming that they had been over-assessed by the Chairman as political retribution, refused to pay their municipal assessment, a situation which threatened the Notified Area with bankruptcy. Tribeni Lal in turn declared that their refusal to pay was only another aspect of their political opposition to him.

Such intrigues and accusations were not unusual to the town; indeed, they are the normal appurtenances of political rivalry. From the very inception of the Notified Area, such internal devices of revenge had been the common stock of the political process. But in 1955 a new aspect was added: the use of external governmental and political machinery to punish an adversary.

In this chapter we will consider the growing influence since 1955 of regional politics and parties in Tezibazar and the increasingly direct merger of the town with the larger society through such political channels.

PENETRATION OF REGIONAL POLITICS

There are now two intermediate colleges (up to the twelfth grade) in Tezibazar; in 1954 there was only one. That school, Hindu Intermediate, from its beginning in 1928 as an elementary school to attainment of intermediate status in 1950, was the creation of Tribeni Lal Umar alone. It was Tribeni Lal's gift to the town and the symbol of the social service to which he had dedicated his life. Tribeni Lal has been the manager of the college since its inception, and he is aided in governing it by a committee selected from and by the Board of Trustees. Any individual who pays Rs. 50 becomes a member of this body. Although the school is a private organization, a necessary percentage of its expenses is met by an Uttar Pradesh government grant.

In 1953 a dispute broke out between Tribeni Lal and the principal, Lal-ji, who had charge of the academic affairs of the school. Tribeni Lal now says that this man began plotting with Sita Ram Dube, the Rampur Thakurs, and other Congress leaders. The latter claim that Tribeni Lal wanted to discharge Lal-ji and assign the principalship to his own son (who is and was at that time the senior "master" in the school). In any case, when Tribeni Lal attempted to discharge Lal-ji, the Board of Trustees, which had been "bought into" by his political opponents, refused to allow him to do so for two years. By 1955, when the discharge was accomplished, the local Congress group was ready.

In that year Hindu Intermediate's government grant was suspended. Official recognition of the school was threatened, and, more significantly, the recently fired Lal-ji was forming a new school whose manager was Tribeni Lal's arch-political opponent, Sita Ram Dube. This new institution, Gandhi Intermediate, was given official recognition for intermediate status in a matter of months and at the same time was guaranteed a generous government grant. The reaction of the town was immediate. Most of the students from Hindu Intermediate turned quickly to the new school and Tribeni Lal, in addition to problems with the N.A. committee, was forced to spend a great deal of his own money as well as all he could collect from others to keep his school going.

That the motivation behind the establishment of the new educational institution was political retaliation is accepted by everyone in Tezibazar. What was novel about this occurrence was not its mundane and (in the town environment at least) hackneyed causation. Significantly new was the use by the Congress leaders of outside political contacts to promote wishes which without this external aid would have been impossible to accomplish. The then Chairman of the Jaunpur district board was the classificatory *cacera bhai* of the Rampur Thakur brothers. It was he who provided the site for the new intermediate college, which at that time was a middle school compound (up to the tenth grade) run by the district board. Further, at that time the Education Minister of U.P. was a Thakur from Jaunpur district, connected by friendship with the Rampur Thakurs and their classificatory father's brother's son in Jaunpur. This Minister recognized the new school and accorded it a government grant. His agency also suspended Hindu Intermediate's government grant and was in the process of annulling that college's official recognition. Thus the town Congress leadership of Sita Ram Dube and Bhanu Pratap had humiliated Tribeni Lal in his most sensitive spot. As

Bhanu said, "Since this [the school] was Tribeni Lal's weakest point, it was the best at which to hit back at him politically," although he claimed that Dube had solely planned the school incident. Not only had the Congress leaders set up their own institution and almost bankrupted their opponent's, but they created additional havoc by means of their positions on the Board of Trustees of Hindu Intermediate and continued their harassment of the Notified Area committee. Internal dissension at Hindu Intermediate continued unabated into 1964.

Finally, in 1956, the Congress organization managed to unseat Tribeni Lal from the N.A. chairmanship. To review the machinations which led to this vote of no confidence would call for too great an involvement in the opportunistic give-and-take of internal politics. It should be said, however, that the school incident played a large role in cutting away Tribeni Lal's supporters. A new election for the interim term was called late in 1956. In this contest, which was officially on a non-party basis, Sita Ram Dube, who in fact represented the town Congress organization, opposed Moti Lal Umar, who made his debut in local politics mainly with the support of his lineage segment and the help of the Leader *khandan*. Dube won and the Congress organization was again in political control of the town.

A new election was called for late 1957, and in it Dube again ran against Moti Lal. A significant change had, however, occurred in a short space of time, for in this election Moti Lal gained the official Congress ticket as well as the support of the local Congress organization led by Bhanu Pratap and the other Rampur Thakurs. Dube, formerly the leading Congress figure in the area, was reduced to soliciting favor from his so recently deposed rival, Tribeni Lal, who was not at all adverse to the combination. The latter's opposition to Dube was quickly melted by the appearance of his lineage rival, Moti Lal, and his long-standing enemies, the Rampur Thakurs, on the other side of the fence. It must be remembered that in this year the system of indirect election of Chairman was again in force, and so when I speak of the opposition of Dube and Moti Lal, I do not refer to an actual electoral contest between these two men. Each party prepared a list of ward candidates, and it was for these individuals that the public voted. Nevertheless, it was public knowledge who would be selected as Chairman if one set of contestants or the other was elected to the committee—so that, although the confrontation of the two leaders was never open, it certainly was never secret.

Dube and Tribeni Lal were running on the Praja Socialist ticket. Moti Lal won, mainly through the support of Akbar and the Muslim community, who were constrained to back the new Congress designate, even though Dube had been their choice in 1947, 1953, and 1956.

This striking change in political alignment and support was entirely the result of supra-town politics. Beginning in 1955 a factional clash developed in the Uttar Pradesh Congress ministry. Two factional groups formed: one led by C. B. Gupta (a Baniya), who was the political manager for the Chief Minister, Sampuranand, from 1955–1957; the other led by Mohan Lal Gautam (a Brahmin), who became Sampuranand's political manager from 1957–1960 after the defeat of C. B. Gupta in the 1957 elections.[1] In Jaunpur district two similar groups appeared: in the C. B. Gupta camp were the sitting M.L.A. from Baragaon *tehsil* and the Education Minister who had helped to start the rival intermediate college; with them on the local level went Bhanu Pratap. On the side of M. L. Gautam stood Sita Ram Dube and various other generally older Congress leaders in Tezibazar.[2] The C. B. Gupta faction was paramount in Jaunpur district, and thus the Thakur, Bhanu Pratap, became ascendant over Dube. Up to then he had been inferior or at most equal. Bhanu stripped his opponent of his post as manager of Gandhi Intermediate College and then, in the 1957 election, he and the

[1] Cf. Paul R. Brass, *Factional Politics in an Indian State; The Congress Party in Uttar Pradesh*, pp. 45–46.

[2] Notice that in Jaunpur district, the Congress factional split saw the Brahmins in one camp and the Thakurs in the other.

Congress party backed Moti Lal, whose slate of candidates was officially chosen over Dube's list.[3]

Tribeni Lal also benefited indirectly by the Congress factionalism. The 1957 state elections in U.P. were won by the Congress, but the former Thakur Education Minister who had so plagued Hindu Intermediate was defeated. Kamla Patti Tripathi, the new Congress Education Minister, was more receptive to Tribeni Lal's pleas for reinstatement of the government subsidy for his school. Tripathi has always been closely identified with the Gautam group and in 1964 became the leader of the opposition to C. B. Gupta in the Uttar Pradesh Congress party elections. Thus in January, 1958, the school grant was returned to Tribeni Lal by what were in effect members of the Congress faction opposing those from whom the Rampur Thakurs drew their support.

The chain of events set in motion by the 1953 election had not yet subsided. Dube resented what he felt had been shoddy treatment at the hands of the district Congress party. The 1961 general elections presented an opportunity for revenge. The sitting Congress M.L.A. from Baragaon *tehsil* had made the decision which gave Moti Lal official Congress recognition over Dube in 1957. This man, a Muslim, had also done much to establish the entente between Akbar and Moti Lal. In 1961 the M.L.A. was up for re-election. His opponent was a Brahmin from Tezibazar standing for election on the Praja Socialist ticket. Through his great influence in the rural area, Dube was able to insure or at least to promote this man's victory over his Congress rival. Of course no proof can be given for this contention, but its main importance is as political truth rather than actuality. That is, people attributed the victory of the present

---

[3] The 1957 municipal elections occurred after the 1957 general elections. In the latter, C. B. Gupta and his faction lost much of their power in the state. Nevertheless, the Gupta group remained dominant in Jaunpur district, at least as far as the selection of candidates for the municipal elections. Brass notes that although the Gautam faction was in power in the state legislature, it lost most of the municipal tickets in 1957; Brass, *op. cit.,* p. 91.

M.L.A. from Baragaon *tehsil* to the support of Dube, and subsequent political behavior in 1964 was based on the acknowledgment of this situation. In the 1961 state elections, Dube was again joined by his old rival Tribeni Lal and the fundamentally Baniya vote later to be utilized by the Jana Sangh.

This lengthy exploration of the meanderings and revolutions of Tezibazar politics has larger meaning than that of merely cataloguing the behavior of competitive politicians and political groups. It indicates the extensive penetration of regional politics into the public life of the town, the use of the latter by town residents to solidify their own positions, and the interest of higher-level bosses in maintaining a sound and loyal grass-roots base. The aspect of town life in Tezibazar which I have emphasized has been the direct merger with the political machinery of the modern state for want of any internal traditional system of social control or cohesion. We have seen such a development in terms of the sympathetic formation on the local level of communal groups which mirror the electorally produced, sentiment-based communal voting blocs of the district and state levels. In the section above, I have noted the structural or institutional aspect of the dependency of the town on external political units: the actual penetration and determination of town political life, of local victory and loss, by the regional party and government structure.

THE 1964 ELECTIONS

The foregoing political description and the political groups previously named indicate the status quo as of early 1964. In this year it was proposed to hold the municipal elections which had been twice postponed on an all Uttar Pradesh basis. The elections were at first scheduled for early May, and before February was very old the politicking had begun in earnest.

At the start it seemed as if 1964 would be a repetition of 1957, with Dube and Tribeni Lal running under the auspices of the Jana Sangh instead of the P.S.P., and Moti Lal getting the Congress ticket and the support of the Muslims, of the Rampur

Thakurs, and, of course, the backing of his faction and the Leader lineage.

Political alliance soon began to change, however. A few years earlier Akbar, the Muslim leader, had lent Moti Lal a sum reported as being between Rs. 7,000–40,000 to cement their political friendship. Moti Lal had been slow in repayment and indeed was involved in financial difficulties. Akbar began to belabor his debtor's tardiness publicly, and Moti Lal in shame quickly paid up his arrears by selling some rural properties. As a result, however, neither cared to be in the same party with the other. Further, Bhanu Pratap and the Rampur Thakurs had grown tired of both Moti Lal and Akbar: the latter because of his degraded moral reputation in the town, and the former because of complaints of his misuse of authority. Thus, the Congress organization was ripe for a change.

The Jana Sangh party was not so shot through with conflict. Sita Ram Dube was rather shy of openly aligning himself with an anti-Muslim group (in 1957 the Praja Socialists had not been openly or even necessarily anti-Muslim), but even this hazardous factor was matched by the newly found electoral unity of many Baniyas behind the Jana Sangh organization. As I have earlier noted, dissatisfaction with the Congress government for its alleged corruption and supposed "extortion" of the merchant, coupled with a dislike for Muslims, helped to bind this party of opposition into an effective threat to local Congress domination.

The Congress leaders felt they could not afford an open split in their party lest the Jana Sangh use it as a road to victory. Akbar, to appease Bhanu Pratap and his own community, agreed to step out of the public political light in favor of a hand-picked successor. Then Akbar proposed that a *détente* be reached with Sita Ram Dube so that he could be returned to the Congress fold and be the Congress candidate for Chairman in 1964. Bhanu Pratap was said to eye the M.L.A. position in the next general election, and because he recognized Dube's power behind the outcome of the 1961 M.L.A. contest, the Rampur Thakur also favored Dube's "redemption." These moves were highly secret, however, and the impression was given out that should the Congress win, either Moti Lal or a Congress Kesarvani would have Bhanu's and Akbar's support for the chairmanship. The mention of the Kesarvani was a move calculated to unnerve Moti Lal, who was his natural opponent, as well as to weaken to some extent the attachment of the Kesarvanis to the Jana Sangh. How many people this tactic fooled is difficult to say, but it did maintain an outward appearance of unity (if also one of nebulosity) on the part of the local Congress organization.

The real infighting began with the drawing up of a list of ward candidates in early and mid-April. It was necessary for Bhanu and Akbar to avoid an open split with Moti Lal which would make the latter and his followers desert the Congress party and set up as Independents—a step which would be beneficial only to the Jana Sangh. There was little fear of Moti Lal's and Tribeni Lal's reaching an agreement; the family dispute precluded that. But in the face of Jana Sangh strength it would be politically unwise to risk a three-party contest. The objective of the Rampur Thakur and Akbar was to reach an understanding with Moti Lal to the effect that each group within the Congress should put up a certain number of candidates and that once the election was over and their men successful, the conflict over the chairmanship could be resolved. Such a method was acceptable at this point to Moti Lal, who understood that his own political status hinged on a Congress victory. The groups then began to haggle over candidates. They agreed on a number of men—the Muslims of Akbar's choice were the ones who would win in any case, and a few other individuals were considered by both sides to be potentially maleable to their own viewpoints. For the rest, each group put up its own "safe" men: Moti Lal chose Umar of the Leader *khandan* and other close associates; Bhanu Pratap chose mostly supporters from Sita Ram Dube's backing.

The dynamic part played by Akbar in bringing about a rapprochement between Bhanu Pratap and Dube should be noted. To be sure, defeat of the Jana Sangh was in the best interests of the Muslim community and there was the matter of bad feelings between Moti Lal and Akbar. Even more directly, when the Congress party won, the man with the effective if not decisive ability to choose the future Chairman from among Dube, Moti Lal, the Kesarvani, or anyone else would be the politician who controlled the unified Muslim vote on the council: that is, Akbar. Thus, the latter was in effect carving out an empire for himself and his community.

While these intensive preparations were in progress, an event in state politics suddenly canceled all political undertakings at the local level. In late April an election was held to fill the main offices of the Uttar Pradesh Congress party. Before and especially after the voting (whose results were contested), a wide factional split again occurred (or reopened) in the ruling Congress party between the followers of C. B. Gupta, and the group behind Kamla Patti Tripathi. The dissension was so open and the recriminations so bitter that the party decided against any idea of contesting municipal elections at that moment. By decree of the Congress-controlled state legislature, municipal elections were indefinitely postponed on May 7, 1964. Nehru's death later in the month provided further grounds for putting off this electoral battle.

As soon as the action of the state legislature was announced, political activity in Tezibazar ceased. The rapidity of its inception once the original election date was fixed and its equally speedy hibernation once the postponement was announced are indications of the total involvement of local politics with that of the region. In May, June, and the early monsoon months, it was as if no politically competitive groups existed in the town—in an active sense.

Finally, in August, new elections were fixed for November 3. Political activity again resumed but in a different form and with different allegiances than before. For many reasons, the hoped-for merger of Bhanu Pratap and Sita Ram Dube had fallen through: the flare-up of state Congress factionalism,[4] Bhanu's

[4] Perhaps, too, the Thakurs feared that Dube, a Brahmin who in the past had been identified with the Gautam-Tripathi (both Brahmins) group, would not be acceptable to the Gupta faction.

distaste for the eventuality of Muslim and Akbar's control over the deciding vote in the committee, and Moti Lal's changed attitude toward a compromise on the candidates contributed to its failure. Further, because the Jana Sangh continually gained strength in the town as the food situation in the area worsened and government control over commodities increased, the Congress had to remain unified in the ensuing election. However, as a concession to Akbar and in order to weaken Moti Lal's political independence, Bhanu Pratap allowed no one of the Umar Chairman lineage to stand and only one from the Leader lineage. This action more effectively cut Moti Lal's caste and lineage backing on the committee. On the other hand, the now-rejected Dube did not choose to rejoin Tribeni Lal and the Jana Sangh, for he preferred to play the role of "spoiler," perhaps in order to gain one or two seats in the committee and thus to reach a fair position from which to maneuver for further political concessions. This decision may have been motivated by fear that Tribeni Lal would become Chairman if the Jana Sangh won. Then, too, as long as the Congress party remained unified, Dube —like most other citizens—felt the Congress party to be unbeatable, and the Brahmin did not want to go down in what he foresaw as a general Jana Sangh defeat. The Jana Sangh stayed pat. They felt their position improved with every passing day, with every rise in prices, with every disclosure of official corruption surrounding the supply of food grains and sugar and every lengthy line in front of a government rations shop.

It is an indication of the extent to which ideological considerations in voting habits (as distinct from communal *group* ideological leanings) had penetrated the town that Dube and his independents gained only about 5 percent of the vote.[5] Dube was in fact committed to old-style politics: of factional power manipulation and personal charisma to bind an ascriptive base; of winning as an indication of opposition, not as an espousal of ideological goal. The Congress party, which won all ten seats on the

[5] I had left Tezibazar before the election. I have, however, these figures and facts from trustworthy informants.

municipal council claimed about 60 percent of the vote, and the Jana Sangh won 35 percent.

The case of the 1964 elections thus presents a picture of how factional dealings and "party" turnover among the component caste, lineage, and communal groups, and outside influences all conspire to determine the outcome of an election. It also demonstrates again the rising importance of national party considerations in the town and the polarization of the urban locale into competitive, ascriptively based communal groups as essential elements of the political process.

Tezibazar is involved and absorbed in the regional political system in two ways: The town fully interacts with the state and district political and administrative organization, and local groups are transformed to fit the style of political development emerging at state and perhaps national levels. I refer here especially to the maturation of the Muslim community and to the rise of the nascent Baniya movement. This development goes hand in hand with the growing importance of regional political parties and ideologies and consequently with the amalgamation of the town with higher and more comprehensive political bodies. As the situation now stands, town-wide leaders emerge from the older level of caste-lineage political groups because of the absence of a complete stereotyping of the political front into communities. This leadership, which in general is parochial or opportunistic as far as ideological convictions are concerned, nevertheless helps amalgamate the town with larger political entities through the pragmatic use of such higher-level structures to chastise local rivals. All political roads in Tezibazar ultimately lead to Jaunpur or Lucknow or, albeit tenuously, even to Delhi.

This discussion of politics extends a step further the characterization of the town as a whole. The apparent absence of social and economic community in Tezibazar leads to the town's total involvement in the modern political process. This process supplies and defines the town's system of social control, power alignment, caste and lineage conflict, communal antipathies, and preferential access to certain economic prerogatives. Further, we have seen how such political conflict motivated the establishment of a second intermediate school in the town, and how in its more generally negative aspects it hinders the internal collection of funds for town improvement. Politics is, then, the community aspect of the town, its source of entertainment, its stage for drama and intrigue, its often all too opportunistic and unbridled life.

CHAPTER 13

The Umar

In the following consideration of the Umar, they are looked upon solely as a representative Tezibazar Baniya caste, and their characteristics as noted serve simply to illustrate specifically the arguments advanced in the preceding chapters. No attempt is made to catalog them and their social structure. Rather, their relevance here is directly proportionate to the degree to which the caste's internal and external organization complements or reflects the structure of the town.

In its recent development, Tezibazar has shown a pervasive tendency toward increasingly direct amalgamation into the larger political and economic as well as social and ideological spheres of the region and nation. Such, too, has been the trend of Umar caste development in the last thirty years, and, indeed, the progress of the Umar caste complements the evolution of the town as a whole. One evidence of this direction is the attempted merger of various local endogamous and commensal castes into a larger Umar unit which encompasses two states, many districts, and an extensive population. This development has been spearheaded by the formation of an All-India (*sic*) Umar Vaisya Sabha (council) with annual meetings, an elective leadership, a newsletter (*patrika*), and regular duties as the symbol of communality of all Umar people.

As this supra-local organization of the Umar has developed, the powers of the local Umar castes have withered. Even though there has been little breakdown in local endogamy or commensal restrictions, various political institutions of the local Umar groups have degenerated. Particularly, the *tat* and its *pancayat*, agencies of social control within the local caste body, are no longer the arbiters of internal caste political action or social conformity. This degeneration has promoted another sort of involvement of the local Umar within a larger social framework. Thus, the town's political arena is increasingly called upon to adjudicate what formerly were internal caste or lineage disputes. Both the formation of the Umar Sabha and the replacement of local caste institutions by town politics highlight the amalgamation of the local Umar caste into novel, larger organizations: on the one hand, into the town as an aspect of regional Indian society; on the other, into the nationally directed, voluntary interest group, the Sabha. Basically, however, the unity is more one of sentiment and elite organization than of popular social mutuality.

THE UMAR "CASTE": SUPRA-LOCAL FEATURES

The Umar have long been resident in Tezibazar. Their local history goes back at least as far as the semi-legendary figure Ganga Visun, who amassed a fortune as victualer to the British army before the Mutiny. The larger and more ancient past of the caste is even more obscure, and there have been various attempts to trace its origin to Vedic peoples. Although this latter historical exercise is the concern of only a few dedicated caste scholars, it does nonetheless illuminate a vital aspect of present-day Umar caste grouping and expectations: the search for a phylogeny which substantiates the single ancestry of all Umar in India.

The Several Types of Umar

The Umar "caste category" [1] on an all-Uttar Pradesh and Bihar state level (there are some Umar in Madhya Pradesh and

[1] I use the term "caste category" to refer to all de jure endogamous groups presently referred to as Umar. The concept is taken from F. G. Bailey, who defines a caste category as an aggregate "of persons, usually in the same linguistic region, usually with the same traditional occupation and sometimes with the same caste name. These are not social strata since, while they are exhaustive . . . and exclusive . . . they are not unambiguously groups. They are categories made up of groups with similar attributes"; "Closed Social Stratification in India," *Archives Europeannes de Sociologie*, IV, No. 1 (1963), 107.

Bengal states, but they are recent immigrants) is an amalgamation of several different social groups which thirty or forty years ago were separate de jure endogamous or commensal castes [2] and which existed in a hierarchical rank ordering. Even now, differential commensal rules are observed although officially disallowed, and marriages between the formerly endogamous units are few. More successful has been the political combination of these disparate groups into a regional "caste" council or Sabha which promotes and symbolizes this new Umar unity. The recent and imperfect amalgamation of these groups was self-consciously pursued by a number of individuals who tried to convince the formerly separate castes of their historical oneness. Even now, there are some Umar who refuse to acknowledge this past identity, although a persistent search is carried on by one or two older members of the community to prove it from historical records and, particularly, old reports by amateur British anthropologists.

These early reports touch closely (and often erroneously) upon the complexity and multiplicity of the groups styled Umar. Two early British would-be ethnologists—W. Crooke and the Reverend M. A. Sherring—accepted the oneness of all Umar historically and give some space to this "numerous and influential tribe of Baniyas." [3] Both agree also in reporting the division of the U.P. Umar into three endogamous and differently ranked bodies which, in order of relative status, are: (1) *til* Umar; (2) *dirh*, or *derh*, Umar; and (3) *dusra, dusre* (*dusar*) Umar. Sherring notes that these three groupings are further divided into twenty sections each, but he does not identify the sections either in name or type of structure. Crooke further remarks upon the existence in Mirzapur city of two endogamous groups—the *khara* and *dosar*, or *dosra*, Umar—but does not specify in what way they are related to the tripartite division of the Umar specified before.

Commonly, in Uttar Pradesh and other parts of India, caste

[2] That is, *bans;* see Chapter 5.

[3] Sherring, *Hindu Tribes and Castes as Represented in Benaras*, p. 298.

categories such as the Umar rank their component castes differentially, with the higher in the western localities and the lower in the eastern region. A developed form of this status system is used by the Umar and accounts for two of the names cited by Sherring and Crooke. *Dirh* or *derh* Umar was a term used by eastern (U.P.) Umar groups to refer to the totality of their historical brethren in the west (central U.P.).[4] Omar is now the accepted designation for the western Umar who have admitted unity with the eastern branches. The term *"dirh"* or *"derh"* may mean a number of things: (1) "stable," in reference to the fact that this Umar section was not influenced by the Muslim conquest or that it did not allow widow marriage, for until recently, all western Umar were distinguished from *most* of their eastern comrades by a refusal to allow the marriage of widows; or (2) "rigid" and "upright," a derivation from the same word but here used in reference to the rigidity of social customs among the western Umar. The term *"derh"* or *"dirh"* was formerly an aggregate category used by the eastern groups to specify the west and was not used by the westerners themselves. The word "Omar," however, is taken from the usage of the Western Umar. Neither term is used to refer to a single group; rather, both are merely employed for convenience in referring collectively to all western groups (or all westerners in the Sabha).

The term *"dusra* Umar" or *"dusar* Umar" has a similar usage and is employed by the western groups to indicate the eastern Umar taken in total. It is not used by the easterners themselves. Thus, two of the Umar "groups" listed by Sherring and Crooke are no less amorphous and no more corporate entities than the mass term "Umar" itself.

As for the third term, the *"til* Umar," no vestige of this unit or group—did it ever exist—now remains. Two schools of opinion hold sway in Tezibazar about this matter, which incidentally show the importance of anthropology in the developing world. The majority of Umar who have heard of the *til* Umar at all (and most have not) say they lived in the eastern districts of

---

[4] The main areas of concentration of Umar in the west are Hamirpur and Kanpur districts; in the east, Mirzapur and Jaunpur districts.

U.P. and engaged in oil pressing and sales (*til* = sesame). Because this occupation is somewhat degrading, they were the *lowest* (contra Crooke and Sherring) kind of Umar. A few historically minded people nurtured on the work of Sherring profess the other opinion. They accept the *til* Umar as the highest status group, but explain that at the present they have somehow merged with the other eastern Umar. Even though anthropological expositions may be of little value to the economic and social advancement of the underdeveloped world, they nevertheless have a consequential impact upon old men reminiscing about caste origins.

Status differences are still considerable between western and eastern Umar, although they are no longer expressed in the traditional terms of differential commensality or in social customs such as widow marriage. Now the criterion is wealth. The western Umar are more urbanized and on the average better off financially. They share in the general economic precedence of central U.P. over the eastern region. The Omar look down upon their eastern kin as unsophisticated and petty, small-town Baniyas. The basis of distinction seems now to be changing so that the wealthy and urbanized Umar of Mirzapur city (eastern) and Kanpur city (western) are becoming progressively more unified and more divorced from their respective rural sections.

Such was not the case thirty years ago. All the western groups, because they did not wish to be associated with their eastern brothers, used the term "Omar" to denote themselves. They derived the name from the auspicious word "*om*" and employed it to buttress a more prestigious background for their caste origins. Since these more urbanized and wealthier groups took the lead in the formation of the All-India Sabha, this body was called the "Omar" Sabha until 1947, when the name was changed to the "Umar–Omar" council. A large dispute continues in the Sabha about whether it should be called the All-India Umar or Omar Sabha.[5]

Within each of the categories of *dirh* Umar and *dusar* Umar

[5] For convenience, I shall hereafter refer to the council as the "Umar" Sabha.

there are further subdivisions. To descend to this subsequent
level is to begin dealing with de jure,[6] prescriptively endogamous, commensally independent castes. The latter are the Umar
bans (although this term is not employed). The two categories
also ranked each other. In the western, or *derh*, Umar were two
castes: the *kanyakubjiya*, or *kanaujiya*, Umar and the *jahanabadi*, or *umre*. The former was named after the region occupied
by the ancient kingdom of Kanauj; and is mainly found in
Kanpur and Fatehpur districts. Further west come the *jahanabadi*s who rate themselves superior to the *kanyakubjiya* Umar.
These two territorial castes were for the most part endogamous
—not only by distance considerations but also by distinct pro-
scription. Some informants reported that the *jahanabadi*s would
infrequently marry hypergamously with the *kanyakubjiya*—
that is, a boy of the former group would take as wife a daughter
of the latter. These two castes would not share *kaccha* food or
smoke the *hukka* together, although they would accept *pakka*
from each other. Two main groups existed in the eastern or
dusar Umar. These were the *khara* ("upright") and the *dosar*, or
dosra, Umar (the latter were sometimes referred to as *dusar*; see
below). The *khara* were so named because they did not permit
widow marriage, whereas the *dosar* did. The *khara*, a very small
grouping, are found only in Mirzapur city or as minute immigrant enclaves elsewhere, and therefore in that city alone is a
term of balance, "*dosar*," applied to the Umar who did allow
widow marriage. For the rest of the eastern Umar, including
those in Tezibazar, the term "Umar" sufficed, because they all
belonged to the group which permitted widow marriage. Neither *khara* nor *dosar* Umar (meaning here all non-*khara* Umar in
eastern U.P., not just those of Mirzapur) would intermarry
except very rarely in a hypergamous fashion, nor would they
take *kaccha* food or smoke the *hukka* together. They did, how-

---

[6] These were de jure in the sense that within these groupings there
were de facto endogamous regions based on convenience and considerations of distance and expense in contracting marriages.

ever, sit down in unison to *pakka* feasts. They were as distinct from each other as they were, in unison, from the western Umar.

There is room for much confusion between the terms *"dusar,"* referring to all eastern U.P. Umar, and *"dosar,"* meaning all eastern Umar who allowed widow marriage. Such possibilities are heightened by the frequent interchange of *dusar* for *dosar* and vice versa. The lexical similarity between these terms stems from their denotation of a similar social positioning; both groups referred to are *"dusra"*—which in Hindi means "lower" or "secondary"—to one or another category. The *dusar* Umar are *dusra* to the *dirh* Umar; the *dosar* are of lower rank than the *khara* Umar of Mirzapur. It should be remembered that these are attributed names not real ones. The fact that the Tezibazar Umar use *dosar* and *dusar* interchangeably in reference to their Mirzapur caste brothers *only* indicates that *"dusar"* (meaning eastern Umar) was an aggregate category restricted in employment to the western branch and only understood there, much in the same fashion that *"dirh"* is used only by the eastern people. In the following pages, *"dusar"* will always denote the reference term for the totality of eastern Umar, whereas *"dosar"* will refer to those Umar of the eastern districts who allowed widow marriage in contradistinction to the *khara*.

The Umar caste category, with its component groupings listed in traditional rank order, is as follows:

Western Umar (Omar)—called *derh* Umar by easterners
    jahanabadi or *umre* de jure caste
    kanyakubjiya or *kanaujiya* de jure caste
Eastern Umar—called *dusar* by westerners
    khara de jure caste (in Mirzapur city only)
    dosar de jure caste (applied especially in Mirzapur city but
        sharing social relations with other Umar, including those
        of Tezibazar, in eastern U.P.)

In the last forty years, all these various types of Umar have been gradually merging into a single de jure if not de facto social unit. This trend has emanated from leading personalities who formed the political voice of this proposed unified entity, the

All-India Umar Sabha. In this case, political identity of a sort was achieved long before social oneness or equality.[7]

The *khara* and *dosar* groups in Mirzapur and the rest of eastern U.P. have moved further in the direction of social unity than have the eastern and western Umar. Informants stated that now *khara* and *dosar* would eat *kaccha* food together. Since I never saw such interdining in Mirzapur, and since, as we shall see, the eating of *kaccha* food together is not interdicted *outside* of Mirzapur (or away from the particular group's home area), I cannot vouch for the truth of such statements. There have been no more than ten marriages between Tezibazar families and the *khara* of Mirzapur or other areas. Local Umar say that more intermarriage goes on in Mirzapur itself, where the wealthy (richer than Tezibazar) *dosar* are fully accepted by the *khara*. This factor of money is indicated in Tezibazar as well. All but four such intermarriages from the town are between wealthy members of the two leading lineages, the Chairman and Leader, and two others occur in another of the (recently) rich families of the N.A. Then too, some of the *khara* women who married into Tezibazar allegedly came from families either outcasted or in bad standing with their natal group. So there are many qualifiers to even this tentative social identity between *khara* and *dosar*. Still, the situation has improved since 1935, when one of the first *khara* girls was married into Tezibazar. At that marriage ceremony only the girl's father attended—both the girl's brothers and paternal uncles absented themselves. It is important to note, however, the factor of money as a leveler of the social path to such marriages.

If the nonpolitical (non-Sabha) ties aligning *khara* with *dosar* are few, those binding *dusar* and *dirh* Umar or Omar are almost nonexistent. As one informant put it, "The restrictions [against intermarriage] have died, but the practice has not yet

[7] There is an interesting comparison here with the Muslim community, wherein also political unanimity has preceded at least one form of social identity—intermarriage between all the component Muslim castes.

begun." Only four Tezibazar marriages have been made with Omar, and although the town families involved have been of the highest status and wealth, the western Umar families involved have suffered reprisals in their own groups. Thus, again, only the Chairman Umar lineage (three marriages) and the Leader lineage (one marriage) have gained access to the Omar. A man whose son married an Omar girl from Hamirpur explained that his *samdhi* (son's wife's father) was now of considerably lower standing in his group because he had married his child with a *dusar* Umar and at the present cannot easily marry his children into his own Omar group. As with the *khara* intermarriages, the wealth of the *dusar* family is quite important in settling the contract. Often, too, the father of an Omar girl need give considerably less dowry to a *dusar* family than he would within his own group, not only because they are of lower traditional status, but, at least in Tezibazar, because their dowry expectations are set at a lower level.

Tezibazaris claim that Omar and *dusar* Umar will now share *kaccha* as well as *pakka* food. Because I never attended a feast where both were assembled, I cannot assess the truth of this statement. In any case, such contacts would be limited to families related or to be related by ties of affinity, and if they were willing to establish such relations, they surely would not hesitate over commensal restrictions. Another interdining situation occurs among Omar and Umar attending the All-India Sabha meetings, but because of the highly sophisticated nature of these individuals and their dedication to the goal of Umar unity, no thought is given to commensal restrictions. In fact, both in the case of Umar-Omar and *khara-dosar*, a statement of commensal regulations is hardly tenable since there are so few opportunities to put these rules to the test. People want to believe that all Umar are one and equal so they say that they can all eat together now. Taken as a statement of ideological conviction, it indicates the creation of supra-local caste thinking; taken as a statement of interactional reality, it is as tenuous as the behavior on which it is supposedly based. The fact that complete freedom of interdining has not yet been accomplished between groups of Umar within Tezibazar itself (see the discussion of *tat* below) makes the unregulated interchange of *kaccha* food at these much higher levels appear doubtful.

The All-India Umar-Omar Sabha

In 1928 the first meeting of the All-India Omar Vaisya Sabha was held in Shahabad, western U.P. Intermittently since then, this council has met in various parts of U.P., primarily in the western districts. No meetings were held in 1930, 1937, 1942, 1944, 1945, 1949, 1950, 1952, 1954, nor from 1956 to 1962. Only five out of twenty meetings have occurred in eastern U.P., and as aforesaid, until 1947 the name of the Sabha was "Omar," and only since then has "Umar" been used in the title. Throughout its history the All-India Sabha has been the elite activity of a few wealthy and interested members of the U.P. Umar caste category. This esoteric base is attested to by the gap in meetings between 1956–1962, which came about because neither of two men—Tribeni Lal, who was involved with school problems, and another man who was besieged by sudden business duties consequent upon his family's partition—was able to give the time needed to organize the Sabha. The 1963 meeting, however, saw the most popular representation of all the Umar congregations when several hundred people assembled.

A meeting of an All-India Umar or Omar grouping had been held as early as 1918, but from lack of support it soon disintegrated. A number of other abortive attempts to establish sectional councils for eastern and western Umar were also organized.

Tribeni Lal of the Umar Chairman lineage attended the 1931 All-India Sabha meeting as the first and only representative from Tezibazar. At that time there were only two other delegates from the whole of eastern U.P. (Mirzapur). Tribeni Lal was later to become President of this council many times and one of the leading figures in establishing its reputation.

The Umar Sabha is composed of individuals from the various locales in which the Umar reside and its organization is along democratic, nontraditional lines. Each man has one vote on the various proposals and for the several officers. The latters' terms are for one year only, and their duties consist mainly of overseeing the annual assembly. Resolutions are discussed and carried or vetoed by majority vote. The delegates then return home and try to convince the Umar in their region of the good sense behind the Sabha's pronouncements. In the early days the main dispute had to do with widow marriage, which was opposed by many Umar groups (and which even now, if necessary because of inability to restrain the widow's sexual impulse or the economic burden of her presence in the household, is often considered demeaning). There was less disagreement on such other main issues as the necessity for all Umar to eat together, the education of boys, an end to early marriage, and the unity of all castes of Umar. At no time did the Sabha take an anti-British or pro-Congress stand. Most of the members were, in fact, passive sympathizers with the colonial regime.

The All-India Umar-Omar Sabha now primarily engages in social work and social exhortation of its membership. The Sabha publishes a Hindi magazine every other month which contains blurbs and pictures about important figures, marriage announcements, articles encouraging the membership to remain vegetarian and abstain from alcohol, and other features along the lines of a "trade" journal. Each copy also contains a list of Umar who subscribe to the magazine—and this list is the emblem of corporateness for this newly-styled Umar caste. Rarely does the Sabha take a political stand or offer a national political opinion in the journal; its single interest lies in binding the Umar into a unitary body.

The journal, as well as the entire Sabha itself, has a heavy urban orientation, particularly toward Kanpur and Mirzapur cities, which have the largest concentrations of Umar. Even though Tribeni Lal and Moti Lal are the only Tezibazar Umar

who attended the 1963 meeting, many of the town Umar subscribe to the magazine and are becoming increasingly interested
in the Sabha's program.

The present actual work of the Sabha is directed toward social
welfare projects, although because it has only resumed on a large
scale again after an intermission of six years, these activities are
hardly more than plans. There is hope of setting up a fund for
aid to poor members of the community or to those sick and
disabled. As we shall see more clearly later, no attempt is made to
have the All-India Sabha perform the duties of internal social
control formerly enjoyed and employed by the local caste bodies.

ORGANIZATION OF TEZIBAZAR UMAR

Tat and Pancayat

Of equal importance with the amalgamation of Umar with
other Umar is the process of integration which concerns the increasing merger of the Tezibazar Umar in the sphere of town
activities and organization. How intralineage and intracaste disputes are moving out of the traditional caste system of social
control and into the realm of competitive town politics has already been described. Primarily one intracaste group organization, the *tat* (caste faction), and its agency of social control, the
pancayat, have suffered a diminution of influence and an atrophy
of use as a result of this town-directed externalization of conflict.

Within the Umar of Tezibazar are two formal divisions of the
local caste group termed *tat*. *Tat* refers to the jute sacking laid
down as mats for guests at feasts. These mats plus eating and
cooking utensils, pillows, tents, and other paraphernalia needed
in entertaining large marriage groups are supplied by each *tat* to
its respective members, who over the years have paid for them
by contributions.

Each *tat* contains several Umar lineages or joint families
within the town. Membership in the *tat* is inherited. However,
an individual could switch to another *tat* at will if it would

accept him. Individuals desiring such transfers were often those who had been thrown out of their former *tat* for breaking its rules or moral code. The *tats* in Tezibazar as elsewhere among Umar were factional organizations of competition and exclusion and as such waged a continuous war for control over membership and therefore over the local Umar caste segment. Twenty years ago, before the present state of structural degeneration set in, each *tat* was a separate commensal unit, sharing neither *pakka* nor *kaccha* food [8] nor smoking the *hukka* with its rival *within the town*. Marriage between the *tats* was by the nature of the then limited geographical area of selection a necessity and not strongly avoided, but a match of this type was not considered the most advantageous.

The *tat* structure was not unique to Tezibazar. Almost everywhere the Umar lived, they were divided into such organizations. In nearby Pratabgarh town there were three such exclusive units, while in Mirzapur city there were no less than four. In all small villages within fifteen miles of Tezibazar where Umar lived, there were also *tats*, and sometimes there was a combination of talents and organization between these rural factions and various of the town ones. The extent of such larger *tat* developments in the Tezibazar region corresponded with the old de facto marriage area.

A generation or more ago, no Tezibazar Umar expected to marry much beyond fifteen miles distance from the town, and the average was considerably less. Now it is not uncommon for marriages to be contracted fifty to sixty miles away, and several relations of affinity span hundreds of miles. What has changed are not prescriptive regulations against intermarriage (since most marriages still take place within the de jure endogamous caste), but rather restrictions by default—that is, based on considerations of distance and expense. The poorest Umar still

[8] Some informants claimed that the *tats* would share *pakka* food but not *kaccha*. I could not obtain a satisfactory resolution of this point, although the more historically minded Umar claimed they did not share either sort of food.

marry close to home, and undoubtedly rising wealth has provided impetus for this territorial extension of marital ties. Even
though there was no caste restriction on marriage outside a
fifteen-mile radius, the formal group organization of the *tat* was
based upon this local endogamous region. As the influence and
importance of *tat* organization began to decline, the boundaries
of marriage were enlarged beyond the geographical limits of this
structured entity into other *tat* locales (within the de jure endogamous caste) which were similarly losing their identity and
social definition.

Each *tat* has a formal, hereditary leader called *panc* who is in
charge of organizing and directing his group, setting its moral
stance, punishing "caste" (that is, *tat*) offenses, and carrying on
the dispute with the other *tat*. The *panc* is selected from the
family of the leading or originating *tat* member, and this position
passes down from father to first-born son over the generations.
If the eldest son is not resident in Tezibazar, the office passes to
his younger brother. Another *tat* position is the appointive post
of *caudhari*, the duties of which are to call the members together
for feasts and other group occasions. The *caudhari* can also
formally "outcaste" (that is, out-*tat*) an individual, but such
powers have not been employed for twenty years, and the
thought of such a happenstance is more an object of humor than
of fear. Even though the social control, competitive, and commensally restrictive aspects of the *tat*s in Tezibazar have died, the
offices of *panc* and *caudhari* remain, but have authority only in
minimal social functions (both *tat*s in Tezibazar, moreover, now
use the same *caudhari*).

The local *tat* groups and the conflicts which gave them rise
have not been resolved but only superseded and vitiated.
Growth of a political realm in the town and the expression of
caste and lineage conflicts within it undermined the appeal and
control of the *tat*. Competition for leadership of the local caste
body which the existence of separate *tat*s symbolized was no
longer as important in the eyes of members as the political world,
which had been suddenly enlarged to encompass first the town

and then the region. Thus, there is a striking difference between the intracaste *tat* structure and the use and valuation of position within that structure as it existed thirty to fifty years ago and its present condition of atrophy: the value of *tat* has been totally superseded by the modern political sphere.

According to the local Umar, *tat*s in Tezibazar are as ancient as Umar occupation of the town. However, the present ones date their origin to about a half-century ago. The larger and wealthier *tat* was represented fifty years ago by Narain Das of the Umar Chairman lineage; this man was the classificatory *caca* of Tribeni Lal and the actual grandfather of the present *panc*, Mahavir Prasad. His real opponent was Mata Tahal of Baragaon (the *tehsil* headquarters fifteen miles away), whose local representative in Tezibazar as leader of the second *tat* was Ram Kumar. The Ram Kumar *tat* (for such is the fashion in which the *tat*s were and are named) was completely autonomous in terms of organization, but it would never have achieved any success in challenging the Narain Das *tat* without the help of the Baragaon group. That is, structurally and in origin the factions of Mata Tahal and Ram Kumar were separate, but in the competitive politics for control of the local (de facto endogamous) Umar grouping, they found themselves advantageous allies, with the dominant and challenging power in the hands of the Baragaon leader.

Ram Kumar's *tat* seems to have originated when it was outcasted from the Narain Das group over some matter of caste morals. At that time, the Narain Das *tat* contained most of the Umar lineages in Tezibazar, including the Leader lineage and, of course, the Chairman lineage—except that Tribeni Lal's father (the father's brother's son or classificatory *bhai* of Narain Das) left his *tat* for Ram Kumar's over a family dispute about inheritance. The Narain Das *tat* also established ties with about ten nearby villages—either with *tat*s within each village or, if they were not so divided, with the entire Umar community therein. Similarly, Ram Kumar's *tat* was formed of Tezibazar lineages (including his own, which is popularly known as the "Medical

Hall" lineage from the present occupation of the *tat panc*)—although to a smaller extent than his competitor's—as well as *tat*s or whole Umar populations in twelve surrounding villages. About six or seven villages in each *tat* overlapped, and it was in these that a division into two groups existed. Therefore originally the *tat*s not only had to do with the allocation of feast equipment and utensils or with a limited commensality based on the outcasting of a group for disobeying caste mandates but also exercised an explicit judicial and, therefore, political function as well. Through the *tat*, a man could become accepted leader of a group. To be sure, once begun the office became hereditary, but the innovator established his own reign. The fact that Ram Kumar was outcasted from the Narain Das *tat* was not politically significant. But when his lineage mates and other discontents followed him in the creation of a new intracaste body and when he further joined his nascent and weaker group with that of Mata Tahal in Baragaon, a definite threat to the leadership of the local endogamous group was mounted. The two *tat*s and their leaders played a game for the political control of the local caste body through their judicial powers in the *pancayat*s (see below). Numbers were naturally crucial in this matter, and the competition for control over the local Umar group most often took the form of attempting to attract the membership away from the opposite *tat*. The different *tat*s would immediately accept whoever had been outcasted or had left a competitor.

One case exists where a transfer of *tat* allegiance was refused. Forty-four years ago, when the Leader lineage supported the Muslim candidates for the N.A. committee in opposition to those of the Chairman lineage, they were outcasted from the Narain Das *tat* (see Chapters 9 and 10). This lineage was also not accepted by the faction of Ram Kumar and for twenty years, or until the time when the *tat* became meaningless and devoid of social consequences, remained an autonomous body. They have now been readmitted into their former *tat*. This lineage is sometimes referred to as a third *tat*, but it seems never to have had the formal functions of *pancayat* held by the other two groups nor was its organizational base ever larger than a single lineage.

Another point worth noting is the degree of unanimity of lineages within the *tat*. That is, Ram Kumar's following was heavily grounded in his own "Medical Hall" lineage. The same is true for the lineage of Narain Das, save for the father of Tribeni Lal. This singleness of direction and action by lineages no longer exists nor can it be employed except in town politics.

The *tats* were commensally separate in both *pakka* and *kaccha* food, although they freely accepted *pakka* from many other *biradari*s: Thakur, Brahmin, Kisan, and other Baniya. The pattern of interdining was used to signify status and identity within the caste even though it was not so regarded in external relations. However, there were many occasions on which these rules were modified. Generally when people left Tezibazar, they felt free to take *kaccha* and *pakka* food with members of the opposite *tat*. Further, since marriage was often contracted between members of the different factions, this relationship complicated observance of commensal restrictions. Mata Tahal, the leader of the Baragaon *tat*, married daughters into the families of both Narain Das and Ram Kumar. At Umar marriage feasts, it is customary for the fathers of the couple to eat a token *kaccha* meal together after the nuptials to symbolize their new affinity. Mata Tahal had thus to eat with the *tat* of Narain Das, but only he of his faction performed this action and it was looked upon as a special dispensation considering the circumstances. Obviously there were necessarily many such dispensations given the relatively limited area of intermarriage.

The demise of the Tezibazar *tats* began about twenty years ago under the influence of the propaganda of the All-India Sabha for unity and, more importantly, the death of the political importance of control over intracaste judicial structures such as the *pancayat*. A decade ago all the Tezibazar Umar began eating together—but in a qualified sense, either not discerned or admitted by Umar informants. For the *tats* did not meet and agree to cease hostilities; they only became of a sudden functionless and their conflicts meaningless; like an ant in an avalanche, they were covered over, buried and dead, but preserved in fossil form. The avalanche of town political conflict and the movement by caste and lineage conflicts into this new world had started in 1922 and steadily increased, especially after Independence. What value was there in maintaining competition for internal caste power through control of the *pancayat* when this office no longer brought anything except a certain ritual station, and even this was slight? What need was there to muster the support of the Umar residents for caste control when it was control of town government which people set as their goal? The caste aspect of politics had been completely superseded, and anyone holding the reins to such organization enjoyed whatever advantage accrues to a buggy owner in a world of automobiles.

There are two indications of the extent to which the *tat* organization was merely superseded, not resolved; merely buried, not eliminated. One is the fact that the factions and their *pancs* exist at the present, only nominally to be sure, but nonetheless this existence is significant in itself. The two *tats* have never reconciled their differences and merged; they have only agreed to a stand wherein each maintains its own identity, and the questions of precedence or rank are left unasked.

The second indication is more complex. Informants claim that now the *tats* freely interdine—but this is hardly a true statement of the situation. Outside of Tezibazar, members of the several *tats* interdine without hesitation—both *pakka* and *kaccha* food. However, this practice is not at all novel. Within Tezibazar one true innovation in *tat* commensality has been made. The factions now are willing to share *pakka* food together—an extension of what applies to most other castes or status categories to an intra-caste grouping. Rarely are any *kaccha* feasts given within Tezibazar where the two *tats* might be forced to sit down together. Such events limited to one *tat* only used to take place and were important for the proceedings of the *pancayat* (see below). However, fifteen years ago, it became customary to give *pakka* feasts so that, for political reasons of cementing advantageous friendships, almost all castes could be invited (see Table 20). The feast given on the eve of the departure of an Umar *barat* (groom's marriage party) is *pakka,* and Thakur, Kisan, Brahmin, and the other Umar *tat* attend and eat in a single line. An Umar

Table 20. Guests at Umar marriages

Guests	Party A *	Party B †	Party C ‡
Direct affinal and			
consanguineal relations §	19	21	16
Lineage mates	21	8	42
Caste mates	25	64	33
Baniyas	16	43	21
Brahmins	16	19	7
Thakurs	7	12	1
Kisans	9	17	1
Kayasths	3	1	–
Sudras	–	1	–
Muslims	20	8	3
Officials	15	7	12
Foreigners	2	–	1
Total	153	201	137

* Marriage party invited for younger brother by leading Congress leader (N.B. figures for Muslims and officials) in economic straits.

† Marriage party for daughter invited by nonpolitical, below average income man (daughter's marriage is always larger; the high figure for caste mates is a result of the small size of this lineage).

‡ Marriage party for son invited by man with above average income and political ambitions (note the large size of lineage, which is the basis of political power).

§ By direct affinal is meant all relations of nonclassificatory nature. Almost every Umar is related affinally to every other one in Tezibazar by classificatory affinal ties.

man who is too poor to afford a *pakka* feast (and these are highly expensive) or does not wish to ingratiate himself politically gives a *kaccha* feast, and here only his own *tat* need be invited. People say such men have small incomes, and the imposition of another *tat* upon their purse would be cruel. Whatever be the popular sentiment, there is still little *kaccha* commensal contact between the *tat*s within Tezibazar. Further, a man is bound to invite members of his own faction to a feast first before he includes any from the other *tat*. Thus, the question of identity as exemplified in interdining regulations has been modified, but not fundamentally: in the allowance of *pakka* interchange between the factions, the Tezibazar Umar accord their separate internal divisions the equivalent commensal status of Brahmin, Thakur, and Kisan.

However, in their avoidance of *kaccha* common feedings, they indicate that nothing exists but a veneer of unity buttressed by sentiment. The situation in Tezibazar is more advanced than the condition of the Umar in nearby Pratabgarh town, where it is said the *tat*s still refuse to interdine under any circumstances within their urban area.

The *Pancayat*

Tat and *pancayat*—that is, the body which supervised social control within the caste faction—were coterminous. Whenever a serious matter required a ruling on caste morals or custom, the *tat panc* would call on representatives from all families in his *tat* to assemble and adjudicate. In the case of Ram Kumar, his *tat* often met in *pancayat* with the Mata Tahal *tat* of Baragaon because of their political and social alliance, although there was no necessity for such joint activity. The *pancayat* did not consist of any elected guardians of the public morality, but contained the *panc* and all wealthy, aged, and otherwise influential *tat* members. Its powers of coercion were extensive. The *pancayat* could levy fines, or require expiatory feasting of the entire faction, or, most seriously, could socially ostracize and outcaste—although the efficacy of the final mandate was vitiated by the existence of another, receptive *tat* group.

Usually such matters of import were not considered in a special *tat* meeting. Rather they were heard at the *kaccha* (thus limited to *tat* members) feasts attendant upon marriages or other celebrations. One informant explained:

In former times the marriage feasts were primarily *kaccha*, and they were more or less limited to caste brothers of the same *tat*.

The feast at the marriage was *kaccha* so that all caste members regardless of wealth could give an honorable meal. Within *kaccha* there were differences in quality and the quantity of food, but even the poorest could afford *dal* and rice, and every man of the caste had to accept this—even the richest. But as people became richer, they preferred to give more expensive *pakka* feasts with fancy sweets for their own *biradari,* and they were also motivated by desire that all castes should eat in the same line. In villages and among poorer Umar people, still primarily *kaccha* feasts are given, and *pakka* given only to non-*biradari* guests.

[At this *kaccha* feast] the assembled party heard all complaints about infringement of caste rules or personal disputes before the food was served. [wryly] This often went on for a long time before people got their dinner. [Interview in English.]

For the last fifteen years the custom of the initial *pakka* feast has supplanted the former *kaccha* institution. Now, too, no time is set aside before the meal for a discussion of caste or *tat* disputes, nor must everyone feel as one before they savor their dinners. The very fact of serving *pakka* food completely obviates the necessity for *tat* unity. Even in the *kaccha* feasts held at marriages on the second day, such tradition is not maintained, and it is merely the feasting of an identifiable Umar mass, not a self-identified Umar group.

Where, then, and when does the *pancayat* exercise its power and duties of social control? Indeed, it never does (except regarding impersonal matters such as the upkeep of the caste temple), and the former sanctions of social restraint are now absolutely defunct. Neither the Ram Kumar *tat* nor that of Narain Das in Tezibazar has met with its rural components in over thirty years. These former entities are now so vague that even the *panc*s are unsure of just which villages were contained in their faction and which belonged to their adversary's. The last man to be outcasted by either Umar group in Tezibazar was Suraj Lal Dalal, who kept then—and still keeps—a prostitute-dancer, but this action took place twenty years ago. This man is childless, but even had he offspring, many people felt that in no way could he be hindered from finding a mate within the caste, and they speculated that even his background would not pose an insurmountable difficulty. Suraj Lal Dalal was, however, cut off from much contact with his caste mates in the town, seemingly more by personal choice than by their avoidance of him. Another case from the Kalvar caste—which is much more unified than the Umar—will illustrate the force of caste interdiction at the present. Prem Nath Kalvar opened a shoe shop twenty-five years ago and was formally outcasted by his local *biradari* on the grounds that such an enterprise was unbecoming a Hindu. However, Prem Nath has never attempted to regain his caste status, for he maintains that the shoe trade is like any other business. In truth, he suffers few disabilities from his outcaste status. He still openly associates and eats with his many friends among his caste fellows. He sees no problem in finding eligible matches for his children. To be sure, he is not invited to public feasts of his caste, but aside from this penalty he pays no further social price for his wrongdoing.

The Umar situation is still more acute, for not even such token form of social punishment is possible:

My *tat* still meets at marriage feasts and such occasions, and previously we would take such opportunities to talk about caste offenses and rules, and so forth. Nowadays no one talks about such matters at any time because the *pancayat* has been obliterated (mit gaya). We have not taken any caste action in ten or twelve years. But we could if we had to, that is, if someone broke the rules.

[Question: Don't people break the caste rules now?]

Surely, people do all sorts of sins against the caste, but no one gives a fig about punishing them. One of the worst [sins] is the breaking of a marriage contract after it has been firmly settled. [This] is very common in my caste, and the problem was put before the *tat pancayat*. But no one listens to the *panc* anymore, and so my attempts to curtail this evil practice are to no avail.

The above statement is by Laksmi Narain of the Medical Hall lineage, present *panc* of the Ram Kumar *tat*. Mahavir Prasad, the leader of the other *tat*, noted: "People are no longer willing to listen to the *mukhiya* [*panc*], or obey his commands." The supersession of the formal structure of the *tat* in terms of its political functions has been accompanied by a resultant reduction in the powers of internal social control exercised by the *tat* or any other caste body. No longer does the fear or even threat of outcasting immobilize behavior considered antisocial. No longer does the *pancayat* act as mediator to quarreling groups or as exegete of individual actions. The bare bones of *pancayat* organization remain, but they are fleshed neither with public acceptance nor, consequently, with power.

Pancayat and Sabha

With the atrophy of the *tat* and its *pancayat*, the local caste and its internal groupings have relinquished control over caste members. Although many people regard the absence of *tat* conflict as beneficial to the new unity of the Uttar Pradesh Umar "caste," almost without exception all Umar regret the passing of the functions of social restraint from the local caste body. They feel that even though the *tat* externally created friction with other such groups, its important duty of control almost outweighed any loss of unity in the local Umar caste.

What replaces the local Umar *tat pancayat*s in a temporal sense, if not in the performance of their duties, is the All-India Umar Sabha—that large, heterogeneous body composed of what are in effect separate castes. Not only is its organization different from the old *pancayat*, but so are its operational techniques and its social methods. It replaces outcasting and caste regulations with social work and substitutes the old kinship-residential corporateness with a "togetherness" based on a conscious recognition of identity by the most advanced and educated Umar. The old *tat pancayat* punished to maintain unity and ostracized to retain caste custom; the new Sabha propagandizes its members to regard each other as brothers and solicits adherence to traditional caste usages. In no way, then, is the Umar Sabha a replacement for the *pancayat* as a caste organ of internal social restraint and behavioral supervision.

These two institutions are clearly of fundamentally different types and operate in intrinsically different ways. The boundaries of the traditional Umar castes were set by endogamy and commensality. The new Sabha does not operate on the basis of such social boundaries; it succeeds only to the extent it is intellectually subsidized by forward-looking, generally rich and urbanized Umar. Membership in the traditional Umar castes was based on coresidence and kinship or birth. Although membership in the new Sabha is also determined by birth as an "Umar" in an exclusive sense, it is more importantly conferred by payment of dues (or magazine subscription) and a conscious desire for membership. Thus, the corporateness of the new Sabha must necessarily depend wholly on its selective, self-conscious membership and the growing sense of "Umar brotherhood" or "Umar caste-patriotism."

The formal organization of leadership between the traditional caste order and the new Sabha is also considerably different. In the former, the opinions of certain men had greater weight than others because of ascriptive criteria such as hereditary leadership of a *tat* or age or because of wealth and local influence. The machinery of decision making explicitly rested on a nonegalitarian principle, wherein, however, every attempt was made to achieve a unanimous decision symbolic of a common purpose. In the Sabha, leaders are elected by open and majority vote. Each man has only one vote. However much in practice the Sabha is run by bosses or local big men or there is consistent pressure for unanimous decision and the avoidance of electoral contests, the formal mechanics of leadership and decision making are based on a democratic electoral principle.

Many Umar in Tezibazar hoped that the All-India Sabha would begin to assume the duties of social control formerly exercised by the *pancayat*.

These people have been necessarily disappointed and left with no hope for future internal regulation of their caste. Tribeni Lal, who, as we have seen, was one of the leading figures in the formation of the Sabha, summed up the present and future situation in this fashion:

The All-India Sabha does not have the organization to do such things as social control. Instead, it must do social work such as helping widows and poor and bringing the Umar together. . . . Since the All-India Sabha cannot manage this sort of social control, and the *tat* in most respects is dead, there will probably be no one to enforce the caste rules in the future.

Clearly, then, local caste organization is breaking down. The emergence of the unified All-India Sabha, the de jure merging of the several regional Umar castes, the enlargement of the boundaries of the previous endogamy of territorial convenience, and the transfer of internal caste disputes into the town political arena are all aspects of the absorption of the local Umar groups into a regional caste or town political structure. The autonomy of the local caste body has been sundered, and its current course is directing it further into organizations and interests of larger scope.

A similar process has been noted for Tezibazar town as a whole, and the tenuousness of internal Umar caste social regulation clearly parallels the situation in Tezibazar itself. After the departure of the zamindars, only the externally organized and externally given political system mediated between the individual and the town. So, too, now with the demise of *tat* and *pancayat* those few caste social control activities not performed in the town political arena come only as noncoercive suggestions from the social-welfare-directed regional Umar Sabha.

CHAPTER 14

Preindustrial Urbanism
and Tezibazar

The picture which we have presented of the present-day community organization of a small urban locality in India and the suggestions we have advanced to explain historically and economically its political organization and social order may well have relevance beyond Tezibazar itself and its mercantile population. Let us now consider what this relevance may be: what significance Tezibazar may hold for discussion of preindustrial centers in India; in what relation the town stands to the wider perspective of oriental urbanism; and how Tezibazar's structure is representative of an urban type intermediate between preindustrial and industrial urban centers.

PREINDUSTRIAL URBANISM

Gideon Sjoberg has convincingly advocated a re-examination of the concepts of "urban" and "city" in the social sciences.[1] Sjoberg feels that many of the theoretical statements on world urbanism have been marred by an ethnocentric preoccupation with the form of the city in the western, industrialized world. He demarcates two types of city, the preindustrial and the indus-

[1] Gideon Sjoberg, *The Preindustrial City* (1960); "The Rural-Urban Dimension in Pre-industrial, Transitional, and Industrial Societies," *Handbook of Modern Sociology* (1964), pp. 127–160; "The Rise and Fall of Cities: A Theoretical Perspective," *Urbanism and Urbanization* (1964), pp. 7–20.

trial, which differ fundamentally in technology, morphology, class structure, function, kinship, and family organization.[2]

We need not here recapitulate all of Sjoberg's criteria and analysis. Suffice it to say that the Tezibazar of a century ago fit neatly into Sjoberg's preindustrial type. One of Sjoberg's points, however, has special importance for the thesis of this book. Sjoberg maintains that urban growth in the preindustrial world is "highly correlated with the consolidation and extension of a political apparatus."[3] The famous cities of the preindustrial world were all formed as a result of governmental initiative into the administrative centers of empires. Commercial function is not a sufficient cause for preindustrial urbanism; rather, it is the very political function of the city which promotes commerce: "Nowhere do cities, even commercial ones, flourish without the direct or indirect support of a well-established state system. We can find no instance of significant city-building through commerce alone."[4]

Max Weber has similarly commented:

Often the existence of a market rests upon the concessions and guarantees of protection by a lord or prince. They were often interested in such things as a regular supply of foreign commercial articles and trade products, in tolls, in moneys for escorts and other protection fees, in market tariffs and taxes from lawsuits . . . . The lord or prince might also hope to profit from the local settlement of tradesmen and merchants capable of paying taxes and, as soon as the market settlement arose around the market, from land rents arising therefrom.[5]

F. Benet has made the same point respecting the Near East:

The Near Eastern city is the result of a political decision. This city is not . . . the *outcome* of trade and merchants. The Near Eastern cities were created "whole," and though they immeasurably strength-

[2] Sjoberg, *op. cit.* (1960), pp. 1–13.   [3] *Ibid.*, p. 68.
[4] *Ibid.*, p. 76.
[5] Max Weber, *The City* (1962), p. 73. Weber, however, believes that market towns unattached to local lords could arise in natural economic zones.

ened the merchant's hand one feels they were not absolutely essential to all the trafficking of caravan trade.[6]

The morphology and class structure of preindustrial cities indicate their political-administrative origins. The preindustrial city has a sharply demarcated two-class system consisting of a political and/or religious elite and a low class-outcaste group (which includes merchants). Sumptuary rules clearly mark the individual's class position, and mobility between classes is exceedingly difficult.[7] What Sjoberg calls the elite and lower, or outcaste, classes respectively might better be termed the politically enfranchised and the politically disenfranchised groups in the society. The elite are not only economically preponderant; they are also the manipulators of political power. Political position and power determine economic class. The morphology of the preindustrial city is an extension of the political power structure. The main business district does not compose the city center. Rather, the political and/or religious edifices of the ruling elite dominate the urban landscape. Markets originate around these as secondary outgrowths, dependent upon the favor if not the outright subsidy of the ruling elite.[8]

Thus, in preindustrial urban centers the governmental apparatus of the state and the city are one and the same:

Throughout the preindustrial civilized world the upper class, and above all the society's ruling stratum, is urban in nature. . . . The writings of Pirenne and his followers, who emphasize the bourgeoisie's control over the European city of the late Middle Ages in northern France and the Low Countries have convinced some social scientists that the nobility of that era were established elsewhere, in rural areas. But this was not the case during the period of bourgeoisie ascendancy (essentially a short-lived one) in selected cities and was still less so in Europe as a whole or the Middle Ages in general. The fact that the nobility rather quickly regained control of the political apparatus in numerous cities wherein the emergent

[6] F. Benet, "The Ideology of Islamic Urbanization," *Urbanism and Urbanization*, pp. 111–126.

[7] Sjoberg, *op. cit.* (1960), pp. 108–142.   [8] *Ibid.*, pp. 96–99.

"middle class" had temporarily displaced them is evidence of their retention of an urban base.[9]

The most distinctive quality of preindustrial urbanism, then, is its political origins. Urban centers grow up around elite political figures, as administrative nodalities, and as habitations for the ruling classes.[10] This point is crucial to the discussion of Tezibazar. Here, too, the market area arose around the political and religious edifices of the ruling zamindars as a result of their direct subsidy. This development occurred in similar fashion twice in the history of the town, in the formation of Old Town several hundred years ago under the aegis of the Khan Muslims and in the creation of Sahibganj by Rai Udai Baks toward the end of the nineteenth century. From its origin until the end of the nineteenth century, the "political class" organization of Tezibazar was sharply demarcated into two groups: the zamindars, who had sole access to political power and the administrative machinery and who were intermediaries between the town and the outside; and the remaining urban population, primarily traders, cut off from the main avenues of administration and enjoying wealth from a source (commerce instead of land) which did not bestow political power or following.

To the extent that Tezibazar fits Sjoberg's model of preindustrial urban formation, it indicates that a main element in the thesis of this book—the role of the (zamindar) founder—is not peculiar to this town but is rather a specific reflection of the norm of preindustrial urbanism. This point need not rest on Sjoberg's model alone. Throughout Hindu and Muslim times

[9] *Ibid.,* p. 113.

[10] I do not see as a problem the fact that Sjoberg talks about preindustrial *cities* whereas Tezibazar is a town. His arguments apply to the nature of preindustrial urbanism in general, not to such artificial entities as "cities" opposed to "towns." The division between cities and towns loses much of its fineness as one deals with the preindustrial world, where the technological and occupational distinctions between industrial city and town did not exist, and where population differentials were also much smaller (due to the small size of preindustrial urban centers in general).

and until the coming of the British, town formation in India was a reflex of state control, the prerogative and duty of the ruler whether emperor or only local zamindar and an essential policy of any size government.

Thus R. L. Singh and K. N. Singh write of town formation in part of the middle Gangetic Valley:

[From 1200–1750 A.D.] it will be seen that the majority of towns and townships were founded by Rajput chiefs, subchiefs or vassals thereof during the process of their conquest and colonization when they needed new footholds for their military needs, or afterwards for security, consolidation, and administration, and still later for stronger political hold on peripheral areas and economic gains through land use extension in the uncultivated waste or forested lands. . . . Foundation of settlements exclusively as trading posts was rare, if at all, until about the later [sic] half of the eighteenth century. Rural weekly markets were held under the aegis of some local zamindars, and one of the causes of the multiplication of markets was the intercompetition among the families of repute for holding markets at their respective seats.

Thus, all the towns and market villages that evolved up to the eighteenth century grew as the strongholds of the chiefships and baronies.[11]

Merchants followed the courts of the local overlords, and their position depended upon the political fortunes of the ruling elite. R. L. Singh and K. N. Singh write, "The Bansi merchants reported . . . that their ancestors had followed the Raja, when the latter was compelled to move." [12] When new towns were begun by subordinate lineages of Rajput chiefs, they stocked them with craftsmen and merchants brought from the parent lineage town.[13] N. G. Jain reports a similar situation for eastern Maharashtra, where the decline of a dynasty signaled the demise of its capital town irrespective of its commercial nodality. Jain

[11] R. L. Singh and K. N. Singh, "Evolution of the Medieval Towns in the Saryu-par Plain," *National Geographical Journal of India*, IX (1963), 9–10.

[12] *Ibid.*, p. 10.   [13] *Ibid.*

concludes: "Most of the towns in the region have historical [political] and religious background. For long time commerce and industry followed in towns located for non-economic reasons." [14]

The creation of the cities of Poona and Azamgarh as well as the small town of Barhaj all take place at the instigation of a local political authority.[15] It is this personage, too, who creates the market and attracts commercial population to it: "Under the benevolent patronage of the Majhauli Raja, there settled [in Barhaj] several families of Kalvars, Baniyas, other tradesmen as well as professionals such as the boatmen, blacksmiths, carpenters, potters, etc." [16] After its destruction by the Muslims, Poona city was rebuilt through grants of *kaul,* or free protection, by the political authorities.[17] Even the later growth of the city was through direct supervision and subsidy by the state apparatus:

The formal establishment of a ward usually took the form of a grant to a person, enjoining him to take steps to populate the ward with artificers, traders, etc. and giving in return the hereditary office of the chief of the ward with certain dues and perquisites attached to it. Usually the newly settled traders and artisans were exempted from payment of occupational and other taxes for a stated number of years after the establishment of the ward.[18]

These references indicate that the distinctive political and social history of Tezibazar was probably characteristic of the great majority of cities and towns in pre-British India. Let us

[14] N. G. Jain, "The Emergence of Urban Centers in the Eastern Districts of Vidarbha (Maharashtra)," *National Geographical Journal of India,* X (1964), 148–149.

[15] For Poona, see Gadgil, *Poona: A Socio-Economic Study, Part I, Economic* (1945), p. 7; for Azamgarh, see Satish Chandra Singh, "Evolution of Azamgarh," *National Geographical Journal of India,* IX (1963), 176; for Barhaj, see K. N. Singh, "Barhaj: A Study in the Changing Pattern of a Market Town," *National Geographical Journal of India,* VIII (1961), 22.

[16] K. N. Singh, *op. cit.* (1961), p. 22; see also Satish Chandra Singh, *op. cit.,* p. 181.

[17] Gadgil, *op. cit.* (1945), p. 7.

[18] Gadgil, *Poona: A Socio-Economic Study, Part II, Social* (1952), p. 9.

now consider what this fact has to say about the internal organization of such urban centers.

ORIENTAL URBANISM

Max Weber in several of his works notes that in the ancient and medieval Orient the formation of an independent and functional urban government or corporation similar to the cities of medieval Europe did not occur. Weber writes:

Outside the western world there were cities in the sense of a fortified point and the seat of political and hierarchical administration. But outside the occident there have not been cities in the sense of a unitary community. In the middle ages, the distinguishing characteristic was the possession of its own law and court and an autonomous administration of whatever extent.[19]

Weber does not find such autonomous administration, independent legal apparatus, or traditional social cohesion characterizing oriental urban areas. He remarks that oriental villages often were more self-administered and independent of the state than were the cities.[20] Weber makes this point with special reference to India. Through the divisive influence of caste and thus the relative impotency of guild organization, through the strict commensal restrictions on public feastings and the self-protective policies of great and small princes, the urban center in pre-Muslim India never developed a sustained independent identity. "In most Indian cities, the king and his staff always have remained dominant." [21]

[19] Max Weber, *General Economic History* (1927), p. 318.
[20] Max Weber, *op. cit.* (1962), pp. 89–90.
[21] Max Weber, *op. cit.* (1958), p. 90. D. R. Gadgil, however, notes that in Gujarati cities during the eighteenth century, strong guild organizations called "Mahajans" existed and transcended caste and kin lines. In Gujarati towns, civic organizations composed of all merchants regardless of caste were also found. The Mahajans are said to have been autonomous of the state, although Gadgil cites several examples of their use by political authorities for tax collection or supervised craft production. Gadgil concludes that trade organization in Gujarat was the most highly evolved in India. "In most other parts such elaborate

A. K. Nazmul Karim has sought to tie what he (following Weber) regards as this uniquely oriental lack of urban community to an irrigation regime (on the model of Marx's and Wittfogel's "oriental agriculture").[22] But the passage from Sjoberg cited above indicates that the comparison of oriental urbanism with the "free" cities of medieval Europe may be unfair, since the latter phenomenon was so temporally and geographically limited. Over the long range, Sjoberg argues, preindustrial urban centers in both east and west were similar in their existence as an extension of the political authority, without any independence or internal cohesion apart from that subscribed from the ruling agency. He notes as one of the qualities of the preindustrial city type, its segmentation into ethnic or caste divisions which exist as self-contained, noncooperative, and sometimes hostile neighborhoods.[23]

Whether this lack of community is a specifically oriental or, instead, a general preindustrial urban trait is not pertinent here. Even if limited to the oriental area, this analysis of community in urban areas has much importance for the findings on Tezibazar. I have shown how Tezibazar lacks a traditional cohesion based on caste ranking or commensality or a *jajmani* system. I have indicated how it is split by caste and communal antagonism and by an economic market which in its impersonality and competition is not hindered by any form of traditional social restraint. The town as a unit has been portrayed as an amorphous commercial enclave structured in the past only by the paternalism of the zamindars, organized in the present only by the tactics of electoral battle. In Tezibazar, then, the lack of traditional community is a product of its political origin as well the prime determinant of the present-day interaction between town and

---

organizations of craftsmen and traders did not either exist at all or were indistinguishable from particular caste or community organizations," *op. cit.* (1959), p. 28.

[22] A. K. Nazmul Karim, *Changing Society in India and Pakistan*, pp. 33–53.

[23] Sjoberg, *op. cit.* (1960), p. 100.

nation. If the lack of community be taken as typical of the (oriental) preindustrial city, then the present analysis of Teziba-zar and its interaction with the larger society is pertinent to urbanism in a great range of nonindustrial or undeveloped complex societies.

Unfortunately, the comparative sociological data which might substantiate this assertion exist in only the most sketchy form. For India, primary historical materials relating to the internal organization of cities and towns are sociologically unsophisticated and fragmentary at best. Weber based his distinction between oriental and occidental urbanism primarily on Indian data. More recently, Karim has summarized historical and modern accounts of the Indian city, although he is still forced to rely heavily on Weber's research. Karim concludes:

The different castes and communities living in the Indian city could never produce a homogeneous community (i.e., a city community standing for political and social rights of its own). . . . The merchants and handicraftsmen, that is the bourgeoisie as a class organized in the guilds, never attained the supremacy which their counterparts in Europe won for themselves when they seized power in the towns. This was . . . because of the social weakness imposed upon the bourgeoisie by the peculiar Indian social stratification and also because the Indian town was nearly always an outpost of the territorial State and as such was governed by prefects or boards appointed from the center.[24]

Better materials on urban constitution exist for other areas. Wolfram Eberhard finds that the traditional Chinese city was sharply divided into self-contained wards which generally did not cooperate in any city-wide activities. He notes, too, the lack of a city law or any legal or social definition of the urban populace as a cohesive citizenry.[25] Eberhard maintains that "the

[24] Karim, op. cit., pp. 73–74; see also pp. 53–86. Karim's interesting discussion is marred by undue reliance on Pirenne's theories for medieval Europe and Marx's for the Orient.
[25] Wolfram Eberhard, "Data on the Structure of the Chinese City in the Pre-Industrial Period," Economic Development and Cultural Change, IV (1955–1956), 262, 264, 267.

city [was] tightly controlled by the government, not as an independent unit, but as part of a territory. There were no municipal institutions, but there were institutions which served the wards of the city. These, however, did not participate in the administration." [26]

G. E. von Grunebaum reports much the same situation for the preindustrial city in the Near East:

[The *polis* was] not an autonomous association of citizens. . . . Self-government with executive officials designated by the full citizens there never could be, for the city constituted not a closed corporation, a share in which defines the citizen, but merely a *functionally unified*, administrative entity with a more or less stable complement of settlers or inhabitants. . . . There were no qualifications to be met to obtain admission to citizenship in the Muslim town for the simple reason that there was no body of town dwellers in whom political or civic authority was seen to reside. [27]

Further on, von Grunebaum more clearly defines what he considers "functional unity": "In its business district (and in a sense in its 'official' section—mosque and governmental buildings —as well) the unity of the town is apparent. . . . For the unity of the Muslim town is functional, not civic." [28] This same limited unity—that of the common market site and administrative center—is the only sort which characterized Tezibazar in the past.

In their analyses of the Near Eastern and Chinese cities, von Grunebaum and Eberhard portray a lack of urban community in these areas which Karim and Weber report in general for India and which the history of Tezibazar represents in specific form.

TEZIBAZAR AND POSTCOLONIAL URBANISM

The preceding discussion gives historical depth and comparative breadth to the portrayal of Tezibazar's social evolution. But Tezibazar has changed in the last fifty years to the point where it

[26] *Ibid.*, p. 265.
[27] G. E. von Grunebaum, *Islam: Essays in the Nature and Growth of a Cultural Tradition*, p. 142.
[28] *Ibid.*, p. 147.

no longer fits Sjoberg's preindustrial type. Gone are the zamindar overlords and the political and economic pattern which they originated and supervised. However, it is also clear that Tezibazar has not been reorganized in an industrial pattern. The technological and functional base, the organization of commerce, the continuation of unified caste and communal groups, and commensal and marital restrictions all preclude such an interpretation. Tezibazar of the 1960's is an intermediate urban center, having grown out of the preindustrial style but not having attained the industrial order. Just as in the past Tezibazar's urban organization represented a widely spread type, so, too, the present postcolonial structure of the town may reflect the reality of urbanism in many of the undeveloped complex societies now studied by anthropologists.

Sjoberg has talked about what he calls the "transitional" urban type to be found in those undeveloped countries of the world now attempting to industrialize. Unfortunately, in delimiting this type, he discusses the *process* of transformation of the city from preindustrial to industrial more than the *structure* of such "transitional" urban centers. Sjoberg refers to the impact of large population growth and urban migration upon the so-called transitional city. He also notes that with increasing industrialization, the ties binding the city to its rural hinterland are increased, and the state intervenes more and more in the life of the peasant.[29] Little light is cast, however, on the actual organization of these "transitional" urban centers.

The portrait of Tezibazar's present social, economic, and political structure herein presented provides a specific example of Sjoberg's "transitional" urban type. These data also suggest certain emphases differing from Sjoberg's formulation (including a preference for the term "postcolonial" rather than "transitional"). Sjoberg does not underline the fact that his transitional urban type is much older than the relatively recent attempts of the nondeveloped nations of Asia and the Americas to industrial-

[29] Sjoberg, *op. cit.* (1964), pp. 143–144.

ize.[30] This type predates any changes in the technological order toward industrialization. In fact, preindustrial cities began to disappear the moment industrial nations came into existence and began to set up colonies. Just as the preindustrial states did not remain unchanged in the presence of industrial nations, so, too, the preindustrial cities were altered by their existence in a world of industrial cities although they themselves were not industrialized. Even the backwater town of Tezibazar was fundamentally altered from the preindustrial type over a half-century ago. Sjoberg's "transitional" also suggests impermanence and implies that the direction of urban change in the nondeveloped countries is toward an industrial form.[31] A broader historical viewpoint indicates, however, that such postcolonial types may be of long standing and may be a relatively permanent urban accommodation by formerly preindustrial cities and societies to colonial and postindustrial existence.[32] The rate of industrial growth may be and may have been so minimal that the society and its urban centers become entrenched in an intermediate status. For many undeveloped countries, the road to modernity has been paved with pious hopes and oratory rather than fundamental economic changes. Even if the postcolonial type is less permanent than either the preindustrial or the industrial, must we assume that its direction of change is toward an industrial urbanism? For these

[30] Sjoberg is inconsistent in this matter. At one point, he identifies the "transitional" urban type with a changed technological order: "The heyday of the preindustrial city is past. A few cities of this type persist in almost pure form, but *in the face of industrialization* they are fast relinquishing their special characteristics. . . . Even where *industrialization is well advanced* . . . survivals of traditional forms crop up on every hand" (*op. cit.* [1960], p. 355; italics mine). In another place, however, he equates the "transitional" urban type with a colonial status: "One result of . . . colonialism has been that the cities of transitional (or underdeveloped) countries in Asia today exhibit a semi-preindustrial, semi-industrial character, industrial traits having been superimposed upon an already existing urban social structure" (*op. cit.* [1964], p. 15).

[31] Cf. Sjoberg, *op. cit.* (1960), p. 337.

[32] See Walter Riggs, "The Theory of Developing Politics," *World Politics*, XVI (1963–1964), 167.

reasons the term "postcolonial" seems preferable, since it implies neither a temporal duration nor a historical progression for these urban centers.

More fundamentally, an expanded historical perspective on such postcolonial urban areas requires a radical revision of Sjoberg's underlying perspective. Sjoberg defines both preindustrial and industrial urbanism in terms of the society's technological base.[33] But in the case of intermediate cities and societies, it is not technology which determines their status (since in most nondeveloped complex societies, the amount of industrialization accomplished has not directly transformed social and economic organization to any large extent). Their peculiar position is that they exist at a preindustrial technological level even though their politics and economics have been highly conditioned by the industrial world. The nonindustrial complex societies of Asia and Latin America have felt the effects of colonialism or economic dependence on the industrial world primarily by alterations in their political and commercial sectors rather than in their technological base.[34] The history of Tezibazar is a local reflection of the process of political change accompanied by technological inactivity that presently defines the peculiar intermediate position of the nonindustrial nations and their urban centers.

[33] *Ibid.*, pp. 7–8.

[34] Marshall D. Sahlins and Elman R. Service (eds.), *Evolution and Culture*, pp. 117–119. Riggs (*op. cit.*, p. 169) writes similarly: "It was specifically the impact of the West, and the externally threatening industrial revolution, which compelled the leaders of Iranian society to launch a program of basic institutional change. Such elite-guided transformations (and these include alien imperialist as well as nativistic transformations) involve the elaboration of bureaucratic instrumentalities to impose economic change."

CONCLUSION

From Zamindar to Ballot Box

The town of Tezibazar is defined as an urban market center by its service institutions, its regional economic functions, and its placement in the political machinery of the modern state, but not by any traditional social conditioners of a community existence or urban cohesiveness. In Tezibazar both the caste rank system and commensal restraints are anomalous; they impose a regime of separateness—a separateness of equivalence with regard to Brahmin, Thakur, Kisan, and Baniya, of inequality in the case of Muslim and Sudra. In both situations the opposition or repulsion of castes is what is primarily structured by the traditional social order in the town. Hierarchy does not exist as a binding force, nor as a dimension of rating within a generally accepted caste status ordering.

The social world of the town is further fragmented by caste and communal antipathies which replace the merely negative rank and commensal systems with positive disavowals of unity and community. The interpersonal tone of Tezibazar, conceived by the local populace as morally derelict and opportunistically derived, further cleaves the urban locality. Even what functions locally as a *jajmani* system is of fundamentally different structure from that of its rural counterpart. In Tezibazar this relationship—even to the limited extent it continues at the present—does not bind caste family to other caste family but rather merely designates territories of control for the various caste functionaries usually required by a Hindu family. Each neighborhood and house site may be advertised as convenient to washerman, barber, and Brahmin priest.

The absence of social cohesion also reflects the economic order. The latter seems to leave no room for a town community of interest or an urban cohesiveness of effort. By the nature of the rural underdeveloped economy and the conservative subsistence attitude of the businessman (both interrelated and mutually derived), a highly evolved price competition exists in town commerce which leads the merchant into extensive adulteration and chicanery. The structure of the market and the competitive interpersonal relations within it disqualify any movement toward town social community. Then, too, the actual familial organization and capitalization of commercial concerns restricts business establishments, practices, and town trade organizations or councils. These general disabilities to a community effort or a supra-familial structure of trade are clearly shown in the absence of all social and group restraints upon the operation of the town market.

There is an explanation partially historical and partially economic for this social and commercial order. The economic determinants concern the aforementioned style and organization of business, commercial ventures, and trading groups. The historical factors have to do with the formation of the town and market by local overlords who provided it with political, economic, and social cohesiveness. As these individuals set the rules for the market and offered inducements to attract commercial settlers, they also created an existence for the town above and apart from the internal interests and internal organization of the populace. Thus, even in the traditional order, the cohesion of Tezibazar was a product of external intervention, of supra-local supervision. In the early part of the present century, however, the old zamindar-overlords were reduced and then finally removed by economic pressures. An interim period followed during which the duty of social control formerly performed by these overlords was continued on a reduced scale by newly affluent merchant-zamindars. Finally, even their role was dissolved by the economic permutations of the Second World War and the changes in legal status enacted with zamindari abolition.

What replaced the old rule of the zamindar was the new legal machinery of the modern state, particularly after independence in 1947. This apparatus became the sole conditioner of local group involvement and unity within a common social framework. It determined the power and prestige structure of the town; it assumed the juridical role in intracaste conflicts previously enjoyed by such corporate group structures as *tat* and *pancayat;* it gave valuable access to certain economic prerogatives and the ears of influential officials in a bureaucratized society. The personal rule of the zamindars gave place instead to the impersonal modern political arena where coordination of effort and alliances are conditioned in large measure by the prevailing winds of individual and group aggrandizement.

With the replacement of zamindar by ballot box came also a novel transformation in the attitude and actualities of the town. The overlords had been local men. The town political arena, especially after Independence, was only a limited aspect of a much larger world to which Tezibazar became increasingly amalgamated as it became more dependent on politics to resolve its internal disputes and order. This merger with a regional political structure has taken an interactional form in the direct determination of local politics by regional issues and groups and the alignment of local politicians with district and state leadership. The other aspect of this amalgamation has been the creation of politically significant communal *groups* on the local level which reflect the unstructured sentiment-based electoral communities of the region. As the local political scene becomes progressively more conditioned by such communal groups, the union of town with region and nation on the basis of party ideologies will increase.

Finally, the Umar Baniya caste concorded in its internal organization with the general processes at work in the town. The growth of the Umar All-India Sabha, the preliminary and still mainly ideological amalgamation of the several regional de jure

Umar castes, the puncture of the previous de facto endogamous region based on distance and expense, and the movement of intracaste squabbles into the town political arena all highlight the absorption of the local Umar group into a regional "caste" or town political structure. The evolution of the local caste body is toward further loss of identity in these organizations and interests of larger scope. This process is advanced by the demise of intracaste corporate group structures like *tat* and *pancayat* as agencies of internal caste competition and regulation. The latter development not only promoted the absorption of the local caste group into the All-India council but also the demise of social controls exercised by the local caste body. In this lack of internal local organization and control mechanisms the Umar resemble the social structure of the town outside of politics. Many Tezibazar people hoped that the Umar Sabha would take over the social restraint duties formerly performed by the *pancayat*, but they have been disappointed, for what comes forth from the noncoercive and social-welfare directed Umar council are only "goodthink" paper exhortations. Just as in the town the ballot box has succeeded the zamindar, so in the caste the suggestion box has irrevocably replaced the black ball.

At first glance, it may seem that the pattern of interaction between Tezibazar and the larger society has changed little in the last century. In the past, the agency of integration in the town was the zamindar, who represented on a local level the governmental apparatus of the preindustrial state. At the present, the modern electoral machinery performs a similar role, although it is part of a wholly different administrative and national structure. To be sure, both these systems effectively bind the town to a larger political and territorial organization. But the structures of interaction, as channeled through the zamindar and as defined in the electoral process show strikingly different natures.

The paternalism of the zamindar meant that the town was a private domain, not touched by the region and nation except as such pressures filtered through the local overlord. The important rules of intercaste behavior, of markets, and of social and ritual proprieties emerged from the mandates of this personage. Conversely, the modern electoral system and the politics of independent (and no longer preindustrial) India have thrown open the town to social action unhampered by traditional or paternalistic restraints and consisting of an individualized and unrestrained competition for power, position, or physical amenities. What is significant is that this political and economic manipulation is increasingly taking direction from similar competition at the regional level.

How valid these generalizations about Tezibazar are for urban centers in other nonindustrialized complex societies is a question which cannot be answered here. A circumstantial case for Tezibazar's relevance can be drawn from the data and formulations of Sjoberg and Weber, but primary materials at hand, particularly for the postwar decades, are scant at best. In many recent surveys of Indian urban areas, the attention given to migration, living standards, family pattern, and other such matters has provided information of great value.[1] These studies would, however, have had much more bearing on this question had they employed a larger historical perspective and a greater comparative orientation. Before more comprehensive hypotheses can be entertained, such studies of the traditional and present organization of towns and cities must be made, both in different regions of India and the rest of the world.

[1] See Radhakamal Mukerjee and Baljit Singh, *A District Town in Transition*; C. Rajagopalan, *The Greater Bombay*; D. N. Majumdar, *Social Contours of an Industrial City*.

APPENDIX I

Survey Data on Business and Businessmen

Both the survey of town businesses and the sample of Baniya merchants were conducted in Hindi with the help of an assistant. I personally conducted all but a few enumerations. The first survey was extensive and short and not intended as a probe in depth. The second survey (of Baniya merchants) was also patterned but purposely contained many open-ended questions designed to elicit opinions at length. This latter material, however, was used only to substantiate or clarify previous extended observation or informant statements. In most cases, the survey questions were designed to provide quantitative data supplementary to direct observation and informal and unstructured interviews. Aside from the quantitative aspect, the surveys were peripheral to other, anthropological techniques for the analysis of social behavior and custom.

Tables 21, 22, and 23, on the pages following, supplement the data on business and businessmen already provided in the text.

Table 21. Caste, family, and population of businessmen

Caste	No. of families			No. of people		
	Resi-dent	Non-resident	Total	Resi-dent	Non-resident	Total
Brahmin						
1 caste	12	14	26	75	147 (25 *) †	222
Thakur						
1 caste	4	6	10	21	81 (19 *)	102
Baniya castes						
Umar	98	–	98	653	22 *	675
Kesarvani	38	1	39	255	– ‡	255
Halvai	35	–	35	191	20 *	211
Bhuj	34	–	34	179	–	179
Kalvar ‖	31	–	31	211	47 *	258
Teli	22	–	22	154	5 *	159
Kasodhan	7	1	8	18	11 *‡	29
Sonar	7	–	7	47	1 *	48
Agarval	6	–	6	43	–	43
Agrahari	3	–	3	5	–	5
Thather	2	–	2	6	–	6
Kasera	1	–	1	9	–	9
Madhesiya	1	–	1	2	12 *	14
Total, 13 castes	285	2	287	1,773	118 *	1,891
Kisan castes						
Ahir	5	5	10	26	34	60
Barai	5	5	10	27	41 (4 *)	68
Koiri	6	2	8	41	29 (14 *)	70
Nau	1 §	4	5	–	33	33
Kurmi	3 §	2	5	9	19	28
Bari	1	4	5	9	33	42
Lohar	3	2	5	20	12	32
Kevat	1	2	3	10	15 (2 *)	25
Mali	1	1	2	5	– ‡	5
Kahar	–	1	1	–	5	5
Pal	1	–	1	12	–	12
Total, 11 castes	27	28	55	159	221 (20 *)	380
Sudra castes						
Camar	12	7	19	82	54 (9 *)	136
Pattahar	2	2	4	6	8	14
Dhobi	3	1	4	24	6	30
Total, 3 castes	17	10	27	112	68 (9 *)	180

Table 21 (cont.)

Caste	No. of families			No. of people		
	Resi-dent	Non-resident	Total	Resi-dent	Non-resident	Total
Other Hindu castes						
Srivastava	1	1	2	2	19	21
Arora	1	–	1	8	–	8
Total, 2 castes	2	1	3	10	19	29
Muslim castes						
Shekh	19	6	25	191	55 (5 *)	246
Kunjra	24	–	24	135	–	135
Julaha	17	1	18	144	12	156
Halvai	10	–	10	78	–	78
Fakir #	9	–	9	45	–	45
Curihar	5	2	7	30	15 (5 *)	45
Darzi	6	–	6	33	–	33
Nau	5	1	6	34	5 (1 *)	39
Khan	2	–	2	11	–	11
Cikuva	2	–	2	13	–	13
Chipi	1	–	1	9	–	9
Kayasth	1	–	1	7	–	7
Bhangi	1	–	1	2	–	2
Other **	3	1	4	34	10	44
Total, 14 castes	105	11	116	766	97 (11 *)	863
Grand total, 46 castes	452	72	524	2,916	751 (202 *)	3,667

* This figure represents members of joint families who now live outside Tezibazar or away from their rural families, but who are still considered part of the joint family (usually either their wives or children or both are at home). This figure is indicated in nonresident totals by parentheses.

† One firm held in absentee ownership by a family of this caste. Family data obtained.

‡ Same as † except that no family data was obtained.

‖ Kalvars claim they are Ksatriyas not Vaisyas.

§ Data on one resident family not obtained.

Fakir includes two endogamous divisions (prestige names: Shah and Shah Kalandar).

** Includes Muslims who refused to give caste, widows who did not know.

Table 22. Firms employing *munim*s and/or servants

No. of employees per firm	No. of firms	Type of firm *				No. of *munim*s	No. of servants
		w	r	m	s		
1	52	10	27	4	11	5	47
2	24	13	5	3	13	7	41
3	12	5	3	3	1	5	31
4	8	2	4	2		6	26
5	4	2		2		4	16
6	1			1		1	5
7	3	1	2			1	20
8	2	1		1		2	14
9	1	1				3	6
12	1			1			12
14	1	1				1	13
Total	109	36	41	17	15	35	231

Grand total *munim*s and servants, 266

*﹐w = wholesale; r = retail; m = mill; s = service.

Table 23. Distribution of businesses among various castes

Caste	No. of businesses	No. of business types
Umar	115.50	32
Kesarvani	44	20
Halvai	40	11
Bhuj	39.67	9
Kalvar	35.50	19
Teli	20.50	11
Brahmin	25.83	15
Thakur	10.50	7
Barai	10	3
Ahir	7	4
Camar	19	3
Kunjra	22	5
Shekh	26	15
Julaha	17.50	8
Muslim Halvai	11	4
Other	123	
(Other Baniya)	(32)	
Total	567	67

APPENDIX II

Transliteration and Glossary of Hindi Terms

TRANSLITERATION SYSTEM

Appendix II. Transliteration and Glossary
of Hindi Terms

Devanagari	Symbol	Devanagari	Symbol
अ	a	ढ	*dh*
आ	*a*	ढ़	*rh*
इ	I	ण	ऩ
ई	i	त	t
उ	U	थ	th
ऊ	u	द	d
ए	e	ध	dh
ऐ	ae	न	n
ओ	o	प	p
औ	au	फ	ph
क	k	ब	b
ख	kh	म	bh
ग	g	म	m
घ	gh	य	y
च	c	र	r
छ	ch	ळ	l
ज,ज़	j,z	व	v
झ	jh	स,श,ष	s†
ट	t	ह	h
ठ	*th*		*n*-nazalization
ड	*d*		
ड़	*r**		

† There is only one "s" phoneme in the regional dialect.
* Only educated persons distinguish "*r*" from "*rh*".

GLOSSARY

Transliteration	Text version *	Gloss
achut		Untouchable, in reference to specific castes
angrez		Englishman or, in general, any westerner
bahan		Real or classificatory sister
banIya	Baniya	The slightly derogatory name given to the traditional merchant castes taken as a unit; by extension, any businessman or individual engaging in sharp practices
basti		A separate dwelling area for untouchable castes
bhai		Real or classificatory brother
bhar		Original inhabitants of Tezibazar; a low caste
bIradari	*biradari*	General term for caste although covering other social entities as well; i.e., status category
bIri	*biri*	A cheap popular type of cigarette with a tobacco leaf wrapper; usually produced locally
brahmIṇ	Brahmin	The name of a status category; a member of that category
caca		Real or classificatory father's brother (as reference and often in address)
carpai		Cot, commonly used as a bed
cabutra		The porch or stoop of a shop
dasahra		The calendrical celebration of the victory of Ram over the demon Ravan, a part of which is the theatrical re-enactment of this event, called the *"ram lila"*
dharmsala		A resting place for pilgrims
dIh	*dih*	A local shrine; associated in Tezibazar with the *bhar*
divali		A festival especially important to merchants on which homage is done the goddess of wealth; also the traditional day for the changing of account books, although this practice is not always followed
gaddi		Sheeting or matting partially covering the floor of a shop upon which the money box is placed and the shop's owner sits

* Text version is given only when it differs significantly from transliterated version.

GLOSSARY (cont.)

Transliteration	Text version	Gloss
gU*r*	*gur*	A crude form of molasses sugar made by the peasantry
holi		A festival at which great bonfires are lit and individuals throw colored water, mud, etc., as tokens of their mutual affection
hUkk*a*	*hukka*	The water pipe or hubble-bubble
Ikk*a*	*ikka*	A two-wheeled horse-drawn vehicle; passengers sit upon a flat platform
Ikkev*a*n		The driver of an *ikka*
j*a*rd*a*		Aromatic tobacco chewed with *pan*
jan sangh	Jana Sangh	A political party
kacch*a*		Anything unripe or unfulfilled; in interdining, food boiled or baked; dirt roads; mud and thatch house construction
kalv*a*r	Kalvar	Baniya caste whose traditional occupation is wine selling; also known as Jaisval
kanjus		A miser; a stronger term is *makhijus*
kesarv*a*ni	Kesarvani	A Baniya caste
kh*a*nd*a*n		Lineage of any depth; sometimes refers to joint family
kIs*a*n	Kisan	One of the status categories
lakhpatti		A man of *lakh*s; i.e., one worth hundreds of thousands of rupees
m*a*lIk	*malik*	The owner of a shop; also used by women to refer to their husbands
ma*ṇ*di	*mandi*	A (wholesale) market place
masjId	*masjid*	Mosque
maz*a*r		The tomb of a Muslim saint or martyr
munim		Clerk in a shop
mUhall*a*	*mohalla*	Traditional territorial division of the town
mauz*a*		Territorial division for land revenue purposes
mlecch *or* mlIcch		Foreign or uncultivated, with the connotation of pollution or dirtiness; often applied to Muslims by Hindus
pakk*a*		Anything ripe or finished; in food, anything fried; paved roads; brick and plaster house construction
pan*ç*ayat		The social control body within the local Umar caste

GLOSSARY (cont.)

Transliteration	Text version	Gloss
paṇḍIt	Pandit	Priest or learned man; a term of address and reference for Brahmins
pargana		An administrative division below the *tehsil*
pattidar		Lineage-mate
pavItra	*pavitra*	Pure, unsullied
pUrohIt	*purohit*	Family priest, in most cases, a Brahmin
puja		Homage or worship to a divine being
party		English word used in reference to any grouping of political or social opposition
picnic		English word signifying informal social outings into the rural area on which men prepare rustic-style meals for themselves
sabha		Council
sUdra	Sudra	One of the caste status categories
talab		Artificial pond or small lake
tat		Factional division within the local Umar caste
tahsil	*tehsil*	Administrative division below the district
thakUr	Thakur	One of the status categories; also a term of address for individuals in this category
thana		Police station
umar	Umar	Caste of Baniyas
usar		Barren land
zamindar		Under the British, (large) landowner and contractor for the government land revenue

Bibliography

Anderson, Robert T. "Preliminary Report on the Associational Redefinition of Castes in Hyderabad-Secunderabad," *Kroeber
Anthropological Papers*, XXIX (1963), 25–42.

Bailey, F. G. *Caste and the Economic Frontier*. Manchester: Manchester University Press, 1957.

——. "Closed Social Stratification in India," *Archives Europeannes
de Sociologie*, IV, No. 1 (1963), 107–124.

Beardsley, Richard K. "Ecological and Social Parallels between
Rice-Growing Communities of Japan and Spain," *Symposium
on Community Studies in Anthropology* (Proceedings of the
American Ethnological Society; Spring, 1963), pp. 55–63.

Beidelman, Thomas O. *A Comparative Analysis of the "Jajmani"
System*. (Monograph of the Association for Asian Studies, Vol.
VIII.) Locust Valley: J. J. Augustin, 1959.

Benet, F. "The Ideology of Islamic Urbanization," *Urbanism and
Urbanization*, ed. Nels Anderson (Leiden: E. J. Brill, 1964), pp.
111–126.

Bouglé, C. *Essai Sur le Régime des Castes*. Paris: Travaux de l'Anné
Sociologique, 1908.

Brass, Paul R. *Factional Politics in an Indian State: The Congress
Party in Uttar Pradesh*. Berkeley: University of California Press,
1965.

Carstairs, G. M. *The Twice-Born*. London: Hogarth Press, 1957.

Cohn, Bernard S. "The Initial British Impact on India: A Case
Study of the Banaras Region," *Journal of Asian Studies*, XIX
(1960), 418–431.

——. "Political Systems in Eighteenth Century India: The Banaras
Region," *Journal of the American Oriental Society*, LXXXII
(1962), 425–430.

Cohn, Bernard S., and McKim Marriott. "Networks and Centers in the Integration of Indian Civilization," *Journal of Social Research*, I (1958), 1–8.

Crooke, W. *The Tribes and Castes of the North-Western Provinces and Oudh.* 4 vols. Calcutta: Office of Government Printing, 1896.

Drake-Brockman, D. L. *Azamgarh: A District Gazetteer.* (*District Gazetteers of the United Provinces of Agra and Oudh,* Vol. XXXIII.) Allahabad: Government Press, 1911.

Eberhard, Wolfram. "Data on the Structure of the Chinese City in the Pre-Industrial Period," *Economic Development and Cultural Change,* IV (1955–1956), 253–278.

Epstein, T. Scarlett. *Economic Development and Social Change in South India.* Manchester: Manchester University Press, 1962.

Fox, Richard G. "Family, Caste, and Commerce in a North Indian Market Town," *Economic Development and Cultural Change,* XV (1967), 297–314.

——. "Resiliency and Change in the Indian Caste System: The Umar of U.P.," *Journal of Asian Studies,* XXVI (1967), 575–587.

Gadgil, D. R. *Poona: A Socio-Economic Study, Part I, Economic.* (Gokhale Institute of Politics and Economics, Publication No. 12.) Poona: The Institute, 1945.

——. *Poona, A Socio-Economic Study, Part II, Social.* (Gokhale Institute of Politics and Economics, Publication No. 25.) Poona: The Institute, 1952.

——. *Origins of the Modern Indian Business Class: An Interim Report.* With the assistance of M. V. Namjoshi. New York: Institute of Pacific Relations, 1959.

Gough, Kathleen. "The Social Structure of a Tanjore Village," *India's Villages,* ed. M. N. Srinivas (Bombay: Asia Publishing House, 1960).

Gould, Harold A. "A Jajmani System of North India: Its Structure, Magnitude, and Meaning," *Ethnology,* III (1964), 12–41.

Gulati, I. S., and K. S. Gulati. *The Undivided Hindu Family: Its Tax Privileges.* Bombay: Asia Publishing House, 1962.

Habib, Irfan. *The Agrarian System of Moghal India.* New York: Asia Publishing House, 1963.

Harrison, Selig S. "Caste and the Andhra Communists," *American Political Science Review,* L (1956), 378–404.

Hazelhurst, Leighton Wilson. "Entrepreneurship and the Merchant Castes in a Punjabi City." Unpublished Ph.D. dissertation, University of California, Berkeley, 1964.

Jain, N. G. "The Emergence of Urban Centers in the Eastern Districts of Vidarbha (Maharashtra)" *National Geographical Journal of India,* X (1964), 146–163.

Karim, A. K. Nazmul. *Changing Society in India and Pakistan.* Dacca: Oxford University Press, 1956.

Khare, R. S. "The Kanya-Kubja Brahmins and Their Caste Organization," *Southwestern Journal of Anthropology,* XVI (1960), 348–367.

Kroeber, A. L. *Anthropology.* New York: Harcourt, Brace, 1948.

Lambert, Richard D. "The Impact of Urban Society upon Village Life," *India's Urban Future,* ed. Roy Turner (Berkeley: University of California Press, 1962).

Lewis, Oscar. *Village Life in Northern India.* Urbana: University of Illinois Press, 1958.

Lewis, Oscar, and Victor Barnouw. "Caste and the Jajmani System in a North Indian Village," *Scientific Monthly,* LXXXIII, No. 2 (1955), 66–81.

Luschinsky, Mildred Stroop. "Problems of Culture Change in the Indian Village," *Human Organization,* XXII (1963), 66–74.

Mahar, P. M. "A Multiple Scaling Technique for Caste Ranking," *Man in India,* XXXIX (1959), 127–147.

Majumdar, D. N. *Caste and Communication in an Indian Village.* Bombay: Asia Publishing House, 1958.

——. *Social Contours of an Industrial City.* New York: Asia Publishing House, 1960.

Majumdar, R. C., H. C. Raychaudhari, and Kalikinkar Datta. *An Advanced History of India.* London: Macmillan and Co., 1950.

Marriott, McKim. "Social Structure and Change in a U.P. Village," *India's Villages,* ed. M. N. Srinivas (Bombay: Asia Publishing House, 1960).

Mayer, Adrian C. *Caste and Kinship in Central India: A Village and Its Region.* Berkeley and Los Angeles: University of California Press, 1960.

——. "System and Network: An Approach to the Study of Political Process in Dewas," *Indian Anthropology,* ed. T. N. Madan and Gopala Sarana (Bombay: Asia Publishing House, 1962), pp. 266–277.

Mukerjee, Radhakamal, and Baljit Singh. *A District Town in Transition: Social and Economic Survey of Gorakhpur.* New York: Asia Publishing House, 1965.

Nair, Kusum. *Blossoms in the Dust.* New York: Praeger, 1961.

Narain, V. A. *Jonathan Duncan and Varanasi.* Calcutta: K. L. Mukhopadyhyay, 1959.

Neale, Walter C. *Economic Change in Rural India: Land Tenure and Reform in Uttar Pradesh, 1800–1955.* New Haven and London: Yale University Press, 1962.

Neale, Walter C., Harpal Singh, and Jai Pal Singh. "Kurali Market: A Report on the Economic Geography of Marketing in Northern Punjab," *Economic Development and Cultural Change,* XIII (1965), 129–168.

Neville, H. R. *Partabgarh: A District Gazetteer.* (*District Gazetteers of the United Provinces of Agra and Oudh,* Vol. XXXIV.) Allahabad: Government Press, 1904.

——. *Jaunpur: A District Gazetteer.* (*District Gazetteers of the United Provinces of Agra and Oudh,* Vol. XXVIII.) Allahabad: Government Press, 1908.

Office of the Registrar General (India). *Census of India, 1951— India.* Part II-A: "Demographic Tables." Allahabad: Government Press, 1952. Tables A-IV, A-V.

——. *Census of India, 1951—Uttar Pradesh.* Part II-A: "General Population Tables." Allahabad: Government Press, 1952. Tables A-IV, A-V.

——. *District Population Statistics, Uttar Pradesh: No. 29 Jaunpur District.* Allahabad: Government Press, 1953.

——. *District Census Handbook, Uttar Pradesh: No. 29 Jaunpur District.* Allahabad: Government Press, 1955.

——. *Census of India, 1961—India.* Part II-A: "General Population Tables." Allahabad: Government Press, n.d. Table A-IV.

——. *Census of India, 1961—Uttar Pradesh.* Part II-B: "Economic Tables." Allahabad: Government Press, n.d. Table B-IV.

Pocock, David F. " 'Difference' in East Africa: A Study of Caste and Religion in Modern Indian Society," *Southwestern Journal of Anthropology,* XIII (1957), 289–300.

Rajagopalan, C. *The Greater Bombay* (*A Study in Suburban Ecology*). Bombay: Popular Book Depot, 1962.

Redfield, Robert. "The Social Organization of Tradition," *Far Eastern Quarterly*, XV (1955), 13–22.

Retzlaff, Ralph H. *Village Government in India*. New York: Asia Publishing House, 1962.

Riggs, Walter. "The Theory of Developing Politics," *World Politics*, XVI (1963–1964), 147–171.

Rowe, William. "Caste, Kinship, and Association in Urban India," Unpublished paper prepared for the 1964 symposium of the Wenner–Gren Foundation for Anthropological Research (Burg Wartenstein).

Rudolph, Lloyd I., and Suzanne Hoeber Rudolph. "The Political Role of India's Caste Associations," *Pacific Affairs*, XXXIII (1960), 5–22.

Sahlins, Marshall D., and Elman R. Service, eds. *Evolution and Culture*. Ann Arbor: University of Michigan Press, 1960.

Service, Elman R. *Profiles in Ethnology*. New York: Harper and Row, 1963.

Sherring, Rev. M. A. *Hindu Tribes and Castes as Represented in Banaras*. Calcutta: Thacker, Spink and Co., n.d.

Singh, Baljit and Shridhar Misra. *A Study of Land Reforms in Uttar Pradesh*. Honolulu: East–West Center Press, 1965.

Singh, Kashi Nath. "Functions and Functional Classification of Towns in Uttar Pradesh," *National Geographical Journal of India*, V (1959), 121–148.

——. "Barhaj: A Study in the Changing Pattern of a Market Town," *National Geographical Journal of India*, VII (1961), 21–36.

Singh, R. L. "Ballia: A Study in Urban Settlement," *National Geographical Journal of India*, II (1956), 1–6.

——. "Two Small Towns of Eastern U.P.: Sultanpur and Chunar," *National Geographical Journal of India*, III (1957), 1–10.

Singh, R. L., and K. N. Singh. "Evolution of the Medieval Towns in the Saryu-par Plain," *National Geographical Journal of India*, IX (1963), 1–11.

Singh, R. L., and S. M. Singh. "Mungra-Badshahpur: A Rurban Settlement in the Ganga–Ghaghara Doab West," *National Geographical Journal of India*, VI (1960), 200–206.

Singh, Rudra Datt, and Morris Opler. "The Division of Labor in an Indian Village," *A Reader in General Anthropology*, ed. Carleton Coon (London: Cape Co., 1950).

Singh, Satish Chandra. "Evolution of Azamgarh," *National Geographical Journal of India*, IX (1963), 175–186.

Singh, Shiw Mangal. "Ancient Bhars and Their Ruined Settlements in Ganga–Ghaghara Doab West." *National Geographical Journal of India*, VIII (1962), 183–196.

Sjoberg, Gideon. "Folk and 'Feudal' Societies," *American Journal of Sociology*, LVIII (1952), 231–239.

——. *The Preindustrial City: Past and Present*. New York: Free Press, 1960.

——. "The Rise and Fall of Cities: A Theoretical Perspective," *Urbanism and Urbanization*, ed. Nels Anderson (Leiden: E. J. Brill, 1964), pp. 7–20.

——. "The Rural-Urban Dimension in Preindustrial, Transitional, and Industrial Societies," *Handbook of Modern Sociology*, ed. Robert E. L. Faris (Chicago: Rand, McNally, 1964), pp. 127–160.

Spate, O. H. K. *India and Pakistan: A General and Regional Geography*. London: Methuen, 1957.

Steward, Julian. *Area Research: Theory and Practice*. New York: Social Science Research Council, 1950.

Von Grunebaum, G. E. *Islam: Essays in the Nature and Growth of a Cultural Tradition*. London: Routledge and K. Paul, 1955.

Weber, Max. *General Economic History*. Trans. Frank H. Knight. Glencoe: Free Press, 1927.

——. *From Max Weber: Essays in Sociology*. Ed. H. H. Gerth and C. Wright Mills. New York: Oxford University Press, 1958.

——. *The Religion of India: The Sociology of Hinduism and Buddhism*. Trans. and ed. H. H. Gerth and Don Martindale. Glencoe: Free Press, 1958.

——. *The City*. Trans. and ed. Don Martindale and Gertrude Neuwirth. New York: Collier, 1962.

Weiner, Myron. *Party Politics in India*. Princeton: Princeton University Press, 1957.

Wolf, Eric R. "Aspects of Group Relations in a Complex Society: Mexico," *American Anthropologist*, LVIII (1956), 1065–1078.

Index

achut, 88
Akbar, 71, 73, 97
Ali, 115-117; *see also* Muslim communal group
Ansari, 85-86
Aurangzeb, 73
Ayodhiya, *see* Kasodhan

bacch (Thakurs), 11, 71, 73-74
Baniya, 4, 11, 39ff., 73, 89, 104, 108, 111; as hinge group, 4; miserliness of, 61; stereotype of, 58-59
Baniya communal group, 203, 215-217
bans, 86-87; of Umar, 246
Barragaon *tehsil*, 10, 221
Benet, F., 267
Bhanu Pratap, 222, 224, 231-232, 234, 236-238; *see also* Thakurs of Rampur *and* United Club
bhar, 23, 71ff., 74
biradari, 44, 82, 87, 89, 111, 202, 257, 262
black market speculation, 150, 153; and business innovation, 159-160
Brahmin, 39, 44, 89, 113
business survey, 33-35, 127-130, 147, 171
businesses: and capital, 156-157; capitalization of, 175; and debt, 176; expenses of, 175; and family, 135-137; and household expenses, 175; longevity of, 150-151; losses, 149-150; profits and sales, 148-149

Camar, 41, 51, 82
caste: and business, 138; definition of, 38, 45; and employment, 139-140; list of, 83-85; and politics, 185-187
caste category, 87; *see also* Umar caste category

caudhari, 99, 254
Chairman lineage, 197-199, 203, 206, 224-225, 238, 248-250, 255-256; conflict with Leader lineage, 201; *see also* Leader lineage
city, conceptions of, 177-178
Cohn, Bernard, 2
commensality, 38-40; and feeding lines, 94-95; and personal choice, 99; and politics, 94, 97-98
commerce: and adulteration, 155, 177; and capital, 177; and credit, 152-155; and family, 160; and family size, 135-137; and inventory, 127; and money lending, 157-158; past, 125; and price, 155; and profits, 175-177; and savings, 176-177; and subsistence ideology, 142-145, 152, 161, 180; and wholesale businesses, 154; *see also* Baniya *and* businesses
commercial dishonesty, 161-162; Cunni Lal-*sonar* dispute, 163-164; Laksmi Narain–Ram Svarup dispute, 164-165; and social control, 162-163
communal conflict, 112-114; *see also* Muslim–Hindu conflict
communal groups, 42, 46-47, 186, 281; and employment, 139; and political ideology, 213-215
communalism, 204; *see also* Baniya communal group, communal groups, *and* Muslim communal group
community study method, 2
complex societies, 1
Congress party, 188-189, 193-194, 200, 207, 211-212, 214-216, 220-221, 226, 230-231; factions of, 189, 232-233, 237
Crooke, W., 243